Gypsy Gossip and Other Advice

Gypsy Gossip

and Other Advice

Thinley Norbu

Shambhala

BOULDER

2016

Shambhala Publications, Inc.
4720 Walnut Street
Boulder, Colorado 80301
www.shambhala.com

9 8 7 6 5 4 3 2 1

First Edition
Printed in the United States of America

♾ This edition is printed on acid-free paper that meets the
American National Standards Institute z39.48 Standard.
♻ This book is printed on 30% postconsumer recycled paper.
For more information please visit www.shambhala.com.

Distributed in the United States by Penguin Random House LLC and in
Canada by Random House of Canada Ltd

Designed by Dean Bornstein

LIBRARY OF CONGRESS CATALOGING-IN-PUBLICATION DATA

Thinley Norbu.
Gypsy gossip and other advice / Thinley Norbu.—First Edition.
pages   cm
Includes bibliographical references.
ISBN 978-1-61180-208-5 (hardcover: alk. paper) 1. Buddhism—Doctrines. I. Title.
BQ4132.T439 2015
294.3'42—dc23
2014042782

CONTENTS

NOTE TO THE READER

Gypsy Gossip and Other Advice assembles four writings that contain Kyabje Thinley Norbu Rinpoche's direct counsel "like fresh rain as an offering to the Triple Gems for the benefit of increasing the pure river of Dharma," to use Rinpoche's own words. As different as the selections may be from each other, they all offer precious teachings, in a language unique to Rinpoche, on a wide range of topics important to both Western and Eastern students of Dharma.

The first selection, "Gypsy Gossip," was originally printed in 1980 as a small book in a very limited private edition. In its present edition it is happily now available to a wider audience. In an informal atmosphere of spiritual openness, Kyabje Thinley Norbu Rinpoche answers questions from Western students about Tibetan Buddhism, including the teachings of karma and rebirth, monastic discipline, devotion to the Guru, and the importance of keeping vows.

"Beyond East and West" consists of Rinpoche's written replies to questions submitted in writing by Melvin McLeod, editor-in-chief of *Buddhadharma* and *Shambhala Sun* magazines, during a visit to Rinpoche's residence in Delhi, New York, around 1999. In this interview, published here for the first time, Rinpoche gives an extensive commentary on how cultural differences have affected the adoption of Tibetan Buddhism in the West, and emphasizes that Westerners' Buddha nature can be rekindled through a greater development of faith and belief.

"A Message for Young Bhutanese" was written for an organization called the Young Buddhist Association of Bhutan. Rinpoche had a close personal connection with the kingdom of Bhutan. In this message Rinpoche urges Bhutanese youth to preserve their spiritual heritage (including study of the Tibetan language) and to carry its blessings onward amid the modern influences of materialism. Rinpoche warns against introducing foreign nihilistic beliefs into Bhutan and creating sectarian conflicts between its indigenous lineages.

"An Introduction to Dharma Dance Offerings" was written in connection with several teaching films directed by Kyabje Thinley Norbu Rinpoche, who was an accomplished practitioner and teacher of sacred dance. Rinpoche contrasts ordinary dancing, which expresses the passions of material reality and lacks the positive influence of wisdom, with the Dharma dances of Tibet, which manifest the enlightened activities of peaceful and wrathful deities.

It is a blessing that these four precious writings have become part of the cherished legacy of this beloved teacher.

Gypsy Gossip

INTRODUCTION

When I went to the West for medical treatment, I met with friends from California, New Mexico, Hawaii, Spain, South America, France, and England who cared for me not only in a worldly way, but also in a deep spiritual way. When they questioned me, they asked in a simple, direct manner and had hopes of a simple, direct answer. Whether they can benefit sentient beings or not, I cannot say, but their style is simple, direct, honest, intelligent, and eccentric, neither like fickle-lover practitioners nor like holy-style practitioners. And most of them are younger than me. Sometimes their pure, direct, and eccentric activity actually tortures me, although mostly they care for me like their most precious and valuable possession. Some are humble, and when they questioned me, I gave answers instantly. Some wrote letters and I responded through the mail.

Even though we couldn't finish due to illness and other circumstances, my friends eagerly made this simple book with the intention to benefit simple people. They printed it in a simple country where Lord Buddha's lotus feet blessed the land; where, when the amber sunrise sends joyous rays to the earth, the golden tower of the splendid Stupa responds with golden light toward the blue sky; where white clouds lightly glide from the sparkling snows of the Himalayas and red earth smoothly forms a landscape of plateaus, hills, and valleys; where young trees rise and tremble with the gentle winds and beautiful cuckoo birds sing tantalizing melodies. They printed it in a simple city when the purple flowering trees shadowed the streets and international gypsies with black and blond hair, blue and black eyes, yellow and brown skin, dressed in feather-light flowing clothes of clear, bright colors that moved gently with the breeze.

Patrul Rinpoche said, "For those who write scriptures with the intention of benefiting others, it is not always necessary to use poetry; through common language you should teach the clear, thorough path. This is the mark of a Bodhisattva."

When we made this book, we didn't care too much to make it "pukka," because no one can attain perfection through a stubborn intellect. If you find the ideas unclear or contradictory, or if you find the English offensive, please don't hate. Hating and criticism would just become the cause of your own suffering. So you can go your own way; there is no need to quarrel like vegetarians and nonvegetarians. Just eat what you want without insult and with a peaceful mind.

This simple book is dedicated to the benefit of all sentient beings, including simple practitioners who like to rest in simple, natural mind without elaborate, complicated suffering.

ASPECTS OF SPIRITUALITY

Rinpoche, would you like to be a disciple?

I would like to be a disciple without being one, without hope of learning. I would like to find through my good karma, auspicious dreams, searching, or through friends, an intelligent and expert, powerful wisdom teacher to show me the truly correct path until the final result. It does not matter if he teaches in a hierarchical style, if he is a gypsy, a beautiful or terrible lady, a monk or nun, a god or demon, a layman or holy man, a janitor or craftsman. And as I would spend more time with this teacher, my actions, seeing, hearing, and thinking would automatically benefit myself and other beings as they would turn into practice. I would become more kind, profound, clear, and trustful. I would like to feel that my teacher is a wisdom sadist and to serve him with pure intention and reasonable masochism.

But I'm afraid that through my bad karma, I might meet a teacher who would not show me the path or would not release me to other experienced wisdom teachers. I might meet one who would only benefit his ego or the ego of his steward, consort, or retinue without benefiting my enlightenment. I might meet one who would use the Vinaya as an excuse to misinterpret my great desire for desireless accomplishment, thus repressing my desireless wisdom mind, which depends on desire. I'm afraid that I might meet an ordinary, lustful teacher who would misuse, for his worldly power, my great desire for desireless wisdom. He might use it only to arouse ordinary pleasure and waste this life without benefiting this lifetime or future lifetimes. And I'm afraid that if I meet a high or famous teacher, I will buzz around him and look down on other teachers, or if I meet a humble one, I will treat him carelessly. So, maybe I'd better try to stay in ordinary mind instead of being a greedy and careless disciple.

Rinpoche, would you like to be a teacher?

I would like to be a teacher if I could realize that all the different phenomena that come from wisdom mind are the cause of omniscience. If through wisdom intelligence I could understand all the different cultures of humanity, I could impartially teach to all the different disciples or students according to their faculties with or without a system, with or without judgment, at the right time, temporarily for the benefit of their present life and ultimately for the benefit of their enlightenment. But I'm afraid that before I really recognize pure wisdom intelligence I might confuse it with superficial worldly intelligence and as a result not be able to teach clearly without properly responding to their different faculties. And I'm afraid that if I only have worldly intelligence, which can be defeated by impermanent phenomena, then I'll turn my open-minded students into pathetic ones; my rich, powerful, and beautiful students will turn me into a servant; or my careless students will drain my energies and use my precious knowledge for their own selfish benefit and finally throw me away like an old mistress when they are through. So I'd better try to stay in ordinary mind without worrying about whether bad students will stay or good students will abandon me.

Rinpoche, would you like to be an expert writer?

I would like to be an expert writer with unblocked mind profoundly expressing all the words I want to say clearly and deeply. But I'm afraid that when one has paper, there is no ink, and when there is ink, there is no paper. When one has both paper and ink, there are no words. We are constantly putting books in and taking them out of shelves, endlessly trying to pick up good words as a chicken pecks at live worms. Finally, we find the right words but cannot construct metaphors that flow. After choosing the proper metaphors, we find the syntax is wrong. When the editor, with prideful paranoia, corrects the syntax and completely changes the meaning, we cannot find a publisher. If we find a publisher, the text is open to misunderstanding due to the numerous preconceptions of numerous neurotic minds. Instead of benefit, this creates problems, attachment and rejection, high blood pressure, hysteria, confusion, and suffering. So maybe I'd better try to stay in ordinary mind without a typewriter.

Rinpoche, would you like to be a philosopher?

I would like philosophy if I could learn the many different philosophical systems through deductive reasoning without mixing them and with open vision like an ocean frog. But I am afraid that if I learn through my rigid intellectual mind, pride will arise and I will never believe the vastness of other systems. I will only constantly make judgments, trying to criticize and reject with a narrow mind like a frog in a well. I'm afraid that my natural mind will be distorted into a conceited mind. So I'd better try to stay in ordinary mind without judgment.

Rinpoche, would you like to be a scholar?

I would like to be a scholar if I could analyze all of the different systems of knowledge through clear discriminating wisdom, without anxiety about rank. But I'm afraid I would be an ordinary scholar, swelling his limited knowledge and holding his chin high with no respect toward other experts or toward wise men. So maybe I'd better try to stay in ordinary mind without thinking of onstage lectures and other scholarly activities.

Rinpoche, would you like to be powerful?

I would like to be powerful if I could have absolute trust in wisdom mind, which is never overcome by ordinary spiritual or technical power. This means I would constantly practice with bad and good circumstances.

When bad circumstances such as poverty, sickness, suffering, bad reputation, or insult arose, I would see that poverty came from stinginess, sickness and suffering from violence toward others, bad reputation from jealousy, and insults from conceit. And I would not want to blame others for these circumstances, but rather would realize that they arose from previous karma and that they are just illusions created by my dualistic mind. I would acknowledge their karmic cause and try to purify them through skillful means.

When good circumstances arose, such as wealth, health, good reputation, and praise, I would see my wealth to have come from previous generosity, my health from love and kindness toward other beings, and my good reputation from praise toward others. As these good circumstances arose, I would dedicate them for the benefit of all sentient beings, and, once more recognizing them to be illusions from my dualistic mind, I would try not to make them real by grasping or boasting about them.

If I were to examine the origin of all these bad or good phenomena, I would discover that they were created by dualistic mind. I would discover that bad or good circumstances appear to be real only in relative truth, and that the difference between them is just like that between black and white clouds; though their essence is the same, they appear to have different aspects. I would see that the objects and subjects of my bad and good experiences are just temporary and illusory, disappearing into selfless awareness as black and white clouds disappear into the sky. Then bad circumstances would not disturb me because I would have confidence through the recognition of my own selfless mind. So, I would no longer create my own suffering by grasping at or complaining about them. In that way, there would no longer be dependence on or influence by bad or good objects.

Thus, my facial expression would be stable and pure, not rapidly changing like a coward's face; my speech would always be beneficial, smooth, and true, rather than loose and senselessly blurting like that of a delirious person; and my mind would be deep, clean, and unfathomable like the ocean, rather than shallow and scatterbrained. And since no one would know what is happening in it, no one could influence it and it would always remain pure.

But I'm afraid that if bad or good circumstances arose before I managed to attain wisdom mind power, my remembering mind, never being on time, would miss the target. I'm afraid that should I achieve power when worldly opportunity arose, I would use it stupidly over others for my own benefit. And I'm afraid that when my impermanent worldly power was finally exhausted, those whom I had oppressed would take revenge. If that happened, I would become so pathetic and my suffering would be so great that even if I ate delicious food, there would be no taste, and if I slept in a comfortable bed, there would be no sleep. So, I'd better try to stay in ordinary mind, rather than use worldly ego power or try to achieve egoless wisdom power.

Rinpoche, would you like to be famous?

I would like to be effortlessly famous, like the Bodhisattvas and saints of ancient times, for the benefit of all sentient beings without any attachment to the worldly rewards of fame. My efforts to be famous, however, would have constantly changing results like the different masks of an actor and would probably pull me between happiness and unhappiness. So, maybe I'd better try to stay in ordinary mind without self-advertisement.

Rinpoche, would you like to be sectarian or nonsectarian?

I would like to be both. First, I would like to be a sectarian because I am only one person with one mind and unique faculties. The Buddha gave many different teachings for as many different individuals, and all these teachings are not necessary for me to practice at one time. I would prefer to follow only the path that interests and benefits me. I would focus on and aim toward one goal and practice to realize goalless wisdom mind. I could realize through this practice that all Dharmas are contained within one pure mind. When I realized goalless wisdom mind, all my aims would vanish into nonsectarian wisdom mind. Sectarianism may seem to be one-sided, but ultimately it is the way to reach pure nonsectarianism. For example, if you want to visit someone, it is not necessary to take the train, boat, and airplane at the same time. The best way to reach a destination without confusion is by one vehicle.

I would also like to be nonsectarian from the beginning if I could learn the different teachings that are all directed toward one target. Then, all these teachings would flow together like the branches of a river toward the ocean of enlightenment.

But I'm afraid that I would be a bad sectarian, encouraging division and increasing paranoia, and I would be a fake nonsectarian, just a sectarian in nonsectarian clothes like an invader inside a Trojan horse. So, maybe I'd better try to stay in ordinary mind, which is beyond both.

Rinpoche, would you like to be a monk?

The pure monks from the Buddha's time kept the two hundred and fifty vows of the Vinaya like their own eyes. On the outside, they wore sunrise-colored robes. In the inside, they were completely weary of samsara and subdued; they looked at morality as the jewel of enlightenment. The Buddha taught them to have aversion toward their own passions as though they were snakes, but also that they should not hate, criticize, or judge others. Yet there are other monks who do not subdue all their passions and instead create a stronger morality ego by disliking and hating women, yogis, and others whom they think of as impure.

I would like to be a monk who, through the Buddha's teachings, has attained a completely tranquil and disciplined mind that is beyond morality or the conception of morality. I'm afraid, however, that my outer side would be clean red robes, my inner side would be my puritanical ego's superior point of view, and my secret side would be masturbation, homosexuality, or the visualization of fucking. So maybe I'd better try to stay in ordinary mind without worrying about vows.

Rinpoche, would you like to be a yogi?

Yes, I would like to be a yogi if I could realize the mandala of phenomena that is pure from the beginning and inherent in nondualistic wisdom mind. I would like to be a yogi if I could indulge in the passions for the benefit of practice without being entangled in those passions. I would like to be a yogi if I could taste desireless exaltation in self-secret unconditioned wisdom mind by uniting with the wisdom Dakini, whose soft magic display is expressed with conceptionless skill and who dances with uncontrived Dharmata wings in the theater of natural mind.

Yet I'm afraid I will discriminate and not see things with a pure mind and so become entangled in the passions and become a slave of demonesses with irresistible bodies. So maybe I'd better try to stay in ordinary mind without trying to become a yogi and without expecting impure or pure phenomena.

Rinpoche, would you like to be a Lama?

I would like to be a Lama if I could attain selfless confidence in the realization that the phenomena of samsara and nirvana are wisdom magic. I would like to be a Lama if I could teach from the highest sublime and pure natural mind, the golden throne of Hinayana, Mahayana, and Vajrayana, knowing the faculties of my disciples without confusion. I would like to be a Lama if I could see how relative truth's effortless skillful means are harmoniously performed for the benefit of all individuals regardless of their different inclinations, just as the moon reflects equally on all pools, and how through absolute truth, wisdom essence never remains in any one Dharma system, just as the moon never remains in its reflection on any one pool. But I'm afraid that before I get wisdom eyes, I would be like a blind man leading the blind, so I'd better try to stay in ordinary mind, on the ground, without any expectation toward a splendid throne.

Rinpoche, would you like to be a Bodhisattva?

I would like to be a Bodhisattva if I could establish the egolessness of self and the essencelessness of phenomena, live according to the six *paramitas* through aimless compassion, and thus benefit all sentient beings without expectation.

Yet I'm afraid that if I only pretend to be a Bodhisattva, then when beings ask even small things of me for their benefit, I would feel they wanted to devour my flesh. So, I'd better try to stay in ordinary mind without an outer smile and an inner black heart.

Rinpoche, would you like to be a siddha?

I would like to be a *siddha* if I could see and decide without judgment that other-phenomena come from self-phenomena, which in turn arise from the mandala of the five Buddha families, self-created wisdom awareness. If I could practice according to my destiny deity's *sadhana* through visualization, wisdom channels, or wisdom mind, my temporary, aging substance body would become light and young and ultimately be transformed into a wisdom body. Siddhas and saints have realized their unobstructed wisdom mind. For them, the display of phenomena has the appearance of wisdom Dakinis with whom they play and sing vajra songs.

If I practiced the untying of my karmic nerves, my scratchy voice would turn into music like the voices of wisdom Dakinis who sing without attachment. Then all sentient beings would wake up in Vajradhara's pureland liberated from our ignorance-obscured samsaric dungeon. But I'm afraid that before meeting a wisdom Dakini, I would have fooled myself and others with the empty magic of my siddha action, and that ultimately my attachment to others' praise would be the cause of suffering. I would use tantric practice as an excuse to chase after lustful women, promoting samsara through this kind of play. So maybe I had better try to stay in ordinary mind rather than be a pseudo-siddha.

What is the meaning of "vajra song"?

For saints who have confidence in their wisdom mind, ordinary phenomena have been completely transformed into pure phenomena. All worldly sounds are automatically transformed through pure phenomena into true and meaningful sounds, which by their nature are unobstructed. The words and songs of the saints are indestructible, like the vajra. Like pure wisdom seduction, they are automatically and irresistibly attractive and sweet.

KARMA

Rinpoche, do you believe in karma? One can understand karma as it manifests in this lifetime but not when relating to past lives. Can you explain?

I would believe in karma if I could realize how different phenomena are created by mind. A nihilist is a person who doesn't believe in karma, hell, or other realms. He thinks they are just illusory creations of the imagination and believes that only this world is real. But if this world is real, then the other realms must also be real because they are also created by one's mind. The mind creates all realms, which appear as reality when perceived. For example, ordinary people think that awake experience is real and that dreams are not real; yet while they sleep, dreaming becomes a reality. Both are true within relative truth and its expression as unobstructed phenomena, and both are untrue as long as there is a deluded mind that grasps at duality. Actually, there is no awake experience and no dream experience.

Shantideva said that when a woman who is sterile has a dream in which her child dies, she experiences great suffering, and yet from the beginning, there was in fact no child and no death. Her suffering was created by deluded mind. It doesn't really matter whether or not you believe in other realms, because you can see lots of suffering among animals and humans right here in this world.

According to the Mahayana, or Great Vehicle, because we do not recognize our Buddha nature, the ego lies like rust on natural mind. Only when we burn it with the fire of accumulated merit does unobstructed Buddha nature reappear. According to the high Vajrayana system, we obscured the knowledge that our Buddha nature is from the beginning unobstructed emptiness and luminosity, which is the essence of the Three Kayas.[1] When we didn't understand the desireless bliss of the Nirmanakaya, we obscured it by ordinary desire. When we didn't understand the luminosity of the Sambhogakaya, we obscured it by hatred, and when we didn't understand the vast emptiness of the Dharmakaya, we obscured it by ignorance. We failed to recognize the essence of the Buddha mind, our own unobstructed luminosity and the skillful means of its display. We clung to self-identity and we divided object and subject. We created bad and good phenomena through the three passions of our dualistic mind. Through these passions, we made various karmas and we wandered in samsara, fooled by essenceless phenomena.

This life's karma depends on our previous lives' actions, and our future lives' karma depends on this life's intention. But even though this is true, most of us do not believe in karma. We don't see that if we wish to be reborn as a human being, we can't choose our genes. They will only be good if our karma is good.

Many of us disbelieve in karma when we see that despite our good deeds our lives are filled with suffering, and that despite our bad deeds our lives are filled with pleasure. But this doesn't disprove karma. The Buddha taught about many different types of karma, which can be grouped according to the three times when they will ripen. One is *karma visible in this lifetime*, in which the causes and results of our actions appear in one lifetime. Another is *karma visible in the next life*, in which the results of our present life's karma appear in the following lifetime. The results of karma may not be immediately evident because they lie dormant and will show themselves only when the power of immediate karma becomes exhausted. Finally, there is *karma visible in the lives after the next*, in which the results of our karma arise two or more lives in the future. In any case, karma must manifest until wisdom mind is attained.

Ordinarily, when bad circumstances such as a car accident or a plane crash arise as a result of bad karma, no one blames it on genes. The car crash is blamed on a defect in the machine or a mistake of the driver, but these bad circumstances are not seen as karma. When a plane crashes, it is blamed on the pilot or the weather, but no one notices that the pilot's deluded mind and the bad weather both arose from karma. In wartime, even though soldiers are fighting together in the same circumstances, some are killed and others survive because their good karma is not exhausted.

Even if we don't believe in hells or in realms that we cannot see, it is still apparent that there is karma, as evident in the misery, happiness, failure, and success of people in this life. Bad karma is illustrated by the fact that all human beings, with the exception of manifested Buddhas, Bodhisattvas, or ascetics, have the same intention and desire for comforts. Still, they cannot always have them. Poor people don't like being poor. In the summer, they don't like to appear unwashed and sweaty in the street, or to eat other people's rotten garbage covered with flies. In winter, they don't like to shiver with frozen snot on their faces. They don't like to sleep in the street or in a shack or to wear other people's filthy thrown-away clothes. They don't like being constantly oppressed by the rich and powerful. They don't like it that they work hard and are never comfortable. They don't like it when even though they have been taught, they cannot learn, and even if they have learned, it brings no benefit to their lives, while others, whether or not they have been taught, automatically learn through their good karma and benefit from it. They live in beautiful houses, come from good families, sit on elegant chairs, eat delicious food, and are venerated by everyone.

Also, we can see how different people's karmic patterns are evident in their different faculties. Dogs have an especially sharp smelling sense; from far away, a male can smell a bitch. Because of karma, vultures have extremely sharp eyes; from far away, they can see their prey. If we think all these characteristics can be explained by genetics, we must not forget that even genes have a cause, and that is karma.

Habits keep us chained to karma, and so bad karma must be changed to good habits or good karma, and then we must try to transfer ourselves beyond bad or good karma. But I'm afraid that if I cling too strongly to karma, I will create more bad or good habits, which will not be beneficial for enlightenment. Without believing in and depending on the concept of karma, how will I be able to find freedom from karma, which is dependent on karma? So, maybe I'd better try to stay in ordinary mind instead of going between believing and disbelieving in karma.

BIRTH CONTROL

Nowadays, birth control is widely used. Is it sinful according to Buddhist teachings?

Buddhism is neither an eternalist system, which believes in a creator of all things, nor a nihilist system, which holds that nothing is real beyond what can be perceived by the senses. In general, Buddhists believe that our mind is the basis and creator of all phenomena, and that all conceptions make karma or habit. Through habit, many phenomena arise, and the cause of these phenomena is conception or dualistic mind. Though conceptions are invisible, they continuously make karma until all conceptions finally vanish into nondualistic mind. Although there are bad and good karmas, Pandita Dipamkara said:

Until all conceptions are exhausted, there is karma.
So, we should believe in the cause and result of karma.

Then we should try to abandon bad karma and make good karma.

According to the Buddhist system, there are many bad karmas, but the worst is killing, especially the killing of human beings who are the support of enlightenment or the source of benefit to other sentient beings. Even though because of our ignorance we can't abandon all bad activity, we should still try to abandon the worst as much as we can. We also can't carry out all the many possible good actions, but at least we should try to fulfill the most important ones as much as possible.

Our children are drawn to us because of previous karma, so if we use birth control, it seems that we create an obstacle to their birth. Their birth is like the repayment of a loan. If we reject it, it makes bad karma and increases the loan interest. So we should try to accept our karma, whether it is bad or good, without disbelief in the knowledge that all phenomena are caused by karma.

As much as we are always praying to be reborn in the jewel of a precious human body, we are constantly doing things to make obstacles for human rebirth. So, mostly, birth control serves the purpose of allowing us indulgence in our passions while avoiding compassion for those with whom we have established previous karmic bonds. In general, people think of having many children only in terms of their present convenience, seeing children as the cause of problems and obstacles to their freedom. At first, there might appear to be some immediate truth to that, but really, if we examine it sharply, we can see that some people who have many children have no problems, others with no children have many problems, some with many children have many problems, and others with no children have no problems. It cannot be foreseen.

We also have a tendency to forget that the mind must take rebirth in one of the six realms regardless of the population in this world. Perhaps it is better to give beings in other, lower realms the opportunity to gain merit and attain liberation through a precious human body. Population control solves some of the material difficulties for humanity, but who is to say that the poor and the wretched cannot attain liberation if given the opportunity? Is liberation only for those of wealth and power? Liberation begins with a first step, and it is best with a human body.

The best way to have sexual relations is to follow the inner tantric system. First, we find a great yogi or teacher who can pass on to us his experience in high Vajrayana practice. We should never have doubts about the tantric system. According to this, we should practice without rejecting human birth and always, with seven exceptions, control ejaculation. If we cannot practice this way, we should adopt the Vinaya system of becoming a monk or nun, or another vow system of abstinence grounded in general weariness with samsara.

Some people may think that monks and nuns practice birth control by their abstinence from sex. That in effect is true, but there is a major difference. Ordinary people who do not understand or believe in the Dharma have sexual relations to satisfy their desires, their motivation being selfish and impure, whereas monks and nuns are weary of samsara and renounce their desires in order to attain enlightenment and thereby help all sentient beings. Vajrayana practitioners as well may seem to practice birth control by using and controlling desire, but their intention is also pure. They do not have sex in an ordinary way. They visualize pure deities in their practice with the intention to attain desireless wisdom bliss enlightenment, and so help all sentient beings.

Intention, then, is what is most important. If we believe in the Dharma, then we should practice in either of these two ways or as normal married couples without forethought of preventing birth.

I don't mean to reject birth control if it is the social custom of a country. For those who don't believe in karma, it is not necessary to follow the Buddhist belief in karma. I am speaking only of my own personal conviction.

REBIRTH

Is the Buddhist rebirth doctrine the same for spiritual teachers and ordinary beings? What about for you?

Buddhas are reborn effortlessly through a most powerful wisdom compassion. Bodhisattvas are reborn due to their great and powerful prayers of aspiration in previous lives. Ordinary beings are reborn simply as a result of their karma.

When great teachers are born, they unobstructedly manifest the wisdom compassion of Buddha's mind of enlightenment through various appearances, in whatever way will most benefit the different faculties of sentient beings.

According to the tantric system, when a Lama or yogi has confidence in the realization of fundamental wisdom, this realization appears as the form of the deity. Through the power of his visualization or pride as the deity and with the wish to be reborn, he can either spontaneously enter the mother's womb, or, through the visualization of the parents as wisdom deities, he can transfer his mind in the form of the deity's seed syllable to the mother's womb seen as the deity's palace.

But ordinary beings are reborn due to the ripening of their karma. The root circumstance for rebirth is their attachment to samsara. The contributing circumstances for rebirth are clinging to the parents and the seeds produced through sexual union.

But I myself do not think that I was reborn through unobstructed wisdom compassion or due to my great and powerful prayers of aspiration. From the beginning, although they were inherent in me, I didn't recognize my father, great pure self-phenomena, Kuntuzangpo, and my mother, unchangeable gentle great emptiness, Kuntuzangmo. So I couldn't suck the desireless bliss milk of my mother's breast. I couldn't rest in her uncontrived, natural, smooth love lap, nor could I discern my father's skillful-means love. Although these great parents constantly comforted me without expectation, I separated from them and met my bad-influence playmate, which is ego.

Exactly when my ego began, I don't remember. Anyway, I didn't recognize the unobstructed clarity of wisdom mind. Instead, I saw all phenomena as separate from myself and I grasped at them as objects. I linked with them as a self-existing reality. When I saw good phenomena, I grasped at them and created more desire, and when I saw bad phenomena, I rejected them and created more aversion. These passions generated my karma. I, the subject, and my playmate, the object, united and sought out more friends to play with. I met the ordinary six sense consciousnesses of seeing, hearing, smelling, tasting, touching, and mind. We wandered together in the turbulence of cyclic suffering, aimlessly producing garbage for schizophrenic rats who dwell in the muck of samsara, roaming through cities for countless lives.

EASTERN TEACHERS IN THE WEST

Rinpoche, is it a benefit that so many teachers from the East have come to the West?

It depends on the teachers, the disciples, and the different cultures. It is very difficult to really do enlightenment's practice because it depends on the disciple's practice and belief, and whether or not the teacher has skillful means and wisdom mind. If the disciples don't have belief or the desire to learn and to practice, but are just grasping on to a holy style, then they have just changed from one social custom to another. There is no enlightenment point of view when mind is always clinging to style. Then, mind can't be sublime nor ever change from ordinary mind to wisdom mind.

If a teacher has powerful wisdom mind, he can conquer his disciples' wild minds and lead them toward the wisdom path. Then the disciples will never return from the wisdom path to the ordinary way. If the teacher doesn't have wisdom mind, but only has Dharma's style, he loses it easily to the power custom of the West, using it for the benefit of worldly success. His disciples, as wealthy, powerful men, will use and conquer him through their beautiful constructions, transparent city houses, bankbooks, centers that are the basic support of the Dharma political factory, presidents who are expert Dharma politicians and have close connections to the Lama or his consort, his steward, or whoever has the most power, vice presidents who are waiting for the presidents to die or be expelled, secretaries who are trying to build the support of their own power base, treasurers who are making reservations to be reborn as hungry ghosts, and through all others in the Sangha who are the pathetic underdogs to the executive committee.

In the midst of these beautiful constructions, the mind of a teacher like me who doesn't have wisdom power would be completely corrupted by their god realms' hook. If a teacher has wisdom mind, he never changes no matter who tries to lure him, because he recognizes his wisdom display. So he never rejects bad phenomena and never clings to good phenomena, is never careless toward the poor or subservient to the rich. He can help all without discriminating, through wisdom compassion.

We cannot see into the future, because the outer and inner character of samsara is impermanent. In this present generation, however, it seems that Easterners are deluded by scientific discoveries and dazzled by styles from the West. Their subtle spiritual qualities have become weakened now through seductive Western phenomena.

Westerners are hoping to discover inward spiritual qualities, digging into all bulges and holes frantically, with aggression and torchlights blazing. Adamantly, they are lecturing, talking, and writing about how to discover spiritual qualities.

Each in a different way is seeking the same goal: to grasp worldly power and gain fame and benefit for themselves. It is no different from homosexuals and heterosexuals who have the same goal of getting in a hole, but each considers the qualities of their hole to be unique, while actually the only difference is that one is round and puckered, and the other oval.

It is hard to say which type of Lama is most beneficial for Westerners, because no matter what his qualities are—whether he has a very disciplined mind according to the Vinaya system, whether he is completely compassionate according to the Mahayana system, and whether he has a pure mind and complete bravery according to the Vajrayana—still, when he teaches generously through these three systems, his disciples don't pay attention and don't put into practice what he teaches. Then, when a Lama adopts the ancient king style, it becomes difficult to distinguish his real qualities. Keeping the Lama distinct from ordinary people and using a hierarchical style that keeps him on the top, all disciples become desperate to be with him, holding him in awe and great respect. The more he removes himself from them, the more precious he appears. So, instead of his real qualities becoming precious, the distance becomes precious.

Most Easterners have the habit and ego of holding the precious teachings in awe, at a great distance, thinking of their enlightenment as far away. If a great teacher says to us, "Your Buddha is looking at you from far away. He is covered with beautiful clean clothes like a monk," or, "He is covered with jewels and surrounded by a vast retinue," that makes us feel comfortable, while if the teacher says, "Your Buddha is naked and alone in you," it makes us very uncomfortable. We cannot get actual enlightenment, even if we practice, when we are stuck in the habits of systematic style. Creating complications makes enlightenment more distant.

Westerners especially like to have a substance Buddha, not too heavy, but convenient, like a light handbag. When the Buddha without substance escapes from the bag, they are confused, lose patience, and without understanding that the Dharma is within them, they blame the Lama and the Dharma. When Westerners see the Buddha as substance, they want to use his power for themselves to benefit their substance power. Even if they don't like the Buddha, they like his power, and although they don't want to abandon him, they still don't want to have him sit above them or on the same chair either. The Buddha's power must be less conspicuous than their own to serve their worldly benefit, so they choose to use a powerful landlord's style and make the Buddha their doorman. When they ring the bell, the Buddha must open the door toward their proud chin. Then they give a nod with a faint artificial smile, as they don't want to bow. Then they adopt a greedy businessman style, never thinking of *samaya* or practice, but only thinking of where the profit lies, of advertisements and new ideas to put on the hook.

Eastern people like to keep their valuable things hidden, protected from other people. Westerners like to show them and use them for boasting, but they do not like to give them away. These are two different styles of greed; one is hidden, the other displayed.

TEACHERS

Some teachers, even high and famous ones, seem dishonest, while others appear to be direct and extremely honest. This makes me confused. How can I judge? And some teachers don't seem to have so many good qualities but have many disciples. Then there are some teachers who have such good and pure qualities but have only a few disciples. Why is this?

Honest activity is not always beneficial. Sometimes it causes pain. Actions and words expressed out of time, too soon or too late, even though they seem honest, can cause great pain. For example, an arrow can kill because it is straight. In general, dishonest activity appears to be bad all the time, especially from a teacher whom we trust. But if his activity is done with the pure intention to benefit others that comes from wisdom mind, then it's not necessary to judge him as dishonest. For example, although most conch shells turn to the left, precious and rare ones that turn to the right are most auspicious.

Some teachers, though not having good qualities, have karmic connections from previous lives with their disciples. They have residual "conquering karma." For instance, in a previous life, the disciples may have conquered the teacher, and so their relationship in this life is the response to the previous one. Even though the teacher doesn't have many good qualities, the disciples' phenomena are like fool's gold. Generally, shit is considered disgusting, and yet so many flies are attracted to it.

On the other hand, a teacher with only a few or many disciples, but who has real wisdom qualities, will link with those disciples who have good karma with him from previous lives. Then, without the teacher having an intention of collecting them, disciples come to him naturally through his wisdom light and attend him. The sweet-smelling gardenia has no intention of inviting bees, but still, without invitation, the bees come.

FAITH

For many of us, faith and devotion are words we would prefer to hide, as we are afraid to use them among our fellow disciples, and much more with non-Buddhists. Why?

I don't understand what you mean by saying "hide." It seems there are two reasons why you say "hide." First, you are saying "hide," but that is not what you mean. How can you hide what you do not have? You don't have faith because we are primarily immersed in samsara, in material things, especially those of us from rich countries who are concerned with progress and things that make life easy.

Even if we think we have entered into the Buddhist path, which is beyond the eternalist or nihilist point of view, still, inside we remain gross eternalists grabbing on to an object and to everything as real. So we don't have faith in that which has spiritual qualities, which is beyond materialism.

Or, we are subtle nihilists, sneaky Buddhist thieves. We don't believe in the Dharma, yet we are forever stealing from the treasure house of the Dharmadhatu; we are constantly grasping, using, and trying to possess the innumerable wondrous phenomena of the inexhaustible display. As nihilists, we believe only what we can see in front of us; we cannot believe what is beyond. We believe only in material phenomena, and not in that which possesses spiritual qualities.

So, we always jump from one extreme to another. One time we are eternalists, the next moment nihilists. We never remain in between. Therefore, we can't say "hide," because from the beginning we didn't have faith to hide.

But if we understand actual Dharma for enlightenment, then we have the desire to practice with faith and will not want to boast in front of others. If that is so, then maybe we can say "hide."

But it is difficult to have hidden faith without understanding the main Buddhist point of view. The main difficulty comes from not knowing whether Dharma exists or not, so we have doubt.

What is Dharma? Dharma is not only some letters on pages of a book on a shelf. It is everything, all that happens, both pure and impure phenomena. Everything conceivable is Dharma. We can perceive the world and all its negative and positive phenomena, so how can we say it does not exist? If we believe that Dharma does not exist, then where do all these phenomena come from? Where do we come from? Where are we now?

So we then agree that Dharma does exist. Yet we think we're the result of chance, of a genetic dice game played by our father and mother on a cozy winter night. That's true, we are the result of sexual intercourse, but where do our perceptions, conceptions, and actions come from? All these are constantly changing and therefore constantly moving.

Where does all movement come from? If you think movement comes from a combination of circumstances, like when the rising wind blows the trees, then who perceives this movement? How can we be certain that this movement or solidity exists outside the perceiver? Without a perceiver, how can you know the tree moves? Then, if you think the tree moves, there must be a perceiver, or else how could we acknowledge the movement? The perceiver is the mind's skillful means, and whether or not you believe in a perceiver, there must be an open-space basis for all existing perception. This is called mind.

When Buddha was enlightened under the Bodhi Tree, he said:

I have found a very profound, peaceful, free-from-mental-activity
Unconditioned luminosity, a nectarlike Dharma.
Even though I teach this for all, no one will understand,
So I'd better stay silently under the leaves of the forest.

Lord Buddha just sat with legs in vajra posture with resting desireless lotus eyes, without disagreeing mind, and he remains constantly in timeless, tranquil time.

Even though we have mind the same as Buddha, we don't believe we do. People keep exploring, examining the most minute details of substance in order to understand mind. Philosophers logically philosophize, astrologers calculate, scientists probe, psychologists express, artists create, and all of them continually suffer and disagree because they still miss the target.

The Buddha did not have a brain-wave machine or any of today's modern and sophisticated instruments to arrive at the conclusion that something was happening. You and I as well can reasonably reach the same conclusion. Something is happening. Buddha said that all phenomena are created by the mind.

The mind may be thought of as the subject creating phenomena that it perceives, as in the Buddhist system, or as an object thinking of itself as a creation, as held by those who believe in a supreme being as the creator. For example, if God created man and woman, then God is the subject, and man and woman are the objects created. But if man and woman think God is their creator, then man and woman create the concept of God and so become the subject creating the object, God. In either case, we have subject and object. Sometimes we are subjects and other times objects. The Dharma is everything, be it subject or object. It is relationship between subjects and objects.

So, no matter what we believe, whether we believe we are subjects or objects, we are still friends within the game of Dharma, and it's not necessary for us to have so many contradictions. We may continue to disagree and fight like enemies, but in Dharma we are all the time friends. Some couples are constantly quarreling while sharing one bed, yet are always loving each other on the same bed. It is a paradox, isn't it? We may quarrel with each other, professing our concepts as the only ones holding the truth, yet all these concepts come from the same Dharmata space. One can compare it to a river that starts from a lone source high up in the mountains. As it descends and grows, numerous other rivers branch in and out, but they still all meet again in the ocean.

Whether we believe ourselves to be objects and thus give rise to the concept of a creator of those objects, or we believe ourselves to be the subjects who create the perceived phenomena, in either case we have dualistic mind. In both cases there are two phenomena, subject and object. Through this dualistic mind, we sometimes create bad objects or conceptions, and other times good objects. Anyway, we are all the time suffering between bad and good. If we don't believe this, we should see for ourselves. From bad intention of neurotic mind, we create impure phenomena. This is worldly dharma. From good intention, we create pure phenomena. This is Holy Dharma. But actually, though seemingly different, the two are closely related to each other. Worldly dharma never benefits, as it is perpetuated by negative intentions and neurotic habits. Holy Dharma teaches that by making use of ordinary, impure phenomena, such as the neurotic games we play, the most relevant and precious teachings are realized. It is important to make use of our own phenomena. For example, without anger, we cannot realize mirrorlike wisdom. When the ordinary, neurotic mind gets angry, we want to fight, to subdue our enemy, the source of our anger. Here we can either use so-called worldly patience to suppress anger, or otherwise we can watch our mind, see its nature, and thus allow the subject-object fixation to disappear and release the space of mirrorlike wisdom. This is Holy Dharma.

Even though we have the basis of enlightenment, we cannot enter on the right path since we do not know how to make the most beneficial use of phenomena. Using phenomena is of benefit only when there is clarity as to the right method. This is Holy Dharma.

By practicing this Holy Dharma, we can go beyond the perception of bad and good phenomena, realizing all phenomena to be of one taste. This is the gateway to the vast open space of enlightenment.

So, we need Holy Dharma to go beyond duality, where both subject and object vanish. We must change useless worldly dharma into useful Holy Dharma and temporary Holy Dharma into the ultimate spiritual qualities that are manifested in teachers who have wisdom mind.

Then the problem with faith doesn't come from hiding it or from fear of using words such as *faith* and *devotion*. The problem lies in our misunderstanding of Dharma. Without a proper understanding, we don't have faith, and consequently we have no devotion for the teacher. Faith belongs only to a sublime person who has these seven wealths: faith, morality, generosity, a mind that is open and subdued through listening to Holy Dharma, discipline in relation to oneself, nobility in relation to others, and wisdom. We are ordinary, so we don't have actual faith.

The Buddha taught many different kinds of faith. We cannot write about them all because it would cover so many pages. So maybe we will only speak of three different types of faith: clearness faith, craving faith, and trusting faith.

Clearness faith is when you see or hear about spiritual qualities and your mind becomes clear and clean without concepts. Like a child going into a temple with beautiful images and tangkas [holy paintings], his mind spontaneously becomes clean and happy even though he has no understanding of the meaning.

Craving faith is based on good spiritual qualities that we see or hear about and that we then try to attain. For example, a hungry person craves food and tries to obtain it.

Trusting faith has no doubt toward the teacher even if his actions are wrathful or seductive, even if he pushes us into hell or leads us to purelands. There is no doubt.

We should have reasonable faith through our understanding mind. But if we cannot have reasonable faith, then we should at least have blind faith with a stable mind.

It is very difficult, however, to have trusting faith in the teacher. For instance, if we have worked with material objects all of our lives, expecting material rewards in return, we now also expect the same of our teacher. But his teachings are substanceless, and though we don't express it outwardly, inwardly we feel deprived. We do not have faith in the spiritual qualities he offers; we only expect material rewards, that which we can see and feel immediately, now, now, now.

Our materialistic habit is very strong. Even if we receive spiritual teachings, we don't recognize or understand the meaning because they are substanceless. Buddhism predominantly speaks of spiritual qualities, which are beyond substance. We are afraid because we don't like to separate ourselves from substance, from heavy habits. Even if we talk about enlightenment, which is light, we are afraid to become light and light. We want to feel the ground under our feet, solid, heavy, dull, and obscured.

Without faith, then, of course, we don't have devotion. With actual faith and a good karmic connection with a Lama, we can have immediate results. For instance, throughout life we experience sorrow at the separation from friends, family, and lovers, and at the loss of material things. At such a time, we become very depressed and are unable to find comfort in anything. But if we have a connection with and fervent devo-

tion to a spiritual teacher, we can learn from him the practice of meditation and the understanding of how to transmute this sorrow into the
wisdom of tranquillity.

If we check, we can find that even in a worldly way, a spiritual teacher
is necessary. We may think that we can learn from books, which are substance, or from teachers who speak of substance, but where do the ideas
about airplanes, automobiles, and such, come from? They do not come
only from substance; they come from the conceiver of the idea, from the
insubstantial spiritual qualities of the inventor. How can we have trust
in the use of these material marvels without some respect for the inventor, the teacher who explains their use?

Because we don't understand that Buddha nature exists within our
natural mind, we must depend on a wisdom-heart teacher to make these
qualities blossom. So we must have faith. Otherwise, we won't be able to
link with him. If we don't link with him, how can we increase our spiritual qualities? From beginningless time until now, we have been unable
to increase and express these qualities, but if we have faith in a teacher,
we can make this link, which is crucial for our development.

Before we link with a teacher, we should examine him carefully to see
if his qualities are bad or good. We must be sure that his motivation is
pure, with the intention to help all sentient beings. But after we decide
to take teachings and link with him, then it is best not to examine anymore; otherwise, we will create obstacles through impure perception.

We all have dormant negative paranoia and positive qualities, which
arise according to contributing circumstances. The root circumstance
of our negativity is the seed of our negative paranoia, and contributing circumstances that can cause this dormant negativity to surface are
the teacher's human activity and his environment. If we begin to examine negative circumstances around the teacher, we will create more and
more negative obstacles. Teachers appear in human form; consequently,
many positive as well as negative circumstances surround them. Disciples with pure and impure intention flock around them and create the
full spectrum of negative and positive circumstances. So it is best that
once we have chosen a teacher, we don't examine or judge, but stay pure
with good intention. Then, automatically, the seed of negative paranoia

is burned out and we are freed from negativity, while the seed of enlightenment, formerly lying dormant, blossoms, making us realize that all appearances are pure phenomena.

It is unfortunate, however, that devotion alone is not enough. It is possible for us to have strong devotion and yet end up more confused and in sorrow than if we had never begun in Dharma. If we jump into Dharma without carefully examining the teacher, we may select one who is not skillful in relating to our unique faculties and problems. The teacher may use the wrong approach and leave us crazy and worse off than before. This is not to say that the Lama is a fraud. The Buddha taught countless different teachings to liberate sentient beings from suffering, and it is beyond a single teacher, unless he is a Buddha, to be skillful in all these teachings. So we must be careful to select a Lama who has wisdom mind and who can relate to our unique paranoia. Only then can we receive the substanceless teachings the Lama offers. Without both devotion and a skillful teacher, there is no connection and the teachings are not transmitted.

Samaya

Nowadays, people everywhere are revolting against hierarchical forms of manipulation and power—king, dictator, guru, etc.—and they seek freedom. Then they want Dharma to help them become free, and when they come to Dharma, they find the epitome of hierarchical structure. Why? How can I adapt to this when I don't believe in it? I hear from Tibetans that they have great suffering and fear because of their samayas. Then what is the benefit when it brings suffering instead of comfort?

The intention of samaya is a plan for agreement. We bow to those whom we consider high and do service to them in expectation of rewards. The purpose of samaya is to protect our interests and keep an agreement so that the outcome is successful.

If we think that samaya exists only within a Holy Dharma system or Tibetan system, then we misunderstand the meaning. Even if we have never heard of the word *samaya* before nor practiced Holy Dharma, samaya is essential to all agreement and communication regardless of our intention to keep vows or samaya. In a worldly way, we are continuously bound by promises, which is the same as samaya. This is to say that samaya is always secretly present within our own mind and in the external world. There is nowhere we can go or stay to get away from laws and rules, which are samaya. In a country, if there are no laws or rules, then how can we progress socially and economically? All would turn into chaos and confusion without laws. Rules and laws are the basis of organization and progress; their neglect is the basis of confusion and failure. Countries sign treaties in fear of invasion by common enemies; this is samaya.

Animals must keep animal samaya; human beings must keep human samaya. Ants must keep their common samaya and stay together in their hole in order to continue to exist. If they went off to the web of a spider, they would get entangled in different phenomena, with different samaya. Then again, there is samaya between animals and humans. If domestic animals just keep their own samaya with humans and stay in their houses, life is very comfortable for them. If they venture out into the jungle where wild animals roam, life becomes violent.

If in a family the samaya is kept, then life remains harmonious and comfortable. If it is broken, however, problems arise. If the samaya is kept between a king and his subjects, or a government and its people, then a comfortable and peaceful existence is attained. If the samaya is not kept, then disharmony, confusion, and revolution result and their country is lost. If we don't keep samaya, everything becomes violent.

Even though some Westerners don't want to communicate with Easterners and some Easterners don't want to communicate with Westerners, they do communicate. They interact in business, trade, politics, and power, so through this communication, they have samaya.

Samaya and the degree to which we abide by it, whether completely, partially, or not at all, depends upon the individual. Throughout the world, jails are full with individuals who disagree with and break the social samaya of their country.

Poor people disagree with the economics samaya of the rich who oppress them, break it, and so are put in jail.

Rich people disagree with the economics samaya of communist countries that oppress them, break it, and so are put in jail.

Bartenders fill your glass with 100 percent pure samaya at ten o'clock and 50 percent at twelve o'clock.

Taxi drivers take you the long way around, while the meter runs up, and break the shortcut samaya with devious mind.

Some lovers kiss with passionate samaya, but the lotus flower remains untouched.

Swaying samaya hips veiled in skintight jeans promise things unseen to frustrated men with bulging eyes.

Doctors prescribe comforting samaya, that never ends.

Border customs officials check the suitcase samaya with one suspicious eye while the other winks at your wallet.

Police enforce the law of samaya with one hand holding a gun and the other with an open palm.

Dignified lawyers in a loud and eloquent manner defend the samaya with their clients and whisper concessions in the judge's ear.

Political leaders wave the flag of samaya high over their head and accept political favors with their other hand under the table.

Voting ballot boxes are sealed with a samaya padlock during the day and are broken at night.

In Buddhism, many different systems of vows and samaya are taken depending on the individual's propensities and practice. The following are some of the most important among them: refuge vows, *bodhichitta* vows, *upasaka*[2] vows, *getsul*[3] vows, *gelong*[4] vows, three outer tantric samayas, three inner tantric samayas, and the four great samayas of Mahasandhi.[5] There are countless other vows and samayas, but it is not necessary to list all of them here; if you want, you can find them in the texts. It is not necessary to keep all of these vows, but only those that you choose for your own practice toward enlightenment. Then you should abide by them.

As practitioners, we also take many tantric initiations and we may get confused, thinking that we must simultaneously keep the samayas of them all; yet this is not necessarily true. For instance, while living in the East, we must abide by Eastern laws and not be concerned with the laws of the West. If we attempt to keep the laws of both places, we only get confused. In one country, it may be good manners to belch after a meal, but in another it would be considered rude. How can you belch and not belch at the same time?

Why is samaya to be kept?

We don't want to keep samaya. We want to go somewhere beyond samaya, as samaya is so complicated, is difficult to keep, and makes us so weary and worries us so much. Yet if we want to go beyond samaya, we first have to keep our samaya.

If we want to live without a target, we must first aim at the target of targetlessness. If keeping samaya seems difficult and painful and a source of suffering, then we must keep samaya aiming at liberation from samaya. As long as we are grasping at concepts, we are bound by samaya, since we are bound by karma, so if we want to avoid excessive suffering and attain temporary happiness, or if we want to go beyond all suffering and attain enlightenment, we have to keep certain rules of conduct, avoiding some acts and performing others as much as possible. If we want liberation from samaya, we must reach liberation from karma, and in order to reach liberation from karma and from samaya, we must keep a samaya system. The highest samaya is the samaya of nongrasping or nonconceptuality, which can be kept only when we rest in natural mind beyond grasping, concepts, karma, or samaya. In order to keep this highest samaya, we must be beyond constantly checking our experience and our actions from the standpoint of some samaya system. When we manage to keep this samaya, we are beyond samaya and so we have reached our target and gone beyond all the suffering and weariness involved in keeping samaya.

But what about all the people who stay away from the Dharma because they hear about complicated samayas and about the hells they will fall into if they don't manage to keep the samaya?

We are thirsty and want water, but we don't want all the work involved in getting the water. We don't want work, complications, or perils. We are lazy and want to be free. Yet we cannot be free, because we are thirsty. And we cannot quench our thirst, because we are lazy. We don't want to go, we don't want to stay—catch-22. All this creates confusion and complications, and we try to remove ourselves from these complications. We have to do what we don't want to do in order to get what we want. If these people don't want to enter the Dharma from fear of the samaya that is to be kept, they should know that they still have to keep their worldly samaya and be subject to the law of karma. If they have to keep samaya anyhow, it is better to keep a samaya that ultimately leads them beyond samaya-keeping and all the weariness involved in it. It is inevitable to do what one does not want to do in order to get what one wants. If we can keep the inner and secret tantric samayas and our intention is pure, then there will always be benefit.

Whatever samaya we have, we must keep it without making complications. Samaya is complicated, and so, since we want liberation from samaya, in order to attain liberation from samaya, we keep samaya. When we practice or depend on Dharma, we must keep samaya, and we must do this correctly without a rigid mind. We must open more and more rather than create more and more samayas to keep and to grasp at. Otherwise, samaya will never exhaust itself.

If we take samayas without practicing, then we only create our own suffering through remorse and worry; we create more and more laws, more and more samsara, and more and more suffering. This is not true samaya. If we really want to take pure samaya, then we must practice with pure intention in order to attain enlightenment. As practice improves, samaya dissolves. We become more and more open and natural, and our intentions and our phenomena also become more and more natural. Then, all samsaric and all lower rigid Dharma samaya conceptions naturally fall away. We reach sublime samaya and then we must go beyond that also, until we no longer need to depend on sublime samaya but can rest in samaya-less samaya. If we want to climb upstairs, we must depend on the ground floor to reach the first floor, and on the first floor to reach the second floor, and so on. Yet, when we reach the second floor, we don't need to continue to think of the first floor. When we reach the top, we don't need to think of all the floors below. When we ultimately rest in natural mind without coming in or out of it, the mind of hoping and expecting disappears, and no conceptions about upper or lower samayas remain.

According to our capabilities, we should decide which samaya is most important and most beneficial for us and keep that. It is also important to remember that lower samayas are automatically contained and kept within the higher samayas.

The teachings and their effects depend upon the individual. If both disciple and teacher have no understanding and their minds are narrow, samaya becomes a jail and the disciple becomes a prisoner, all because of the teacher's own grasping and paranoia. If the teacher has wisdom mind and the disciple is very pure and stable, this is precious; then, by keeping samaya, the disciple will be able to go beyond samaya.

Unfortunately, nowadays there are ordinary-minded teachers who don't keep their samaya with their disciples. They have great self-seeking concern for the students' samaya and may say, "You must not do this or that; otherwise, you'll break your samaya." They forget their part of the trust, however, and the relationship becomes corrupt. Of course, it is very important for disciples to keep their samaya, as it is something very precious and necessary for enlightenment, but at the same time, the teacher should keep his samaya with his disciples. If our teacher is a wisdom teacher with a sublime mind, then every act he does is unobstructed wisdom spontaneously manifesting for our benefit and that of all sentient beings. He is saying and doing everything without attachment. But if he is an ordinary person like us, then he must have samaya with us.

Why do we go to teachers? It is because we don't want suffering. We seek liberation from samsara, from suffering. We want to be free, to become simple, not more and more complicated and entangled in samsara.

If, for the benefit of his consort or retinue, the teacher breaks samaya with a disciple, this can be harmful for those who trust him. For instance, leaders of countries and people who are very influential must take care of their responsibilities and keep their laws. They cannot expect their underlings to do everything without direction; otherwise, their position is in jeopardy.

There are also close disciples of Lamas who misuse their position by manipulating others for their own benefit. In their greed for power, they threaten humble disciples with a samaya gun. They say, "Rinpoche wants you to do this or that. If you don't do it, you break your samaya, which will result in obstacles, illnesses, or even death and rebirth in vajra hell." If you want to be of real benefit to your teacher, all sentient beings, and yourself, then you should keep samaya. It is not necessary, however, to feel intimidated by or afraid of these samaya guns. In spite of threats, karma must manifest anyway. Consequently, obstacles, illnesses, and even death will touch us all. Yet it does not follow that this karma comes as a result of breaking samaya. Some of the greatest Bodhisattvas have faced many obstacles even though their intention and activity were pure. They purified the karma of their past lives and used these bad circumstances to teach others through example about karma and suffering. If the threat of broken samaya comes to you with the samaya gun loaded and a black intention bullet pointed at your superstitious-mind target, at that time, if you tremble with fear, you may create a narrow-mind target and the bullet can penetrate. Instead, relax your mind in clear, vast freedom space like the sky, and let them shoot; then the bullet can only fall back down.

Rinpoche, what about the problems with hierarchy and kings, with Dharma's hierarchical style?

Hierarchical systems are not found only in Tibetan Dharma custom. Wherever there is a group, the most powerful one, whether in physical strength or in intelligence, will become the leader. In countries, cities, schools, villages, hospitals, armies, political parties, religious groups, etc., there is always some kind of king and a hierarchical power structure under him. The powerful become the dictators of the weaker. We can find dictators everywhere. If we like the democratic, the fascist, or the communist system, we must be aware of the fact that within all of these, there is some kind of dictatorship. Where there is power, it is used. Where have we seen someone with power who says, "Oh, I don't want to use it, as that would make us unequal"? In a democracy, the ones in power who have been elected by the people give orders to those beneath them, and those who don't follow the rules and orders may be put in jail by armed policemen. According to the law, they cannot resist arrest without creating a further offense that will result in an extended jail sentence. The ones at the top rule and dictate; the ones at the bottom must obey. In communism, dictatorship is more obvious; they even call the socialist government "the proletariat's dictatorship," although the dictator is one man or a group of men whom the proletariat must obey. In fascism, dictatorship is perhaps even more obvious.

Until enlightenment, we cannot live outside of hierarchy or de facto dictatorships. If children become more powerful than their parents, they will become dictators over them. If parents are more powerful than children, they will become dictators over them. If a wife is more powerful than her husband, she will be a dictator over him. If the husband is more powerful, he will be a dictator over her. Until we reach enlightenment, there will be a dictatorship. As long as there are two, one is stronger.

So, we cannot judge the Eastern Dharma customs as being altogether wrong. They arose from social customs and they will change according to how social customs change. Even now, we have a hierarchical totalitarian structure in our own psychological makeup, which we internalized through conditioning from our families, schools, and social structures in general. Thus, even nowadays, we need Dharma to be taught in a hierarchical way so that we may be freed from the net of our internalized hierarchical structures.

If we have faith in Dharma, we must have respect toward any teacher who has wisdom mind, who is a sublime person, who has compassion, or who can lead sentient beings in the right way. Until we have acquired all of our teacher's spiritual qualities, we must hold him in great respect since otherwise we won't acquire them. And even after acquiring his qualities, we should show respect and great devotion toward him.

Respect toward the teacher is necessary in order to establish a difference between the enlightened state and samsara. The distance and respect show that there is a difference between samsara and nirvana, that nirvana is most excellent and highest, and that we must strive to transcend samsara and attain nirvana. We must learn which qualities are enlightenment's higher qualities, and why they are higher. Then we will be inspired to strive to attain these qualities, and our respect to the teacher who embodies them will help us to attain them ourselves. When we attain them, we will be respected by others, and we will have to accept their respect if we want to help them to attain the same qualities.

We tend to think, "Oh, these Tibetan customs, all this respect toward Lamas ... Tibetan customs are very difficult." Then we become pathetic, experience great suffering, and lose ourselves. There are many ways to show respect, however, not only prostrating or bowing. A facial expression, a smile, or a "hello" can be a sign of respect. Respect exists everywhere in all aspects of life. Our bewilderment comes from the fact that in Tibetan customs, respect is expressed in ways that are different from those we are used to. Students must have respect toward their teacher; otherwise they won't learn and they won't trust or believe what he says or put it into practice. Good manners are a sign of respect. We cannot exist harmoniously without respect.

This is not to say that all teachers have qualities worthy of respect. Some teachers use distance and respect to make themselves precious even though they don't have good qualities.

DHARMA CENTERS

Do you think that Vajrayana can really be practiced properly by Westerners, whose minds are often lacking the basic stability that comes with the training and discipline of the Tibetan monasteries or Dharma centers?

Padmasambhava said to King Trisong Detsen, "In my tantra or Vajrayana teachings, the essential thing is point of view. So don't lose your activities toward point of view. If you do, you will have neither virtue nor sin, and you will remain in nihilism. Also, don't lose your point of view toward activities. If you lose your point of view by being constantly involved in activity, you can never have time to become liberated. So practice with point of view and activities inseparable."

Individually, I cannot judge the differences between Westerners and Easterners because, as Buddha Shakyamuni said, "No one can make judgments about individual faculties except for me and those like me." Nevertheless, in the light of my perception of the social habits of the affluent West, if I make a rough judgment through my contradictory mind, then I must say that in general, Westerners, especially Americans, might be inclined to lose their meritorious activity toward point of view, through their "take-it-easy" and "push-button" habits. They might go grasping after high Vajrayana teachings and, before reaching the target, fall in the gutter. Then meritorious activity is lost and they sleep on nihilistic beds without a merit blanket.

Easterners, especially those who talk about Mahayana and Vajrayana, tend to neglect the point of view and are predominantly attached to external Dharma activities with an attitude of expectation and craving. Wherever there is craving, automatically, more samsara is created. So they sleep enclosed within small-aim boudoirs, covered with enormous, rigid, pure Dharma activity blankets without a point-of-view pillow.

All this stuff about Westerners and Tibetans is a matter of different karmas, and it is because there are so many different karmas that the answer to this question is not obvious. Some people who appear to have holy karma turn out to have bad karma, as in the case of the monk Lekpe Karma. After many years of studying directly with Buddha Shakyamuni himself, he had one bad conception. He thought that other than the arm's length of light emanating from the Buddha, there was no difference between them. This idea caused him to abandon the Buddha and resulted in many difficult and unhappy lifetimes for him.

Other people may appear to have worldly karma, but in fact, through worldly karma, they have the opportunity to make good karma. An example of this is King Indrabodhi. Although he appeared to have samsara's karma, when his good karma ripened, he was able to practice Dharma without abandoning his royal position.

As to whether or not monasteries in the Tibetan fashion are beneficial, the answer again is not definitive, as it depends on the karma of individuals. Rigdzin Jigme Lingpa said, "If you really aren't weary of samsara, monasteries and centers become just like a big house. If you really want to have pure practice, then you'd better not go from a small house to a big house."

Wherever there are monasteries or centers, there are also Lamas, directors, and systems. If they don't set up classical systems, then they are not a benefit to the monastery. If they do, then they create a bureaucracy involved in very much work, secretly whispering behind closed doors and conspiring to oust those outside their clique who have pure Dharma intentions, offering extravagant banquets with inner black intentions, and in general being constantly overwhelmed by worldly business. In this sense, the only difference between a monastery and a government are the clothes and the name; otherwise, everything is the same. So don't make spiritual gangster groups with the retinue and sponsors of high Lamas who by their conniving are more dangerous than Hitler or Mao Zedong. Murder kills the body of one lifetime; wrong intentions destroy innumerable lifetimes.

Nevertheless, I don't mean to criticize monasteries or centers. If we can keep our inner practice and pure motivation within the center's traditional environment, then they can be the basis of Sangha and an opportunity to benefit all sentient beings. Moreover, in such places we may encounter sublime individuals, and associating with them and assimilating their spiritual qualities can lead even ordinary persons toward enlightenment. For instance, in ancient times there were many famous centers such as Nalanda in India and Samye in Tibet. Many great scholars became siddhas after being involved in these centers. They were led to enlightenment, like flocks of white geese, by their sublime teachers. Yet not all who passed through these centers became siddhas. We cannot make general judgments about the practice and the qualities of those who have spent time in a monastery or with a Lama because, as we have already seen, the results they obtain will depend on their individual karma and skillful means. If their karma is bad, then even the disciples, retinue, or family of a great Lama who spend their whole life with him may never come to understand his goodness or his real qualities. Such people only appear to have good karma, as they misuse their positions and make bad karma. Other disciples might have real faith and pure practice, even though they are not so close to the Lama.

Even though I can't make judgments, in one way, what you asked about the monasteries in the East and practice in the West seems true. This is because, although Westerners have highly developed scientific systems based on progress and can do many things very easily through substances and materials, Dharma cannot be "done" through material things. Natural mind, which is the support of the Dharma, is beyond substance. Because there is no substance to grasp, it is not easy to recognize and it is not easy to teach or to learn; consequently, wisdom teaching cannot be seen or found easily. People have a strong materialistic habit, which makes them want to perceive only in terms of external objects. Because people have this habit, they don't believe in or recognize the transcendental nature of their own minds. Even if they do recognize it, they become impatient and can't practice, as practice is not easy and they have the habit of doing things easily. All samsaric worldly phenomena are impermanent; since things can change, we cannot say for certain that all Westerners are unable to practice. But neither can we say that all Tibetans are experienced about Dharma. Westerners who previously had greedy minds searched out all material methods for gratification. From their earliest childhood, whether or not they are poor, they are surrounded with material inventions, such as televisions, cars, and stoves; they are used to everything and there is not much more to use. Many among them have become tired of all this substance and are ready for something else. Of course, I can't say for certain whether their substance-habits are too strong, in which case it is very difficult to practice because of residual habits; or whether they are really tired, in which case they can practice with tired mind and are ready for Dharma.

Previously, conditions were good for Dharma in the East. In ancient times in Tibet, there were many good teachers and saints who had wisdom mind. This was passed on through many generations of teachers and parents so that now there are many people whose habit is Dharma. But the times have changed and the minds of some may have become more materialistic. Also, while some among them appear to be more experienced with Dharma, practicing constantly, pushing their beads, they are actually just practicing substance-habit without substance. Real practice is in general very difficult for Westerners. Of course, Easterners and Westerners have the same mind based on wisdom intelligence, but there are different systems of intelligence. One relies on the mind while the other relies on materialism.

French, English, and Central Tibetans have similar mind styles, although their social customs are somewhat different. In some ways, Eastern Tibetans and Americans also have similar habits, but Eastern Tibetans tend to be too stable while Americans tend to be too unstable. Each of these has good and bad sides. Stability, for instance, can be either a benefit or an obstacle. It is an obstacle when it does not move, only staying on one level and never acquiring new good qualities. Real stability begins with a big decision to practice until the result is reached. Even though phenomena or experience may change, the decision of the mind is completely stable. People with good stability can automatically develop their qualities and become sublime. Stupid stability occurs when people resist changes even if they are beneficial. This only looks like stability but is really an obstacle to achieving good qualities, as it makes one always remain on one level or stage. There are also two different kinds of instability: useful unstable mind, which is a temporary benefit for this present life and an ultimate benefit for enlightenment, and obstacle unstable mind, which is constantly jumping and completely lacking the patience to examine the teachings. The first kind of unstable mind helps one to change from bad to good habits, and from good habits to beyond good or bad until the result of enlightenment phenomena is reached. People with the other kind of instability are constantly changing from good to bad habits without examining everything. The ultimate benefit can never be reached because they are constantly changing with no stability or purpose.

Solitude

If you really want to practice with pure intention, would it be more beneficial to be in a solitary place?

This depends on the individual's intention. If your intention is not clear, if you aren't really weary of samsara, then going on retreat is just another game. Even if you stayed for your whole life, you would just be wasting time and you would not learn anything. Many animals spend their lives in caves or in the ground like groundhogs, just eating and shitting without practicing Dharma. The Buddha said that people who go on retreat without first understanding real Dharma have the solitude of a demon's hook. The same is true for those who understand Dharma but have no intention of benefiting sentient beings, just wanting to go from samsara's suffering to samsara's vacation. When people who have spent time in solitude without understanding come out of retreat, only hair, beards, and fingernails are longer; otherwise, everything is the same. When they come out, they have more ego than before and they boast about their accomplishments with saintly pride or siddha arrogance. A person who has the maturity to be in solitude can progress and develop through solitude's beautiful appearances—deer, trees, green meadows, cool running springs. Until our dualistic mind has dissolved into nondualistic mind, we must depend on these beautiful appearances, because good objects make good feelings, good-habit phenomena, and good karma.

According to the higher tantric system, the outer and inner elements come from the potential essence of secret elements. Until all the secret five elements blossom into the wisdom deity's mandala, we must practice with the inner elements. If we live in a samsaric city or monastery where there are many people involving us in anger, desire, jealousy, and confusion, where the surroundings are very dirty and the air is not clean, then our inner elements become more impure because of these bad external circumstances. The potential of the inner five elements becomes obscured. If we go to a hermitage or isolated place, then all the impure external five elements are far away from us and the pure ones are near.

External fresh air cleans our inner breath, which is related to the element air; pure sunshine without smog purifies our body's warmth, which is related to the element fire; and fresh food and water clean our blood and the body's fluids, which are related to the element water. All of these good circumstances combine to make a healthy body whose solidity is related to the element earth, and the clean country space or open blue sky unties the natural mind, which is related to the element space. Even if conceptions arise about your enemies, there is no actual enemy-object there, and so no cause exists for quarreling. Your mind automatically becomes peaceful when you are surrounded by beautiful deer and other tranquil animals who wander by with peaceful mind. Even though there are no friends, the peaceful animals keep you company with harmless expressions, and if you like to gossip, the only response is the song of beautiful birds. Compassion naturally increases in these surroundings.

If it is winter, when all the leaves are blown away by dry winds, these circumstances remind one of impermanence and mortality, and one becomes weary of samsara. If there is a river, then all of samsara's mental chatter drowns in the river's soothing roar. If snow or gentle rain falls, then you remember the graceful blessings of the deity. When the sun and moon shine, memories arise of the warmth and glow of your Guru's blessings. There are so many good qualities in solitude.

Buddha Shakyamuni said that whoever takes even seven steps toward a solitary place with the intention to attain enlightenment brings about immeasurable benefit.

In ancient times, many sublime individuals like Padmasambhava gave blessings in sacred places for the benefit of future practitioners. In the present time of the *kaliyuga*, we can receive these blessings from those sacred places. Because of this, we can automatically realize many qualities if we can do our solitary practice with pure intention.

If you are separated from ordinary-desire mothers, never mind; you can meet the discerning-wisdom-mind mother who plays with her display children through these sacred places.

If you are separated from ordinary-anger fathers, never mind; you can meet the mirrorlike-wisdom father through these sacred places.

If you are separated from your ordinary, ignorant children, never mind; you can meet the fresh, open Dharmadhatu wisdom-mind children through these sacred places.

If you are separated from your ordinary, proud teacher, never mind; you can meet the equanimity-mind wisdom teacher through these sacred places.

If you are separated from your ordinary, jealous friends in the Sangha, never mind; you can meet the all-accomplishing-action wisdom mind friend through these sacred places.

If you are separated from your ordinary sponsor, never mind; you can find all the jewel-like phenomena that are the treasure of the Dharmadhatu in these sacred places.

If you are separated from hunterlike disciples who use their teacher for their own selfish benefit, never mind; you can find countless obedient skillful-means disciples who are never distant from your awareness wisdom mind teacher.

If you are separated from your ordinary, fickle lover who is uncertain like summer weather, never mind; you can find a wisdom Dakini who always has desireless wisdom love in these sacred places.

CHANGE

Some people say that change is good; some say it's unstable activity. What do you think?

Really, Dharma is for changing: from a lower space to a higher space, from a narrow space to an open space, from a bad space to a good space, from an artificial space to a natural space, from heavy space to light space, from substance to substancelessness, from suffering to happiness. But what a sad story it is. The teachers are teaching, and the listeners who are listening, are they really listening, are they really accepting Mahayana and Vajrayana teachings?

If we try to change, then Mahayana Buddhists don't like it, especially Easterners. They think that it is bad to change, that it is reversed activity, something contrary to Dharma. Of course, it is bad to change from high to low, from open to narrow, from good to bad, from natural to artificial, from light to heavy, from happiness to suffering. What is the benefit of Dharma if that's the change?

The Buddha continually went through changes until enlightenment. Was he bad for changing from samsara to nirvana, from impure phenomena to pure phenomena?

If we don't like change, then there is no need to eat fresh food; let's just wait until the maggots have made their homes there, the food is rotten, and we're sick to our stomach. If we don't like change, why bother with clean clothes? Let's just wait until the lice have made their homes there and gone to war with each other. If we don't like change, let's try to deny that phenomena are continually changing. How are we going to control this change? Buddha taught that change is the way.

Show me a place we can stay without changing. If we want to rest and stay in the Dharmakaya, we must change. But if all we want is dullness and stupidity, then what can anyone do for us? What can we do for ourselves?

Nowadays, it is said that activity is very important, even if we are Mahayana or Vajrayana practitioners. Many teachers have told this to their disciples and many disciples believe it. Is this pure activity created by dualistic mind or by nondualistic mind? If it is created by dualistic or deluded mind, then the mind becomes increasingly uptight. We always depend upon dualism and so we create more and more neurotic power and conceptions. When are we going to liberate the mind from this?

More and more, we are hoping for pure activity and rejecting impure activity. Because of these continuous hopes and fears, increasingly we create impure phenomena. Nevertheless, changing depends on our own capacity, and it develops through our intentions. We cannot, however, measure with our own capacity the abilities of others. How can we measure another's intentions or another's mind? Let us not get caught up in judging.

Whether we desire worldly knowledge or Dharma knowledge, we must make our pursuit true to our own capacity. If we act beyond our capacity, even though there may be temporary rewards, finally we will destroy ourselves through this indulgence. For example, one donkey lusted after crops, but he was afraid that if he approached them in his natural state as a donkey, he would get beaten. So he wore a tiger's skin to appear more dangerous, but the villagers, fearing the dangerous tiger, killed him.

I am not saying we should be radical and jump in the water with clothes on for the sake of change. It's fine to change dress style for entertainment, but we must be careful, because if our intention is to change toward enlightenment, we must not concern ourselves too much with our own bodies or we might miss the great desireless body.

It seems that our point of view toward change comes from the mouth only. We say that we want to change toward nirvana, but actually until this day, we have never wanted to make such a change.

It does not matter if we don't want to change; we can stagnate until our eyes become dim and we continually have to adjust our glasses at the end of our nose. What to do?

When people are motivated toward outer change, they easily become excited and proud to change. But really to change from dualistic mind to sublime mind, from sublime mind to high mind, from high mind to supreme mind, one must increase the display of wisdom qualities and continually acknowledge wisdom mind, which does not necessarily excite people so easily.

In ancient times, there were many siddhas who attained enlightenment. They were considered outcasts by society due to their unorthodox actions. But by these fearless activities and changes, they were able to attain realization, whereas we who have taken many vows, made promises, and taken initiations still do not have the intention to change, but would rather make excuses as to why we can't practice. We take more vows, which ultimately restrict change.

ARROGANCE

Rinpoche, I observe many disciples who have contact with famous Lamas, yet they appear obviously arrogant. Then what is the benefit?

It is not necessary to think of the disciples of famous or unknown Lamas as either bad or good. They may have the good fortune or karma to meet with the Lamas, but unfortunately, some will go one way and others a different way depending on the disciples' skillful means. Like a sharp knife coated with honey, you can either lick it clean and derive the benefits of taste and health, or you can cut your tongue.

The problem is that some of us cannot adapt in the right way to the teachings of our high teachers.

If the high Lama lives in a scholarly style, we, the disciples, only take on the outer or visible appearance of the Lama, the way he acts, lectures, and teaches, etc. We don't know how to take on the teacher's inner qualities, because they are so profound and deep that our ordinary mind cannot recognize them.

If the teacher appears in yogic style, we, the disciples, only imitate the outer form. Though it looks as if we have entered the Vajrayana and have taken the samaya vows, we don't really see pure phenomena, due to our neurotic mind. We only adopt the yogi image.

Even if the Lama is pure in morality, both in intention and conduct, we cannot discipline our minds.

From the very beginning, even if we say to our teacher that we want enlightenment, we actually have only wrong worldly intentions. We go to the highest scholars, yogis, and Lamas, but we don't want to change or relate to their inner qualities because we don't know that all material qualities come from immaterial, substanceless qualities. Even if we do know this, we don't want to accept and use these pure qualities because they are distant from our impure intentions. We only want to acquire and use outer material qualities as quickly as possible to make us feel powerful and comfortable in a social context.

Of course, we should meet with high or famous Lamas, but if we are not careful and we cannot learn from them in the right way, it makes us more black of heart and enlightenment more remote.

If the qualities of scholarly Lamas are very vast and if disciples can relate to them properly, then all can be used to create vast knowledge. But by comparing and judging, by thinking, "Our Lama is very knowledgeable and others are not," etc., the vast qualities of the teachers are only used to create narrow-mindedness, thus closing the door to knowledge with the latch of arrogance. Those who are swollen with arrogance have the greatest obstacle for acquiring knowledge. Since their bloodshot intellectual eyes are completely blinded by their arrogance, they can never see good qualities in others, and as a result, their own good qualities can never develop, just as water can never enter a solid iron ball no matter how much you pour on it.

Even if we have a teacher with a pure lifestyle like Buddha Shakyamuni, if we cannot learn from him in the right way, through this association our mind might become impure. Automatically, we give rise to negative feelings toward other teachers; we want to boast all the time about our relationship with a famous teacher. Sometimes, from our boasting, we get praised by others who aspire to attain the same identity with high Lamas. If we possess some good qualities, we want to parade around showing off like a proud cock. If we are disciples of unknown Lamas who possess good qualities, no one will notice them. We prefer to be associated only with those who will bring us recognition. If an ordinary person wears real diamonds, everyone thinks the jewels are fake. If a rich person wears fake diamonds, everyone thinks they are real.

But this is not to say that we cannot praise our Lama; of course, we should praise our teacher. We can derive much benefit from this, but only if our intention is pure, without expecting praise or rewards from this association. Lord Buddha Shakyamuni said, "Without a Lama, there are no more Buddhas, not even the name of Buddha. In a golden age, a thousand Buddhas come through relying on the Lama." So, the Lama is more precious than all the Buddhas whom we cannot directly contact in body, speech, or mind. We can receive teachings from the Lama and link with his wisdom mind. Therefore, we must pray with good intention until our wisdom-lotus blossoms under the rays of blessings from his sunlike wisdom.

But because of spiritual vanity, our humility and compassion wane and become mere words from the mouth. We don't like the humble, those who remain low-key, and those who practice with less famous Lamas. We are afraid to lose fame and position by showing respect to them. We want only to mix with high-standard society people. We think we are like snow lions high up in the mountains, pure and majestic, so we fear to descend and mix with lowly street mongrels.

Anonymously, we hide our relationship with less well-known Lamas from whom we receive teachings and pretend to be disciples of V.I.P. Lamas. This is like some arrogant young fashion-lovers who buy their stylish clothes in the backstreets and tag them with the label "Made in Paris." We become dog shit dressed in brocade. Our ego never respects the Dharmas of other teachers, and so we create more arrogance, which is the cause of samsara.

So, we might have a teacher like Buddha Shakyamuni, but if we cannot learn with good intention and skillful means, then the Dharma is of no help, just like feeding clean grass to a dog.

It is funny that we think we are perfect according to Vinaya vows, while we create a more puritanical ego. We think we are perfect according to the vast scope of Mahayana, while our minds cannot see through the haze of swelling arrogance, which blinds us to the Buddha's boundless teachings. We think we are perfect according to Vajrayana, keeping the samaya of the pure mandala with our Guru, but we don't have directionless, impartial pure phenomena that pervade everything like an illuminating sun; we only have the petty pure phenomena of a firefly.

The problem is that we have lied to the teacher from the beginning. We said, "We want enlightenment, please teach us." We cheated the teacher and enlightenment cheated us. We like substance; enlightenment doesn't like substance. We don't like light; enlightenment doesn't like heavy. We like wealth, fame, and power. If we don't meet high Lamas or famous teachers, then we think that we cannot get the special qualities of the lineage. That is just an excuse. Lineage doesn't mean high social status. Real lineage comes from the wisdom qualities within oneself as shown to us by a Lama of high or low status.

Anyway, everything depends on intention. If we have pure motivation from the beginning, whether the teacher is humble, simple, famous, or high, then there will always be benefit and never waste.

FEAR

Most people have fear. Where does it come from? How can we use it?

The origin of all the passions, including fear, is ignorance. From the beginning, we didn't recognize and couldn't remain in stainless confidence clear space. Instead, we became deluded toward appearance. Appearances are constantly changing from pleasant to unpleasant and unpleasant to pleasant, but still we continue to accept and reject them, hoping for a perfect unchanging reality.

The mind never rests and so it becomes small and ordinary even though we may not be aware of this. Like a feather in the wind, it is pushed from object to object back and forth, back and forth, and so it becomes weary. This lack of stability is expressed as fear. Then we are reborn with karma whether we believe in karma or not. If our karma is not so good, we may acquire parents whose natures are erratic and bodies weak, and who fluctuate between conflicting emotional states. Then children are born and grow in these unstable circumstances, acquiring these tendencies at the very beginning. Children are surrounded by fear expressing itself. We are all continually propelled by fear, often hidden in praiseworthy qualities. For example:

If we see a high person and become shy, this doesn't mean we are noble; it is fear.

If we see ugly people and feel repelled by them, this doesn't mean we are superior; it is fear.

When we talk like a blue streak and miss the target, this doesn't mean we are fluent speakers; it is nervousness and fear.

When we write fancy words and leave out the meaning, this doesn't mean we have lucid realization; it is fear.

When we eat with roundtable groups and use fashionable manners, this doesn't mean we are sophisticated; it is fear.

When we eat with funky people, slurpy and dribbling, this doesn't mean we are siddhas, but that we are afraid to use good manners; it is fear.

When we are gliding smoothly among people, this doesn't mean we are glamorous; it is fear.

If we stumble hurriedly from place to place, this doesn't mean we are on time; it is fear.

If we are smiling, this doesn't mean we are kind; it is fear.

If we are glaring boldly, this doesn't mean we are brave; it is fear.

And so fear continues, and like a contagious disease it spreads from parent to child and flourishes. So, if we are not careful from the beginning, even though we look as though we are mature, we are really always having fear.

There are ways, however, to develop fearlessness in children. Both conception and infancy are important for nurturing fearlessness. It is especially important when parents make love and conceive a child that they remain relaxed and totally free in a place with light and beauty. Then, when the act is over, the mother shouldn't jump up or drink or eat harsh kinds of food. She should stay warm in the afterglow. She should not become involved in elated or depressed talk or concepts but stay even and relaxed like a mute person eating chocolates.

Then, with your babies, don't bounce or set them down abruptly; be gentle and smooth. Protect them from shocking sounds and, as they get older, advise them with warnings in a gentle, clear way. When their minds have matured, adapt to their mental capacity and allow them to learn through risk.

If the child is hurt in any way from accidental circumstances, this can be used in a good way; it is not necessarily bad. Sometimes, for a disobedient child, one accident is much better than one hundred words of advice. From this, the child can learn for his future. If circumstances become really bad for the child, as when he loses a friend, parent, or relative, comfort him with beautiful stories to inspire and uplift him. Lead him gently to the sky.

When he is too elated, push him down slowly through telling him stories about impermanence and illusoriness until he is guided back to earth. Thus, the mind becomes balanced, and with balanced mind, he cannot be lured from object to object. Then, if he can practice meditation with a good teacher, he can gain natural confidence and ultimately his mind can become like the vast sky. Then his mind won't depend on objects and yet it will pervade all objects without clinging. That is fearlessness.

Male Supremacy

Why are men historically more important than women?

Most mammals, such as dogs, deer, monkeys, and humans, have a strong competitive tendency. The one who proves to be the strongest, either through physical strength or through mental skill, becomes the leader or master of those around him, and is looked up to as a hero. Humans were able to feel superior to animals because of their greater power, which came not from greater physical strength but from greater intelligence and inventiveness. Among humans, the male was able to feel superior to the female because his physical strength was greater and grew greater as he dedicated himself predominantly to hunting, war, and heavy labor.

With the passing of time and the development of human civilization, man's supremacy developed into hierarchies with large bureaucratic systems in which the king was the most powerful, followed by the queen, courtiers, servants, cleaners, and so on. From this worldly point of view, the king desired for himself the most beautiful and special queen. On finding such a rare and precious queen, he constantly feared he might lose her to a more powerful king, a wealthier prince, or simply a handsome younger man. Generally, from the king on down, people followed this pattern of behavior. And so it is often the most precious objects that are kept secretly in low places, like jewels that are hidden underground in vaults beneath the open gardens and official decorations.

In this way, the king kept his queen locked in a splendid palace in order to have her for himself. Eventually people believed women to be actually lower than men, while the superior, precious nature of women that had originally caused the king to keep the queen lower than himself was forgotten.

At the time of the Buddha, the group phenomena of the people had arisen from their karma in such a way that they were born into this type of hierarchical social structure. For this reason, through his unobstructed compassion, the Buddha's teachings skillfully took the form of the hierarchical system in which men had power over women.

The Buddha taught various systems. In the Sutra system, where attachment to sexuality is viewed as an obstacle to enlightenment, women are considered the basic support of desire and so are seen as the basis of samsara. This is because, through desire, men and women connect and make families and children, who are seen as great obstacles to practice, causing them to remain constantly within samsara's plan.

According to the higher tantric system, there is no liberation for those who abandon women. When King Indrabodhi asked for teachings and the Buddha appeared with his retinue of monks telling him that first he would have to renounce his kingdom and all his desirable worldly possessions, the king did not want to accept these conditions. He wanted enlightenment without rejection of samsara. At this point, the Buddha, recognizing the superior qualities of the king's mind, miraculously made his retinue of monks disappear and transmuted the social hierarchy into a mandala. The king and queen became the deity and consort in the center of the mandala, and those who were within the social order under the king became the retinue surrounding the deity and consort. The hierarchical structure remained the same, only the point of view was different.

WOMEN'S QUALITIES

All of these questions define a woman in relation to a man. Doesn't a woman have any inherent good qualities?

We have already talked briefly about how endless phenomena are contained within pure and impure phenomena. Countless pure phenomena come from the desireless bliss of wisdom emptiness. Men are symbolic of phenomena, and women of emptiness, so automatically countless good qualities are contained in their wisdom mind. What I have said was real praise made with an open mind and not with the intention to disparage women. This description of women is not made from the hierarchical point of view of social oppression described before, but from the point of view of the mandala in which the consort is symbolic of wisdom emptiness and desireless bliss. Without linking or mutual dependence, there are no phenomena, there is no *shunyata* without dependence on phenomena, no nirvana without dependence on samsara, no samsara without dependence on nirvana, no women without dependence on men, no men without dependence on women. Male and female are mutually dependent; without dependence on bad qualities, there are no good qualities.

If women discriminate and wish to have a life independent of men, they may, for example, choose to masturbate. Then it will seem that they are not depending on men or anyone else. But emptiness cannot play with emptiness. It must have phenomena to play with. Because mind is both clear space and phenomena, it is male and female. Substance quality comes from phenomena. It is not emptiness. Even if women think when they masturbate that they are not dependent on men, their hand being substance is symbolic of the male's penis-phenomenon.

Women may choose to be lesbians, but even then, if they examine their bodies carefully, they will discover that male organs are contained within the female body; ovaries are like testicles and the clitoris like a penis. If you don't believe this, you can ask a doctor or a specialist in the *Kama Sutra* or anyone who has experience about male and female characteristics. So lesbians, who are female, have within them characteristics that are male. But if a woman thinks that because the male and female characteristics are complete within her, it is not necessary to depend externally on men, this is also not true. The thought of having the male characteristics within oneself automatically creates dependence on the male because there is the subject female creating the internal male object. All internal elements are dependent on external ones.

According to high Vajrayana, the female is most important because she is the symbol of emptiness wisdom, which is the source of phenomena in the sense that space is the potential container of all phenomena. Phenomena exist within space and would not exist without it. It follows that if there were no space to contain them, there would be no mountains, rivers, trees, flowers, and so on.

On a more tangible level, all the countless wonderful inventions filling this world, such as culture, medicine, logic, mathematics, music, dance, sports, philosophy, and arts, are the inventions of human beings who all come from women, and without women, none of these things would exist.

BLISS

Rinpoche, is it necessary or not for a vajra master or Vajrayana practitioner to have a consort?

People living in great poverty with begging hands and pitiful eyes are struggling to find bliss. People living in great wealth with sagging bellies and greedy eyes are hoping to find bliss.

Old people feebly walk about with stick in hand to find bliss. Young people proudly walk about with cock in hand to find bliss.

Lowly clerks, though they don't like their position, lick the boots of high executives to find bliss. High executives, though they fear revolution, continue to abuse lowly clerks to find bliss.

Some couples meet and marry in order to find bliss. Some couples separate and divorce in order to find bliss.

Some people insult each other in order to find bliss. Some people praise each other in order to find bliss.

Some people commit suicide to shorten their lives in order to find bliss. Some people become health fanatics to live a long life in order to find bliss.

Feculent pigs wallow in dirty mud to find bliss. Beautiful swans glide in clean pools to find bliss.

Some people are very narrow-minded in order to find bliss. Some people are very open-minded in order to find bliss.

Some governments are fascist in order to find bliss. Some governments are democratic in order to find bliss.

Some people, including monks, keep short hair in order to find bliss. Some people, including yogis, keep long hair in order to find bliss.

Some ritualists ring the bell from inside and beat the drum from outside, creating noise to find bliss. Some meditators sit alone watching their mind inside and their noses outside, creating silence to find bliss.

Hermits go to a fresh-air hermitage and shit warm turds in cool, pleasant meadows to find bliss. Socializers go to stuffy Dharma centers, the cool thing to do, and meet warm lovers to find bliss.

Nonreligious persons hate religious persons in order to find bliss. Religious persons hate nonreligious persons in order to find bliss.

Some sectarians expose their hard penis for all to see and debauch prudish doctrines in order to find bliss. Some supposed nonsectarians bend their harder penis in nonsectarian jockstraps and seduce open-fly sectarians in order to find bliss.

Hinayana followers try to abandon desire to find bliss. Inner Vajrayana followers try to use desire to find bliss.

Hot steam ascends to form clouds that condense into a cool, pleasant rain. Cool water descends to turn generators that convert its power into warm, glowing lights.

Bodhisattvas are praying and manifesting activity, sometimes in a masochistic style, sometimes in a sadistic style, in order for all sentient beings to find bliss.

Lord Buddha taught in countless different ways so that all beings with countless different faculties can find bliss.

Anyway, wherever they go, all sentient beings from insects to wise men appear to be competing, running a race to find bliss. So, to find bliss, all you have to do is choose your target; don't bother about anyone else's target.

If you think Buddha taught that desire is the cause of samsara, this is the Vinaya system. So, stay in this system, with pure mind like the Buddha's disciples of ancient times. Don't create aversion toward others or become aggressive toward those who don't follow the same system. Rest with a tranquil mind.

The root of desire is attachment to desirable objects. Desirable objects are not only women or men. There are so many different objects of desire: houses, toys, wealth, fame, power, etc. Consequently, if we have aversion to sex objects, we must also have aversion to all desirable things and isolate ourselves.

In isolation, if we find that we cannot directly benefit all sentient beings and therefore cannot practice the Mahayana teachings so that we must once again relate with worldly objects, then why should we condemn sexual desire and not all the other objects of desire? We must not misrepresent the Buddha's vast teachings through narrow-mindedness.

If we don't have desire, we cannot even practice the Vinaya system, for even in the Vinaya, when one object is rejected, another is created. The Vinaya teaches one to create a disgusted attitude toward the physical qualities of a woman or man in order to suppress desire toward her or him. When we are no longer attached to women or men, we have fulfilled the desire for nonattachment to desire. Through this sublime desire for nonattachment, we can find the desireless Arhat state.

For a supreme Vajra Master like Padmasambhava, it is unnecessary to have an external Dakini because he is already in desireless wisdom bliss and does not need to do consort practice. Although he may manifest as having many Dakinis, he has realized his own phenomena as the pure wisdom Dakini who is spontaneously manifesting. These many Dakinis manifest from the essential innate consort, symbolic of wisdom itself, *prajna*. All these Dakinis are very pure because they are his own wisdom phenomena. Through these phenomena, he is helping sentient beings effortlessly. So even if we ordinary people think that he and his Dakinis are separate, in actuality, his own phenomena are inseparable from the Dakinis, as all are only his own manifestation of wisdom.

For inner Vajrayana practitioners, however, contact with an external consort is necessary. If we don't believe contact is necessary between two things, then how can we turn on the light switch? Without a link, there is no light. How can we nourish the body without a link between food and body? How can lovers experience pleasure without a link? How can a doctor benefit a sick man without a link from nerve to nerve? How can transmission take place from a wisdom teacher to ordinary people without a link?

There are two different kinds of bliss: temporary bliss, which is worldly, and ultimate desireless wisdom bliss. If we practice casually, just for pleasure or temporary bliss, then it is necessary to rely on the *Kama Sutra* system. Within this system, there are many shastras, some slightly colored by tantric ideas, others purely for pleasure. Many expert and wise saints like Nagarjuna taught the *Kama Sutra*. If we think that the wise men and the Buddha never taught sexual practices, then we must think the Buddha is not omniscient. He taught this path, but some uptight religious people associate the Buddha with puritanical morality, which in their minds means rejecting pleasure. Their nerves and muscles are tense because of their sexual fears. They do not see the Buddha's effortless compassion manifested in clear, open-minded teaching that in its vastness reflects all the different stars, planets, suns, and moons for the benefit of sentient beings.

According to the inner tantric system, ultimate desireless bliss can be found through temporary bliss using skillful means. Following the system of our particular sadhana, our knotted channels untie themselves and thus purify the mind and allow the circulation of air. In this way, our wisdom mind blossoms.

If we like to keep outer Hinayana appearance, observing its vows, then we may not wish to make use of an external consort. In this case, it is not necessary for us to bother about an inner or outer Dakini. If we have devotion toward Vajrayana but still wish to keep Hinayana discipline, we may learn from a Vajra Master the skillful means to unfold the inner wisdom Dakini.

As Vajrayana practitioners who have not yet realized our inner wisdom Dakini, it is necessary for us to seek advice from our Vajra Master in order to find a consort with the good characteristics that are explained fully in certain tantras. Some women, for example, have special wisdom channels. If we can meet that kind of Dakini, it is a great benefit in our practice to reach desireless bliss. So, if we can find a really qualified Dakini, she can make our wisdom Dakini blossom, who lies dormant in our natural mind. There are countless different types of Dakinis, but according to the inner tantric system, these different kinds are contained in the five Buddha families. Some Dakinis are symbolized by the lotus, others

by the conch shell, deer, elephant, and others. They can be recognized by their color, shape, smell, marks, the way they move, and how they speak. From these, we choose and then practice impeccably and secretly. How long we keep our consort depends on the accomplishment of our practice.

When Yeshe Tsogyal was in upper Western Tibet, in Shampo Gang, and was raped by seven bandits, she introduced them through her blessing to the four exalted wisdom states of initiation. She sang this hymn to the bandits:

I bow to GURU PADMA SIDDHI HRI!
Many accumulated merits in your past lives have caused this meeting with an excellent consort like me; so now, through these good circumstances, accept these four initiations.

When you see the beautiful mandala of my body, your perception desire is strongly aroused and so you receive the vase initiation. You must visualize us as your deity and use your desire inseparable from the deity; watch the essence of desire and practice with it. There is no Yidam different from your own desire, so you should concentrate on this desire as the great wisdom deity.

When you join in union with my secret mandala through my great blissful pathways, all universes are moving in glowing bliss. Now dissolve your anger and aggression into love. Use the essence of enjoyment and mix it with your vital airs and keep it for some moments. Now there is no different Mahamudra, so should you practice this great gesture.

When you join my vast bliss mandala space, effortless diligence emerges and your mind mixes in my wisdom heart. This is the blessing of *prajna jnana* (knowledge-wisdom) initiation. Don't let your mind wander; sustain the essence of bliss and blend it into *shunyata*. Desireless bliss is bliss and emptiness, which are inseparable. So should you practice this great bliss.

You join my vital wisdom mandala of desire. Then, when two nectars meet, there is no self-and-other phenomenon; this is the awareness great skillful means initiation. You should sustain this state of unending great phenomena and mix all afterglow into emptiness and rest. Now there is no different Mahasandhi. You should practice inherent desirelessness in exaltation. This is the sublime precious teaching. It is so wonderful that just by our meeting, you are liberated; you are so fortunate. You have received four vast initiations just here in this one place. You are ripened through the four exaltations.

After this, they all became great yogic practitioners. They were enlightened in Oddiyana without abandoning their bodies.

Just for receiving blessings, this translation has been done briefly from Yeshe Tsogyal's life history, focusing on the meaning and leaving it very simple.

Could you give a brief description of the required characteristics of a Daka?

A Daka must have all of the following nine characteristics:

He must be young rather than old.

He must at least have a youthful body because of his good karma, even if he is not young in years.

He must be free from diseases.

He must have a fresh, vital, and flourishing body.

He must have noble channels (*nadis*).

He must be brave.

He must be very devoted to tantric teachings.

He must have had the four initiations, especially the *prajna jnana* wisdom initiation.

He must have practiced with his inner consort before taking an outer one.

In general, youth is necessary, but as a result of good karma, some special persons have a youthful body even though they are not so young.

It is not necessary to count age only. His body should be very straight with high shoulders and open chest. His body must be masculine and attractive. If he is too young, he cannot increase bliss. If he is too old, even if he has desire, his substance of bliss is weak. If he has disease, it is harmful to both him and his consort, and his seed, which is the source of bliss, is impure. So he must not have disease. If his body is not healthy, he cannot practice continuously until the final result. If he doesn't have vitality, he cannot progress toward desireless bliss through desire. He should have vitality. If his veins, channels, and nerves are knotted, then breath and fluids, which are the contributing circumstances to development, are blocked and it is no good. So he must have very noble, straight nerves and channels, open and clear. If he has a narrow mind, then he cannot take risks, which is a precious tantric teaching. So he must have courage. Even though he has a brave mind, if he is a wild, barbaric tantric practitioner, then he will misuse tantric teachings as a game, for pleasure, and this might be harmful for his and his consort's enlightenment and also for Vajradhara's high teachings. So he must have a vast mind with the intention to attain enlightenment. If he doesn't have familiarity with inner tantras, especially the secret initiation, he cannot have the blessing of wisdom, and he cannot practice without the blessing of the lineage, so he must have initiations. Before practicing with his outer consort, his practice with his own natural consort should be developed through visualization.

Anyway, if we want to do consort practice, but cannot find a consort with the suitable qualities, we can practice with our inner, stainless, natural awareness Dakinis or Dakas through the guidance of an experienced teacher. It is obvious that meditation is for the ultimate benefit of enlightenment; there is no question about that. But also, this present life is benefited through meditation. If we meditate with our natural inner Dakinis or Dakas, our minds become blissful and calm, and our bodies become healthy. In fact, meditation is the greatest support of health.

If we are able to meditate through recognition mind, then our sufferings dissolve and our inner luminosity, which comes from potential luminosity, arises. With peaceful mind, our complexion blossoms.

Most people depend on material things to enhance their beauty, never recognizing that wisdom mind or natural mind has the potential to enliven complexion and vitality. When inner mind is not peaceful, then no matter how much the body is made up externally with substances, it is never naturally sweet or radiant and it eventually fades into dust.

One person may have beauty through external means only, another through meditation and peaceful mind, but if examined carefully, it will be clear that the beauty of the second is deeper. Many people, even arrogant ones, are conquered through the natural complexion and peaceful mind of this kind of beauty, which comes from meditation.

THE SEVEN-LINE PRAYER OF GURU RINPOCHE

HUNG orgyen yul gyi nubjang tsam
pema gesar dongpo la
yatsen chok gi ngödrup nye
pema jungne zhe su drak
khordu khandro mangpö kor
khye kyi je su dak drup kyi
jin gyi lop chir shek su söl
GURU PADMA SIDDHI HUNG

The Seven-Line Prayer originated directly from the speech of a Dakini. It came to this world during a debate at Nalanda when heretics were defeating Buddhist scholars. Shiwa Chok, the Dakini called the Great Excellent Peaceful One, appeared to the scholars in their dreams, saying, "You will never be able to defeat the heretics by yourselves. I have a brother, Dorje Töthreng Tsal, who stays in the darkness of the graveyard. If you invoke him there, he will come to your aid." But the Buddhist scholars said they did not know how to find Guru Töthreng Tsal.

So, the Dakini taught them the Seven-Line Prayer and then said, "It is not necessary to go to the graveyard, because Guru Rinpoche has a rainbow body and will come to your aid if you recite the Seven-Line Prayer."

The scholars prayed, and Guru Rinpoche came to them. They were able to win the debate, glorifying the Buddha Dharma and helping it to prosper.

Later, when Guru Rinpoche went to Tibet, he taught the prayer to his twenty-five disciples and it benefited them greatly. Afterward, as it was included in many *termas*,[6] *tertöns*[7] found it in many of the hidden texts they discovered. The first *tertön* to discover it was Guru Chöwang.

The Outer Meaning of the Seven-Line Prayer

LINE ONE

HUNG orgyen yul gyi nubjang tsam

HUNG! On the northwest border of the country of Oddiyana.

HUNG: The prayer begins with HUNG, the seed syllable of the mind of all Buddhas.

orgyen yul gyi: The land of Oddiyana was, people say, in the Swat Valley. All the schools and traditions of tantra agree that all the high Vajrayana teachings originated in Oddiyana.

nubjang tsam: On the northwest border.

LINE TWO

pema gesar dongpo la: On the pistil of a lotus flower.

Guru Rinpoche was born on a lotus on Dhanakosha Lake, which has eight qualities. The lake symbolizes the *yum*, the mother, the consort, and it represents wisdom.

pema: On this lake there were five lotuses, symbolizing the five wisdoms of the five Buddha families. Guru Rinpoche was born on the pistil of the central red-petaled lotus, which represents the Lotus family.

When Guru Rinpoche was to be born, all the Buddhas of the three times and ten directions concentrated the blessings of their body, speech, and mind into the wisdom heart of Amitabha Buddha. The collected blessings emanated from Amitabha's heart in the form of the syllable HRI. The HRI came onto the pistil (*gesar*) of the lotus and transformed into the form of Guru Rinpoche.

There are three main reasons for Guru Rinpoche's, appearing on earth:

For the sake of all sentient beings.

Because of King Indrabodhi's prayers for a son. (By his generosity and vast offerings, the king established a karmic claim for a son.)

To bring the secret Mantrayana teachings to the world, as the Buddha had given very little tantric teaching.

LINE THREE

yatsen chok gi ngödrup nye: The marvelous, supreme accomplishment has been attained.

There are two kinds of *siddhis* (Tib. *ngödrup*) or attainments, ordinary and supreme. Besides the ordinary siddhis, Guru Rinpoche had the marvelous supreme siddhi of having the qualities of a Buddha, being the same as the Buddha.

After his youth as a prince, Guru Rinpoche abandoned his royal position and became a yogi. He stayed in the great graveyards and obtained all the spiritual powers. Even though he was born with all the siddhis, Guru Rinpoche practiced them progressively and attained them all in order to help other beings by his example.

LINE FOUR

pema jungne zhe su drak: You are renowned as the Lotus-Born.

So Guru Rinpoche was given the name Lotus-Born (Pema Jungne).

LINE FIVE

khordu khandro mangpö kor: Surrounded by a retinue of many Dakinis.

Guru Rinpoche had a vast retinue of all the Dakinis, Dakas, Lamas, Yidams, and Dharmapalas. All surrounded and followed him.

LINE SIX

khye kyi je su dak drup kyi: Following you to be like you.

This is a prayer to follow Guru Rinpoche's path, to obtain his siddhi.

LINE SEVEN

jin gyi lop chir shek su söl: I beseech you to come and bless me.

This is a prayer of invocation to Guru Rinpoche asking that the blessings of his body, speech, and mind permeate one's own body, speech, and mind, transmuting them into union with Guru Rinpoche. We implore him to come and bless us in this way.

GURU PADMA SIDDHI HUNG

GURU: The Lama who possesses the excellent qualities of body, speech, and mind. There is nothing higher than this. So the Guru is absolutely precious.

PADMA: His name.

SIDDHI: His supreme spiritual attainment.

HUNG: A supplication: Please give me this realization. So be it.

The Outer Meaning of the Line Sequence of the Seven-Line Prayer

Line one: Where Guru Rinpoche was born.

Line two: How Guru Rinpoche was born.

Line three: The qualities of Guru Rinpoche.

Line four: His actual name.

Line five: His retinue, the manifestation of unobstructed wisdom mind.

Line six: How we must pray to him (*kyerim*).[8]

Line seven (including the mantra): Gathering of all the power. Bestowal of the blessing. Transmutation into union with the Guru (*dzogrim*).[9]

The Inner Meaning of the Seven-Line Prayer

LINE ONE

HUNG orgyen yul gyi nubjang tsam

HUNG represents the direct perception of the unity of awareness and emptiness, which is the true nature of our own mind. If we practice this prayer, visualize Guru Rinpoche, take his blessing, and rest in *nyamshak*,[10] the quintessence of awareness beyond conception, then we can see our own mind at that time, and this is symbolized by the syllable HUNG.

orgyen yul gyi: According to the secret meaning, the land of Orgyen is one's own wisdom mind. It is inherently secret by its own nature.

nub: west, here meaning sinking, by analogy, into samsara.

jang: north, here meaning rising or purifying, by analogy, into nirvana.

tsam: Literally means border, but in this case means that beyond the duality of those two, there is a middle path. The phrase means that the inherent wisdom mind (primordial wisdom) does not fall into any extremes.

LINE TWO

pema gesar dongpo la

pema: tongpanyi, shunyata, absolute emptiness, Dharma space.

gesar: rigpa, awareness, one's own naked awareness.

dongpo: Union, inseparability. The union of the expanse of emptiness and awareness is primordial wisdom or wisdom mind. So the union of awareness and emptiness is enlightenment.

LINE THREE

yatsen chok gi ngödrup nye

The supreme siddhi is the direct understanding of one's own mind as the same as the mind of Guru Rinpoche. It is wonderful and marvelous because it is naturally present. The wonderful quality (*yatsen*) of the attainment (*nye*) of the supreme siddhi (*chok gi ngödrup*) is being praised here.

LINE FOUR

pema jungne zhe su drak

The source or ground of this renowned quality of supreme siddhi is the Trikaya, the three bodies of the Buddha: the Dharmakaya, essence (*ngowo*);[11] the Sambhogakaya, luminous self-nature (*rangshin*);[12] and the Nirmanakaya, unobstructed compassion (*tugje*).[13] This is the actual meaning of Lotus-Born. The ground (*jungne*)[14] of all the Buddhas (*pema*)[15] is wisdom mind (the union of awareness and emptiness), which is renowned (*zhe su drak*)[16] as the source of all Buddhas.

LINE FIVE

khordu khandro mangpö kor

With (*kor*) numerous manifestations (*mangpö*) spontaneously appearing unobstructedly in wisdom mind, in the absolute Dharma space, or Dharmadhatu (*khordu*). One's own awareness, as openness or emptiness, is like space in which unobstructed manifestations spontaneously appear, and these are called Dakinis: the spontaneous manifestations of clear space, or *rigpa*. Dakini, or *khandroma*, means the following: *kha* or *ying* means sky Dharmata, or *chönyi*, emptiness; *dro* means goer or awareness mind; and *ma* means [female] consort, or *yum*. So awareness mind or skillful means arise in emptiness and are inseparable from it. This is the true meaning of *khandro*, the sky-goer. So countless Dakinis are the effortless display of wisdom. Guru Rinpoche, wisdom mind, is surrounded (*kor*) by a retinue (*khordu*) of countless (*mangpö*)

Dakinis (*khandro*) because the manifestations of emptiness and awareness are unceasing and unobstructed.

LINE SIX

khye kyi je su dak drup kyi

khye kyi je su: The absolute view that the true nature of one's own
mind is primordial wisdom, wisdom mind.

dak drup kyi: May I be established in this view by the practice of
meditation.

As Guru Rinpoche is our own mind, the practice of meditation is to
recognize him as such. This line is a prayer to attain that view.

LINE SEVEN

jin gyi lop chir shek su söl

shek su söl: Without doubt and with complete certainty, may I realize
the true nature.

jin gyi lop chir: And in so doing, may I understand that the Lama's
body, speech, and mind are identical with my own, and thus may I
realize the three mandalas of the Trikaya.

If we thoroughly understand the nature of our own mind, then all
phenomena become pure, the mandala of Buddha body, Buddha speech,
and Buddha mind. So this is the deep prayer to attain this blessing.

GURU PADMA SIDDHI HUNG

GURU: Wisdom mind is the supreme Guru. If we have faith and pray
and dissolve the Guru in our own mind, then there is not any other
Guru besides our own mind. The qualities of all the Buddhas are
born in the Guru, our own wisdom mind.

PADMA: Wisdom mind is desireless, uncontaminated like the lotus
that springs forth perfectly pure. If we actually understand our own
true nature, there is no fault, regardless of the ground.

SIDDHI: The four bodies and the five wisdoms,[17] all the qualities of all the Buddhas, are contained in our own mind. If we recognize this, that is the supreme siddhi.

HUNG: May we rest in the understanding of the true nature of our own mind. So be it.

DANCES OF THE EIGHT MANIFESTATIONS OF PADMASAMBHAVA

The following is a brief description of the Dances of the Eight Manifestations of Guru Rinpoche.

I. Guru Rinpoche was named Pema Kara or Pema Jungne at the time of his birth in Oddiyana. The dance is called *Tsokye Shepai Tang Tab*, or *Gesture*[18] *of the Lotus Blossom*.

II. Guru Rinpoche was named Padmasambhava in the cemetery of Lanka Tsegpa, where he displayed the qualities and aspects of a monk in his dress and imparted teachings to Dakinis. The dance is called *Yönten Gi Balab Yowai Tang Tab*, or *Gesture of the Wave of Knowledge*.

III. Guru Rinpoche was named Guru Loden Chogse in the cemetery of Dhe Dhel, where he imparted teachings to Dakinis. He was given outer intellectual and inner Dharma knowledge by Dorje Chang. The dance is called *Mongpai Munpa Selwai Tang Tab*, or *Gesture of Clearing the Darkness of Ignorance*.

IV. Guru Rinpoche was named Guru Pema Gyalpo in the country of Zahor, where he married the king's daughter Mandarava, helped rule the country, and taught Dharma. The dance is called *Kham Sum Wangdu Kyi Tang Tab*, or *Gesture of Conquering the Three Realms*.

V. Guru Rinpoche was named Guru Nyima Özer in the cemetery Kula Zogpa, where he acted as a siddha and gave teachings to Dakinis.

Like the rays of the sun, he subdued and dispelled the dark ignorance of sentient beings. So the dance is called *Drowa Dulwai Tang Tab*, or *Gesture of the Subjugation of Sentient Beings*.

VI. Guru Rinpoche was named Guru Shakya Seng-ge when he received the *bhikshu* vows from Kungawo and dressed and acted as a monk. The dance is called *Dud Pung Jompai Tang Tab*, or *Gesture of Destroying the Assembly of Demons through Wisdom Compassion*.

VII. Guru Rinpoche was named Guru Seng-ge Dradok, or Lion's Roar, in the cemetery Lhundrup Tsekpa, where he imparted teachings to the Dakinis. He heard the Mahayoga teachings from Dorje Sempa.[19] Because he subdued the nonbelievers in Buddhism through wisdom compassion, the dance is called *Si Sum Yowai Tang Tab*, or *Turbulent Gesture of the Three Realms*.

VIII. Guru Rinpoche was named Dorje Drolö in the cemetery Pema Tsegpa, or Lotus Mound, where he imparted Dharma to the Dakinis. He obtained the teachings on Anuyoga from Rigden Dewa Sang Kyong. Because he annihilated evil demons harmful to sentient beings, the dance is called *Drekpa Tsar Cho Kyi Tang Tab*, or *Gesture of the Annihilation of Arrogant Demons*.

Beyond East and West
An Interview with
Kyabje Thinley Norbu Rinpoche

Questions posed to Kyabje Thinley Norbu Rinpoche by Melvin McLeod, editor-in-chief of *Buddhadharma* magazine, in an interview published here for the first time.

How is Buddhism doing in the West?

Of course, the aim of any Buddhist doctrine or theory from the Hinayana, Mahayana, or Vajrayana is to attain fully enlightened Buddhahood, which is liberated from self-samsaric phenomena forever, according to each *yana's* view of enlightenment. That is the meaning of any studying, practicing, contemplating, abstaining from nonvirtue, accomplishing virtue, visualizing, and meditating. Even if one does not have the faith and capacity to practice the higher vehicles of the Mahayana or Vajrayana up to the swift path of Mahamudra and Mahasandhi, there is still a big difference between believing in general Buddhist theory and believing in other religions' theories.

For example, according to the Mahayana, all sentient beings, including human beings, have Buddha nature inherently, which is dormant from previous thick habit, but is potentially capable of being rekindled. Even though one is born in a human being's body, if one's Buddha nature is not being rekindled but one is just being human, it is called *just the name of a human body*. If one can recognize one's own Buddha nature, believe in negative and positive karma, try to cleanse previous negative karmic habit, accumulate merit and wisdom, and practice according to a qualified[1] teacher's instructions to attain the fully enlightened state of

Buddha, it is called *a precious human being's birth*. The reason human life becomes precious is that it is made meaningful not only by using it for the temporary aims of this present, momentary life, but by depending on it for one's practice in this life and throughout other lives until enlightenment is reached.

In Mahayana theory, whoever has mind has Buddha nature, including even insects, so of course both Eastern human beings and Western human beings have Buddha nature equally. The only difference between beings' Buddha nature is whether it is dormant or being rekindled. The diversity of circumstances experienced by beings within time and place that influence the recognition of Buddha nature is due to karmic results, such as the fortunate circumstance of being born in a place where a Buddha and sublime beings[2] have manifested and revealed holy teachings, and where Buddhism flourishes so that Buddha nature can be rekindled, or the unfortunate circumstance of being born in lower realms such as the animal realm, or even in the human realm but without belief in spirituality, or in a place where only materialism is developed, so that the rekindling of Buddha nature is delayed.

As the result of karma, even in the East where Buddhism is taught, there are many people who believe in Buddha and have faith, but there are also many nonbelievers. Even when people are believers, there are many who believe in eternalist religions that temporarily can lead to uncivilized behavior among followers, and logically, from the Buddhist view, can never ultimately lead to liberation because habit is not surpassed, since obscurations are not totally purified. But it is much better to be a believer than to believe in nothing, because even though there is Buddha nature, there is no hope to rekindle it for a while if there is no belief. One will still take rebirth continuously, but it will be without choice about where or when, since one will have no confidence about how to self-direct one's rebirth. Beings do not want to take miserable rebirths, but they may do so unintentionally when there is no influence of pure spiritual virtue due to lack of belief. Belief opens wisdom.

In the Hinayana, wisdom opens through detachment from existence, which is said to be the lineage of sublime beings. In the Mahayana, Buddha nature is revealed. In the general Vajrayana, absolute inherently born wisdom deity is revealed. In Mahasandhi, self-occurring wisdom is revealed. These are all views of wisdom according to the different yanas.

From not recognizing wisdom, beings are first born in samsara, and then from the phenomenon of a self, the phenomena of what is other than the self are created, and this is the duality of ordinary mind that causes all deluded samsaric existence. Still, according to Mahasandhi, the nature of mind is Samantabhadra,[3] even though that is not apparent to beings within duality. As Kunkhyen Longchenpa said:

> Self is Samantabhadra, other is Samantabhadra, eternalism is
>   Samantabhadra, nihilism is Samantabhadra.
> In the expanse of Samantabhadra, there is no self, other, eternalism,
>   or nihilism.

So, actually, not all of these different aspects of self, other, eternalism, and nihilism exist from the beginning in the sole stainless state of Dharmakaya, which is inexpressible; but from lack of sentient beings' recognition of this state, it becomes *alaya*, the basis of mind. In alaya, many different phenomena are seeded, and whatever phenomena appear can be synthesized as being nihilist or eternalist. Among these infinite phenomena, many different beings can be born in many different realms, including the fortunate birth of the high realm of human beings, who are much more capable of recognizing wisdom than beings in other realms. When human beings begin life with predominantly nihilist habits, however, they focus on their survival within their momentary lives, considering only conspicuous material phenomena and not considering inconspicuous spiritual phenomena.

Most people in the West believe primarily in instantly apparent material phenomena and rarely believe at a spiritual level, so inherent spiritual qualities recede. The worst obstacle in the West is excessive skepticism about spirituality, particularly the spirituality of Eastern religions such as Buddhism, from not seeing truth or having positive spiritual habits and experience. The ability to have faith is undeveloped, suppressed by material attachment from totally relying on temporary compounded phenomena, which means spirituality is absent and the practice of religion is lifeless. In this atmosphere, even if there is a spark of spirituality, it soon disperses.

Since you are asking me about Buddhism in the West, I have to mention that Buddhism in the West originated in the East. The place where I was born and what my individual life has been like can be known from reading *A Brief Fantasy History of a Himalayan*, but here it is enough to say that my life began in the East. So, to assess Buddhism in the West, as you asked, I should compare it to Buddhism in my early years in Tibet, with explanations judging these momentary phenomena and the differences between them.

In the country of Tibet, throughout the reigns of many Dharma kings, the teachings of both the sutras and the tantras of Buddha Shakyamuni flourished fully at the same time, which is very rare in the world, including during the time of the great living Bodhisattva Shantarakshita, an emanation of Avalokitshvara; the Vajra Master Lopön[4] Padmasambhava, an emanation of Vajrapani;[5] and King Trisong Detsen, an emanation of Manjushri. All of this history is in libraries everywhere and can be known from the historical writings of great Masters.

I have not been in Tibet for many years and I do not know what has happened there lately politically or religiously, but in my time, although there were different sects of Buddhism, the followers of these sects believed with certainty in their own spiritual traditions and theories. Whether they were sincere practitioners or simple people who did not know very much, this belief was definite. Although there was sectarianism, and there was a small minority group of Muslims, almost the entire country was Buddhist at that time, so it was a different situation than in the West. From the time that Buddhism first spread from India and flourished in Tibet throughout many generations who had been historically Buddhist, people in Tibet had been mentally engaged in studying and practicing Buddhism, dealing with a spiritual level through both logic and experience, which automatically influenced them to be more incisive and deep because of being familiar with a spiritual way of thinking.

In Tibet during my time there, I do not remember there being Buddhists who did not believe in karma, the next life, or the state of enlightenment, or that students revolted against and betrayed teachers the way some Buddhists have done in the West. Although Tibet has changed very much, and refugees are living around the world in many different foreign countries, older Tibetans who are around my age still have kept their faith traditionally in whatever sect of Buddhism they follow. New generations of young Tibetans, however, are very affected by the extreme materialism and nonspirituality of Western culture, copying its fashions and admiring its ideas about liberation. They do not like their own traditions, and think of their parents and ancestors as too conservative or as having what is called a green brain, which means being stupid.

From the habit of nihilism, the way of beginning and establishing life in the West is totally different from the way this was done in Tibet during my time there, where great importance was given to first considering the Triple Gems, holy teachers, Dharma, and karma, which are unknown or disregarded in the West. These days in the West, life generally begins with the development of only material matters. If people in the West hear about the spiritual beliefs and practices of Buddhist tradition, they may even think of them as irrelevant or as potential obstacles to using one's time and energy for what they consider to be practical purposes or material gain.

In the West, from early childhood when the senses start to connect with objects, they connect with television, technology, and entertainment. Culturally, learning is not connected with a Buddhist view. If there is any religion, it is with an eternalist view, and generally materialism is still strongly and predominantly emphasized. When parents or teachers start to teach children, they only teach materialistic ideas about what exists that is apparent to the five senses and how to develop materially, so children start to learn to be nonbelievers who only accept obvious material reality, although the nature of material reality is that it has no life and no truth. That is how Westerners begin to cause the delay of the rekindling of Buddha nature. Even if they have good intentions to help others or improve society, it is only materially for their momentary present lives, and they routinely disengage the power of the immaterial from material phenomena, although the material and immaterial actu-

2

ally always go together according to relative truth. That is the basis for the accumulation of merit according to the Buddhist view. Wherever material reality exists, the immaterial incidentally exists. The only difference between the ways that the material and immaterial exist is in the way that beings perceive them, and in whether beings are misusing phenomena by the misinterpretation of only materializing them,[6] or using phenomena in a correct way for accumulation [of merit] by recognizing this interconnection.

Most people in the West, including supposedly religious people, become nonspiritual and excessively materialistic through their unbearable attachment to the power of reality. Everyone deals with the material and thinks the immaterial is deceptive or does not exist. When children are taught to relate to the material phenomena of reality and to ignore immaterial spiritual phenomena, they begin to misinterpret phenomena in the early years of life. If they perceive what others do not perceive, they are told their perceptions are not real, while whatever is seen or heard by everyone is confirmed and substantiated. They learn that just talking about immaterial phenomena can alienate others, because everyone around them functions within material reality. Therefore, these days, from an upbringing due to karmic results, Western mind is often not deep enough to connect with Buddhism, although I am hoping this will change in the future through the recognition of spiritual qualities. At this point, even when Westerners study Buddhism, they are often not sincerely engaged with actual spirituality, meditation, or a vast view according to the many different levels of Buddhist theory, but are only interested at an intellectual or cultural level. Their greatest fear is to have faith. They use Buddhism superficially as something that can be shown to others and for their personal material comfort, but they are not actually affected by Buddhist spirituality with faith. Everything that is truly spiritual about Buddhism is left as ink and paper in books on a shelf or conceptualized, which is really not enough for dealing with an actual Buddhist view.

Previously in Tibet, since positive Dharma habits had existed for many generations, children grew up with faith blossoming toward positive objects naturally. Faith itself was called one of the seven jewels and considered most precious, along with morality, the positive habit of generosity, liberating the nature of mind through hearing Dharma, being ethical oneself, being embarrassed to do anything wrong in relation to others, and being wise. From early childhood, when the senses began to connect with objects, parents would teach their children that there are sublime beings who are to be worshiped and praised. They would show their children statues and tangkas of Buddhas, altars, holy teachers, and texts of the writings of sublime beings, and with good intentions they would influence them or even impose on them to respect these objects of worship, to hold their clasped hands in the gesture of prayer, and to do prostrations before them with humility about oneself, which causes spiritual qualities. Toddlers starting to mumble their first words were taught the names of the Triple Gems, the names of the Buddhas and Bodhisattvas, and the mantras of deities, and they would start to repeat them. Of course, they may not have known the meaning of the Triple Gems, but they were raised so that the rekindling of Buddha nature was started through establishing the positive habit of beginning to believe at an early age. Later, as children's minds developed and they were able to understand teachings about Buddha, Dharma, and Sangha, they began to learn Dharma their parents had received from teachers.

Children naturally had to act in accord with the attitudes of others, so they could not be against Dharma, temples, statues, teachers, and those who were elder, respectable, or wise, including their own parents, because it would be against Buddhist beliefs and they would become outcasts. Because everyone, from laypeople up to learned scholars, was influenced by Buddha's speech and believed in the Buddhist karmic system, they paid attention to cause and result, which prevented them from doing what was wrong. Whether or not young children understood the karmic system thoroughly, at least they would consider what their parents and others would think, and they would not immediately act on negative thoughts. Even if they were naughty and wanted to do something wrong or did not want to do something right, they thought about the consequences of their actions as they had been taught to do. Therefore, in my time, Buddhist children generally were not wild, because they were in Dharma and they would naturally behave in a disciplined manner unless there was someone who had especially bad karma. Even if children had a bad thought, a second thought would come because of their belief in karma. From the beginning of life, people's attitudes were formed within this Buddhist atmosphere, and the entire culture was influenced by the spiritual basis of Buddhism.

The upbringing of Western children and the general attitudes of Westerners have a different basis. Westerners are not taught in the same way about sublime objects or about humility, because there is a fear of losing selfhood, or "I," to anyone else. Even when children are taught about religion, the main cultural view is still conveyed, which is to construct a self and to make that self powerful. Instead of cultivating humility, children are taught to have self-confidence without a point of view, that self-determination is positive, and to build enormous self-righteousness.

In the West there are many people who have no idea about considering cause and result. They do not think about how to create positive consequences because they are preoccupied with how to exploit circumstances for their own benefit and are afraid to miss any chance to do that. From not understanding the karmic system, there is no ingrained hesitation that stops one from doing something wrong if a bad thought comes. At least those who are believers in karma will hesitate, since even someone who has an intention to harm can still think about the consequences of this intention and stop negative actions because of their belief. Without this belief, however, people can cause unbelievable negativity. Many wars, including World Wars I and II and other wars of the three previous generations, have been caused from a lack of belief in the next life or karmic consequences. By only considering one's own existence and trying to live as though one's life could be permanent, and then trying to be victorious over others by conquering one's enemies as though one could occupy their lands forever, genocide has occurred. Without belief in karma, even the beliefs of religions can cause negative effects in the same way that nihilism does, leading to what are called holy wars that are fought for religious reasons but actually cause suffering.

When the general basic habit is not to have a spiritual view but to rely only on materialism, even if one becomes Buddhist, one can still retain one's former material habits and even materialize Buddhism with a nihilist view. That is why many Westerners who go to Eastern countries to study and take vows according to the Hinayana tradition can be found criticizing the Mahayana and especially the Vajrayana. This is a misuse of Hinayana morality for self-identification rather than practice, which also happened in ancient times in India and still happens in some countries in the East among doctrinaire Hinayana followers. Also, if Westerners study Vajrayana Buddhism, receiving many teachings and initiations, their energy does not necessarily become softer, lighter, or more refined, which occurs naturally as a sign of practice from the positive influence of faith, belief, and meditation. Instead, they often become extremely hardened and indifferent to spirituality, only causing unjustifiable, disproportionate pride about what they think they have learned. For Westerners, due to the habit of too much materialism, the result of taking vows as nuns and monks or of receiving Vajrayana initiations from many teachers can be to build up more egoism instead of subduing their minds. Then they expect to be treated with respect, although they strangely do not like to respect others who are worthy of respect.

Buddha Shakyamuni taught to be disciplined, humble, and reduce ego, but if someone is humble in the West, people think it means that person is pathetic. In the West, even Buddhist teachers can have a conceited attitude and boast about themselves without embarrassment, and it is not even perceived as conceit. Arrogance is considered to be confidence, although it is actually fragility; humility is considered to be a lack of confidence and perceived as self-degradation. It is seen as positive to have a strong sense of self-respect and self-worth and to promote oneself to others. People are supposed to simulate confidence even when they are in the process of learning, and keeping their noses in the air is a sign of that confidence. For previous Tibetans, assuming a hunchbacked posture was considered to be a positive sign of humility, although sometimes people were said to have too much stress and tension about their practice that also contributed to this posture. These days, Westerners who stay with Tibetans in the East often try to use the same physically hunchbacked posture of humility, so that when they return to their homes in the West, they have to go to chiropractors to straighten out their backs again. Of course, it is not the outer expression of humility that is important, but the mind's quality of humility that comes from less consideration of self, as well as from recognition of sublime qualities, which inspires reverence and respect. Also, it is hard to say if someone is being sincerely respectful. Sakya Pandita said:

> Tricky ones respect others for their own purposes. It does not actually mean they are respectful.

In the West, from belief in the value of egalitarianism, people try to show signs of social equality instead of trying to show signs of respect. As an example of this, when the media or others in a lesser position meet with the president of the United States, they sit in a noticeably casual position, leaning back in their chairs and stretching their legs out in front of them or crossing their legs broadly to expose their equality and emphasize their lack of deference. I have seen on television that even when their legs slip out of that position, they immediately try to push them back into place, reinstating their personal right not to use a more formal way of sitting as a way to demonstrate their equality. It is very strange to me for the public to show these disrespectful postures as a gesture of classlessness, since it is a different conception and manner than that of Buddhist tradition.

Many Tibetans used to stick out their tongues as a way to show respect. The use of this gesture began at the time of King Langdarma's death, when the king's ministers tried to find his assassin, the great yogi Lhalung Paldor, who was known to have a white syllable HUNG on his tongue. As everyone was checked in this search, they each had to show their tongues, and it became a custom that whenever one saw Lamas or officials, one showed respect by sticking out one's tongue. Even though the time of Langdarma is over, this custom continues among older Tibetans, although there is no longer any reason for it. It is very hard to change habits. In another Tibetan custom, people showed their respect for others in higher positions by scratching their heads, symbolizing that they had goose bumps as a sign of fear in response to those they were respecting, as a way to acknowledge their higher and more powerful position. This custom is disappearing, but still exists among older people. Of course, respect depends on intention, but I like a unique custom still being used in Bhutan to show respect when sublime beings, teachers, or noble people ask those who are younger or of lower status to do something. They immediately start to run. This running is very funny for people of other countries, but Bhutanese consider it to be a way of honoring others, thinking of whatever has been asked as a command and of themselves as commandos. It is a sign that they are being respectful, not arrogant, and not holding self-righteousness.

In any religion, bowing, kneeling, and prostrating are ways of showing respect, but Westerners often do not have a habit of making a connection between respect and spirituality because of their ideas about equality. Young people are always revolting against teachers, parents, and knowledgeable people, which they think is an assertion of their equality, although it actually comes from their lack of discipline and impertinence, which shows a bad example for others. Respect is actually a form of humility. In Eastern Buddhist countries, humility is not only a custom, but an indication of a connection with Holy Dharma, because the perception of holiness causes natural reverence and respect for sublime spiritual qualities, which benefit oneself and others. Khenpo Ngagchung said:

> Someone who is arrogant is like an iron ball that cannot absorb the nectar of any positive qualities.

In my time in Tibet, there were many students of great teachers whose minds had been disciplined according to traditional ways, and who had studied and done retreat under the guidance of sublime beings. Sometimes, however, even if students studied under sublime learned scholars and became knowledgeable, if they could not practice in a pure way, they could cause additional egotism, but this was considered obnoxious. Respectfulness, humility, and lack of arrogance were considered to be not only refined behavior, but necessary for spiritual blessings to be able to enter one's mind. Particularly for those who held a special title of monk, nun, Lama, or Rinpoche, it was not considered noble to be arrogant or overly attached to power and reputation, and if this happened, others would be disrespectful to them out of disapproval. Tibetans would abstain from seeing even intellectually knowledgeable teachers who were arrogant and would say to each other, "I would like to learn Dharma from that teacher, but I am afraid because he has a huge ego." In Tibet, the development of spiritual qualities through practice was considered most important. There were institutes for learning, which were called *shedras*,[7] and places established for practice, which were called *drupdras*.[8] In *shedras*, however, it was actually uncertain whether someone would only study, because it was also possible to practice and accomplish one's practice, the same as was done in the histories of ancient *shedras*. This was because it was recognized that the reason to study is to practice, and the essence of knowledge is realization.

I often heard about Buddhist scholars who had faith in highly realized practitioners and valued their spiritual qualities. As one can read in the life histories of Buddhist scholars, there were many Asian scholars in India and also in Tibet who saw that there was no essence to intellectual knowledge alone, and finally ran away from their high positions in universities in order to practice to attain the fully enlightened state. These included great scholars such as Nagarjuna, Aryadeva, Vajragandhi, Busuku Shantideva,[9] Sarahapa, Ratnakara Shantipa, and Naropa, as well as countless other Tibetan scholars. From their high realization, their previous inferior intention and behavior ceased, and they entered a new performance of superior activity with wisdom, which is the meaning of the Tibetan term *tul zhuk*.[10]

Even if people today could not attain the same miraculous accomplishments as previous sublime practitioners, they should still believe in enlightenment and Buddha with faith and reverence, but it is rare to hear about anyone with faith and reverence among those who are learned in the West. Famous scholars do not want to give up their scholarly titles in order to practice, but try to hold on to them forever, ambitious about being successful and seriously attached to working for their worldly life. In the West, where capitalism and the freedom of the individual are emphasized, there is a strong influence of a habit of self-sufficiency and independence. People are pushed to stand on their own two feet and strive to enhance their reputations and positions only for this life's rewards while displaying what they think is self-confidence.

With this background, Western Buddhist scholars or professors are often not interested in actual practice, overusing their knowledge for temporary material benefit within this short life. Although they study, they do not connect spiritually with what they study, owing to their lack of belief and faith. The meaning of what is learned disappears and the mind becomes depressed when learning is only conceptual and not integrated with practice. Because these scholars rarely have faith in Buddha, rarely believe in karma, rarely believe in practice, rarely believe in the next life, and therefore, of course, rarely believe in enlightenment, they just use their knowledge to identify themselves as superior within society, with fear of losing a self even though they cannot keep a self.

Even if one studies Buddhism, if one does not have faith, there is no choice except to be born, to waste Buddha nature during one's life, to die, and then to be reborn again from the strength of karmic habit, with no confidence about where to be born, where not to be born, and where to abide. It is necessary to practice, which means believing in Buddha, praying, being indivisible with faith, and meditating. If whatever is learned is not connected with actual practice, everything becomes fabricated. This problem has also existed in the East. As Patrul Rinpoche said:

> Alas, the intelligence of scholars is stuck in dullness.
> From experience to experience, they go from one delusion to another delusion.
> By not seeing that the nature of stainless Buddha is within one's mind,
> They expect to find something special by counting each particle of existence.

The Western academic tradition has a legacy of not encouraging people to have faith or belief in the accumulation of merit and wisdom according to pure Buddhist tradition, which contributes to the conceptual objectification of the study of Buddhism in the West. When Western universities recruit new faculty members, they can find Buddhist scholars who are not believers in Buddhism, so there are even people teaching Buddhism who hold the lineage of nonbelief. Also, in some Western universities in Europe and America, I heard that there is an unspoken expectation for scholars of non-Judeo-Christian religions not to practice the religions they study and not to teach others how to practice. It is a sign of nihilism or extremist eternalism that instead of Buddhist spirituality being valued, it is discouraged. For example, there is a well-known university professor and Buddhist scholar who telephoned the father of one of his students to warn him that the student was becoming overly involved in Tibetan Buddhism. Also, although it is unusual for scholars to be engaged in pure Buddhism with faith and belief instead of just in its intellectual study, if they are engaged, it can jeopardize their jobs. How can this dislike for holding an unbroken Buddhist lineage help people become actual Buddhists and open their Buddha nature?

Of course, it is very hard to be like the saints and wisdom scholars of ancient times with a highly realized view of discerning wisdom, but those who hold the name of Buddhist scholars and are studying and teaching Buddhism should at least not prevent others from having faith and belief in enlightenment or actual Buddhist views. It is unsuitable with pure Buddhism to begin studying with no belief or intention to reach enlightenment, but only to become academics who teach and write books to sell for material gain within one's present life. If one is predominantly connected with materialism and not pure spirituality, even though the terms one uses and the object of one's learning seem to be connected with Buddhism, the essence of one's knowledge becomes fragmented and the same as pure nihilism, and there will be no actual depth or profound meaning to what is known. I wish that these people would do better than that. These days, it has become fashionable to be a Buddhist scholar, and there are many everywhere in the East and the West. I hope and pray that they can become authentic Buddhist scholars who will seed the flourishing of the teachings of Buddha by realizing them through learning and practice, with reverence and belief.

Since the study of Buddhism in the West has often been disconnected from the development of pure spiritual qualities because it is primarily associated with society, even Westerners who consider themselves Buddhists are often very afraid to speak publicly about believing in Buddha, the Triple Gems, karma, and practice with the worship of deities. This makes it difficult for Buddhist theories and practices to flourish in a pure way in the West. Most people are non-Buddhist nihilists and the rest are eternalists, although the essence of the views of either group is usually to believe only in material existence, and without even conversing, they agree with each other. Overpowered by these two cultural tendencies of disbelief and eternalist belief, people just adapt to the response they receive from others instead of internalizing the actual teachings of Buddhism. This is not only mistaken, but illogical. There are so many different theories and ways to practice in Buddhism, from the most elaborate to the most simple, as revealed by the omniscient Buddha, and people can choose whatever is appropriate for them, but they miss this chance if they go back to materialism.

If people are believers, even if they do not know how to describe who Buddha is or how to visualize, they can still receive blessings from Buddha because of their belief. In the West, it will be important for those who learn about Buddhism to have faith so they can truly recognize their own Buddha nature and be able to guide others to reignite their Buddha nature. If one just has faith, even if one does not know anything about Buddha, Buddha will know because Buddha is omniscient and one naturally will receive blessings, just as if one pushes open a white parasol, its white reflection comes back onto one's body. It is so beneficial to even simply think about enlightenment and Buddha and stay in that state for one moment. By thinking of Buddha, one can see stainless Buddha. If one sees or experiences something, it is seeing or experiencing wisdom form. Through that momentary experience, one can transcend to the immortal state. What is wrong with that? It does not cause depression, which is common in the West; it causes the blessing of spiritual energy, which dispels depression.

If people do not have faith and belief, it is a problem not only for studying Dharma, but also for practicing Dharma. When people practice in retreat without a basis of faith and belief, they can have excessive expectations for instant results, so they become easily frustrated and only keep their previous material energy. In the West it is very hard to find people who have developed more faith toward sublime beings or deities through their practice, and who, by seeing truth, have developed more compassion toward others who are not seeing truth. Instead, they have developed their material energy by only thinking about what is materially usable, which comes from not thinking about impermanence and not seeing the truth of immaterial wisdom emptiness.

There are some books, including *A Path with Heart* and *After the Ecstasy, the Laundry*, that blame Buddhist teachers, teachings, and traditions, such as going into retreat, for causing problems. This is illogical. As a simple example, if unskilled mountaineers climbing Mount Everest slip and fall down, they cannot blame the mountain. Practicing Buddhism does not cause problems, even though people would rather say Buddhism has caused something to go wrong than acknowledge their own lack of faith, belief, and experience. If people practice correctly within body, speech, and mind with a relaxed attitude, it definitely leads to attaining immaterial body, speech, and mind. The problems some people experience are not at all from Buddhist traditions or practices, but from a lack of a correct view and method. Problems come from grasping and materializing the immaterial practice of meditation and visualization without having faith or belief, but just wanting to use their involvement in Buddhism to receive acknowledgment from others due to their excessive attachment to their own self-identification, which makes them pressure themselves and causes disturbances in their energy. Actually, one is supposed to practice without expecting instant rewards or signs. When one sincerely practices, even if one does not display miraculous signs such as lifting off the ground or flying in the sky like the Arhats or saints of ancient times, there should still be signs of accomplishment. One should at least develop much more detachment and weariness toward the compounded wheel of samsara, much more compassion not just for family and friends but for all sentient beings, much more faith and devotion in Dharma, and much more serenity, humility, and mental stability. Even if from an ordinary perspective there seems to be something different about someone who is actually practicing, it should not be something negative, like a black crow, but positive, like a white cuckoo.

The body, speech, and mind of those who do retreat with a correct view actually change from the positive influence of practice, so they have much more positive spiritual energy from receiving blessings; and by accomplishing the deity of their practice, they have much more wisdom. Practitioners with these signs are praiseworthy. In the West, though, because of the expectation of an immediate material result and the habit of self-promotion, even after studying Dharma or practicing in retreat, people can have a negative outcome instead. From their frustration, they can develop hatred and resentment instead of appreciation and gratitude for teachers and Dharma; they can become tired, bored, and full of regret from their reversed version of practice; and they can build tremendous egotism and paranoia. These are actually signs of being disconnected from pure Dharma and misconstruing practice because of being haunted by one's own inherent evil. As in an example mentioned by Patrul Rinpoche:

> With mouths hanging open, eyes exorbitantly staring, and
>   visualizing deity,
> They transform into demons.

Patrul Rinpoche also said:

> Without even practicing one session of contemplating bodhichitta,
>   which is most important,
> Pretending to be visualizing, meditating in the completion stage,
> And reciting mantra, and thinking that these are enough,
> The mouth of this kind of Dharma practitioner must be blocked by
>   the excrement of nine towns.

All of these problems predominantly come from a great attachment to self and too much expectation for an immediate material result. From lack of belief, lack of faith, lack of receiving blessings, lack of opening wisdom energy, and lack of realization due to overly grasping and materializing practice, karmic airs and vital energy are overpowered and controlled by passions. Therefore, even for those who go into retreat for practicing the accumulation of virtue, visualization, and meditation, there can be a reversed result because of mistaken intentions and views.

These can be corrected with faith, belief, and the guidance of wisdom teachers.

Instead of practicing according to pure Buddhist traditions that actually open wisdom, Westerners are trying to change Buddhism. Although the Vinaya tradition is very strict, Buddha said that one could adjust its tradition according to time and place. Also, in Buddhist theory, it is said to be good to adjust to guide nonbelievers to become believers. In my experience and from what I have heard, however, Western versions of Buddhism try to adjust to nonbelief without considering how to adjust according to time and place for actual spiritual development. If Buddhism is adjusted to the nihilist framework of Western society, it interferes with spirituality, and even with happiness and prosperity in this life. In the West, even some Asian teachers are adjusting the pure traditions of Buddhism to make them suitable to nihilist society, and ignoring or discarding the supports of pure practice; their intention is based on material attachment.

Buddhist teachers should give a positive example of what is worthy of respect by their own actions with good intentions, influencing others to cause the positive phenomena of virtue and to meditate. They need to be more concerned with immaterial spiritual phenomena instead of commercializing Buddhism. They should at least have signs of spirituality, such as less egoism and more humility and faith. Ego has to be subdued into wisdom Heruka to establish an actual positive Buddhist legacy. The word *Heruka* means one who drinks the blood of samsaric karma and passions from immense compassion, annihilating them in the dustless state of wisdom. As Rigdzin Jigme Lingpa said in *The Roaring Laugh of the Wisdom Dakini Cutting Through Objects:*[11]

> I, a fearless yogi subduing samsaric phenomena and entering the
>   path of enlightenment,
> By the view and performance of leveling samsara and enlightenment
>   in evenness,
> Dance on the gods and demons of grasping mind.[12]
> Dualistic mind, the evil of samsara, is crushed into dustlessness.

In Vajrayana Buddhism, the Sanskrit term *tantra*, or *gyu* in Tibetan,[13] means continuity. This continuity, which is the basis of inherent wisdom deities that exist potentially within beings' minds, is connected with tantric *sadhanas*; sadhanas are connected with categorizations of practice in a proper way; categorizations are connected with tradition; and tradition has to be connected with the *upadesha*[14] of holy Lamas. So far in the West, there is no acceptance or even understanding of the importance of having faith in and receiving the blessings of spiritual lineage, which are imparted by one's holy teacher and actually open wisdom mind. Eastern Buddhists value lineage; Western Buddhists devalue lineage. Buddha Shakyamuni said:

> For human beings without faith, Dharma phenomena will not occur.
> If a seed is burned by fire, it does not sprout.

Also, as Drigung Kyobpa Jigten Gönpo[15] said:

> If the sun of your devotion does not shine
> Upon the Lama's form, the snow mountain body of the Four Kayas,[16]
> The flowing water of blessings will not fall.
> So therefore, you must persist with earnest devotion.

If a subject does not have positive intentions, it is impossible for a positive object to appear. Until full enlightenment is achieved, interdependent relative truth will occur, so it is necessary to have faith subjectively in the objective pure appearances of sublime beings in order to develop spiritual qualities until inner and outer appearances become inseparable.

The Western habit of dismantling subjective appearances from objective appearances and material phenomena from immaterial phenomena is a great obstacle to spiritual development. Separating the absolute from the relative is not beneficial for attaining Buddhahood and is the opposite of the actual Buddhist view. If Buddhism is adapted to a culture based on attachment to reality without considering a genuinely spiritual view of the meaning and importance of Buddhist traditions for people's minds, it will keep people from using Buddhist traditions in a proper way, which is completely wrong. It will be much more beneficial even within this life, and of course for enlightenment, if one can really follow and practice actual Buddhism according to one's individual capability in a simple way, which definitely opens wisdom. Even if one does not practice in an elaborate way, at least one can believe what is actually taught in Buddhism, which is necessary for establishing Buddhism in the West. A sign of not believing and having less faith is the dismantling of Buddhist teachings. It is good to dismantle nuclear weapons, but not Buddha's speech.

In recent history, as everyone knows, the country of Tibet was destabilized through the overpowering effect of sectarianism and racism between different regions, and from these karmic winds blowing, it was easy to cause the waves of the red flag's five-pointed star. At the time of war, many Tibetan teachers who held the lineages of the four sects of Tibetan Buddhism went to India, where they gave teachings and transmitted these lineages. There were many different people among those who received these teachings and lineages, including Western students of these teachers. At that time, I was hoping that even though Buddhism was in danger in the East in this *kaliyuga*, it could be restored in the West from the kindness of these teachers bestowing the teachings and lineages of the Hinayana, Mahayana, and Vajrayana.

In the time of Buddha Shakyamuni, there were many racist ideas about the ancestral lines of brahmins and kings. In the Vinaya system of the Hinayana, which came from that time, it was said not to give vows to blonds, as the body of the one taking vows was supposed to be respectable and suitable to the people of that time and place. In the Mahayana and Vajrayana, however, there is no discrimination over race or color in relation to vows, and vows have to be given to those who have faith. So, I appreciated that many Tibetan teachers gave many vows, teachings, and initiations without racism. I felt very positively that maybe someday in future generations, the teachings of the three yanas could flourish again through the West, and that Westerners could give teachings and initiations to Easterners or any others in this existent world later on.

Temporarily, however, this seems very unlikely because of the

materialistic basis of Western culture. It is sad that the previous traditions of Eastern countries are decaying very seriously in the West due
to an attraction to the power of materialism. Instead of restoring the
teachings of Buddhism, some Westerners who are considered intelligent and knowledgeable are trying to reduce them in many ways, and
are even misusing the speech of Buddha for this purpose. Their conceptual structure is racist and only oriented toward eternalist religion. Con-
descension toward non-eternalist Asian Buddhism demonstrates this,
as well as attempts to de-spiritualize Buddhism by adapting Buddhist
teachings to nihilist thinking in order to complement the nonspiritual
perspective of Western culture. An underlying racist conviction that
their own culture is intellectually, psychologically, and technologically
superior actually keeps Westerners from being able to comprehend the
teachings of Buddhism. This is particularly true of Vajrayana teachings,
which are pricelessly valuable but are being misinterpreted in the West.
Although what will happen in the future is indefinite, it is very sad to see
what is happening temporarily now with Buddhism in the West. Even
though Buddhist traditions have decayed for a while from the impact
of politics and technology in Eastern countries such as China and India
that have a history of spiritual traditions, I hope that they can again be
restored, like gardens that fade according to the season, but have seeds
scattered in the ground that can flower again.

In Buddhism, lineage is essential. It has nothing to do with race or
nationality, because it is a lineage of impartial compassion and stainless
wisdom that is imparted by transmission. The main key for assessing
Buddhism in the West is to notice that many Westerners do not want
to accept any tradition from Buddhism in a pure way; they want to create their own form of Buddhism, which becomes non-Buddhist. Many
Western Buddhist teachers do not accept the importance of Buddhist
lineage, and that nonacceptance has become their lineage. Like Henry
VIII, who broke away from the lineage of Catholicism to form his own
church just so he could divorce, the intentions of these Western teachers
have nothing to do with benefiting all beings through the victorious lineage of wisdom. They have not made a spiritual connection to Buddhist
lineage, so they leave it out of their versions of Buddhism, which are

not based on faith and belief in actual Buddhism or any phenomena of enlightenment, but on the ordinary concerns of human beings. Whatever they write about Buddhism is only for themselves personally or for others with the same cultural perspective of rejecting reliance on sublime beings, which makes a lineageless lineage with no blessing to open wisdom.

In contrast, in the history of previous Buddhist lineage holders, there were practitioners and saints who were not only from Tibet, but from other lands such as India and China, who searched for unbroken lineage holders from whom they could receive Buddhist lineage. They did this without considering race or nationality, but considering how they could receive the blessing of wisdom from sublime beings with realization in order to be able to hold the lineage of the teachings of Buddha and for these teachings to be able to flourish. They were not trying to find a way to be personally acknowledged or materially rewarded, but to attain enlightenment for all beings.

Due to belief, Tibetans during my time were concerned about being able to receive teachings, blessings, and lineage, and many traveled long distances searching for highly realized teachers who could bestow these. If there were good practitioners or teachers, people supported them in whatever ways were necessary, but here in the West, there is no certainty about the importance of receiving the blessings of lineage, accomplishing the meaning of Dharma, or believing in the accumulation of merit. This country is so young about all these things, including understanding how students follow and support teachers or how teachers guide students in a correct way to open spiritual qualities according to their capacity. In Tibet, if students or sponsors did something against Dharma or betrayed their teachers, people felt they were treacherous and not good containers for Dharma. In the West, if someone is treacherous in this way, people are interested and want to hear about it, feeling it is revolutionary and heroic. In Buddhist spiritual tradition, however, when one begins on the path of enlightenment and from then on, one can never give up faith and compassion and one can never betray one's teacher and Dharma. In the West, not only is defiance admired as courageous, but also people are primarily concerned with their own freedom, individual

rights, and what will be good for them personally. Through a misinterpretation of individual rights and freedom, Westerners can betray their
religion, country, parents, and teachers out of opportunism and lack of
respect, morality, or spiritual belief. This misinterpretation only hardens
belief in selfhood.

In the West, the self is examined to understand its formation, development, and function, but this examination occurs with ordinary conception and within the delusion of ordinary existence. Of course, it is
taught in Buddhism that wisdom is only found from delusion, but the
delusion of ordinary existence has to be surpassed. This is absolutely not
suitable for the ears of Westerners, because from attachment to ordinary
reality and wanting to keep a self firmly, even though this is impossible,
Westerners do not like to hear about what is beyond reality, including
enlightenment.

According to the Hinayana teachings of Buddhism, one must discipline ego and destroy the enemy, which is the passions, since the root
of the passions is the self. These teachings reveal that there is no self. If
one annihilates the self, the root of the passions will be cleansed, which
cleanses karma and the root of karma, which is the passions, and does
not make more selfness or cause more suffering.

According to the Mahayana teachings of Buddhism, whatever
appearances are seen from beings' habit and experience are only appearing from grasping mind and previous reality habit, so Buddha showed
there is no actual reality of self or the phenomena of self. Therefore,
there is no belief in a self, which only comes from interdependent relative truth but does not itself exist independently. It is just a momentary
appearance that has no reality but occurs when compounded circumstances come together, like a magician's performance of magic before an
audience. There are no self-existent independent phenomena; they are
all just appearing from habit, which Buddha revealed to purify cognitive
obscurations and to make transparency, the phenomena of stainlessness.
According to the Vajrayana teachings of Buddhism, the ordinary habit
of self, or ego, is wisdom deity. These teachings introduce primordial
wisdom emptiness, and since the essence of wisdom emptiness is stainless, its appearance is naturally unobscured, with many variations in

aspects, which introduces wisdom deity. To be wisdom deity means there is no self, so there is no way to cause any negative phenomena, but immeasurable wisdom qualities unobstructedly and naturally manifest as wisdom deity because there is no grasping at a self. There is only I-less wisdom and its immaculate illumination. Not relying on any ordinary self is called vajra pride, which has no self, so there is no other—there is not even a name of either an object to be vanquished or a subject who vanquishes—so everything is a manifestation of wisdom vajra. That is why any phenomena become wisdom deity.

Western philosophy, psychology, and religion deal with the construct of a self, but from a Buddhist view a self does not exist. They are dealing with what does not exist yet trying to make it exist from the perspective of ego, even when they are supposedly acknowledging its non-existence. If there is no realization of selfless wisdom, the result will be self-full, which causes self-deceit and frustration, not spiritual certainty. To talk about the self and selflessness in order to make oneself feel that the self is stronger and more substantial, and therefore to increase the phenomena of selfness, is negative. This is because it is based on grasping at and belief in a self, even when selflessness is intellectually accepted. From a Mahayana and especially a Vajrayana view, this self is called *rudra*, or evil.[17] From being too full of a self, and attached to that self, there comes too much of what is other than self, and from solidifying a separate self and other, oneself and others cannot be compatible with each other, which causes anger, hatred, and harm. That is why many religions that have caused actual self-ness have the result of violence.

Because there is a focus on this momentary life in the West, everything is used to support this focus, including Buddha's speech. This has led to Western misinterpretations of Buddhism that do not encourage people to worship sublime beings, to have faith, or to believe in what is beyond the ordinary phenomena of existence. This is compatible with a Western liberal intellectual perspective of disbelief in what is not obviously apparent to nonbeliever perception. Whether or not one worships, until attaining enlightenment, there are phenomena, except if one is in the five mindless states of deep sleep, the culmination of union, fainting, the unawareness of intoxication, or indifferent stupor. The duration of these states, whether short or long, depends on the awakened mind of the individual. Within phenomena, one must choose a pure view and decide on one's own which phenomena to create or cancel in order to go beyond nonbeliever phenomena. It is inappropriate to use the teachings of Buddhism with an ultimate intention of surviving in this world and remaining within nonbeliever conceptions, as this supports and concretizes a self, even when selflessness is being discussed. This is why the view of Buddhism cannot be understood from Western perspectives of science, religion, philosophy, and psychology. Not only is Buddhism misrepresented when this is undertaken, but sometimes there is an attempt to remove actual pure spiritual qualities from Buddhism. Although there are books that seem to agree with Buddhist teachings and quote Buddha and famous Asian teachers such as Nagarjuna, some of them contain an insidious neglect or disapproval of actual Buddhist spirituality and try to stop people from being influenced by an actual Buddhist view or anything that is not related to a nihilist orientation that protects and retains a self within this present life. These books are damaging because they misconstrue authentic Buddhism while misusing Buddhism as a source for Western adaptations that Westerners then erroneously assume are truly Buddhist. Some of these books seem to endorse Buddhist methods such as meditation, but indirectly discount the importance of correct views of Buddhist spirituality and Buddhist traditions of faith in sublime beings and wisdom teachers by emphasizing what is presented as compatible with Western psychology, such as increasing awareness, calmness, insight, and peace of mind, while underplaying, criticizing, or avoiding Buddhist beliefs about what is beyond an ordinary self and ordinary reality.

Buddhist methods go beyond ordinary reality because they are spiritual. From a habit of nihilism, many Western Buddhists are actually often not thinking about spirituality. They discard it with negative intentions. That is why they can eventually react to Buddhist teachings with fear and frustration and give them up, and why they can even try to prevent others from being Buddhist. Even though it is obvious that their bodies are compounded and that in one way or another, they are going to leave their bodies and die, they are shockingly unconcerned about this, and only worried about how they are going to live. They need a positive image that is beyond what exists before their senses, since the existent reality they perceive can never comfort them in a deep and long-lasting way, but anything beyond their experience of reality is denied.

I am hoping and praying that in new generations, when people are fresh, they can find out more about authentic Buddhist views, and there will begin to be many Buddhists practicing Dharma in the West in an uncomplicated way who have not been ruined by studying many conceptual ideas without trying to realize them through practice, or by following people who excessively materialize spiritual teachings only to obtain their own material power within this life. At this point, these are problems for Buddhists in the West.

Those who can learn, practice, develop spiritually through Buddhist methods, and teach correctly in a simple way with skillful means about practice with Buddhas, deities, and meditation will never harm people's minds and only benefit them. If someone has no sign of spiritual development, however, it is inappropriate to write books full of misconceptions about Buddhism that will confuse others. The nature of mind is immaterial, but without dealing with the immaterial, including the relation between immaterial mind and material phenomena, a relative connection is not made between mind and immaterial wisdom, and there is no ability to use authentic skillful means within the material.

The consequences of extreme materialism and disbelief are seen not only inwardly in undeveloped spirituality, but also outwardly in the way that Westerners deal with the people of other cultures at both personal and political levels. For example, in the West, there is a general lack of knowledge about other religions. If leaders in Western democratic countries studied the views of the religions of other countries, they could adjust more wisely to what would benefit and what would harm their countries. Just as by seeing a profile of a face, one can understand what the whole face looks like, learning a little about the beliefs of others can be a great help in understanding what they are actually thinking. It is not enough to decide that certain ideas are from religion and therefore not important, or that these ideas should be protected by freedom of religion and therefore are not to be touched, which are the two approaches of Western culture. If one does not understand other religions, it can be dangerous because it can continuously cause misconception, misinterpretation, and conflict, and one will not know how to deal with this conflict. Also, religions do not have nonconflicting ideas. That is samsara. Generally, whatever is discussed about any spiritual view uses logic, unless one is abiding in the nonconceptual stainless state, and any spiritual view can only be analyzed through conceptual phenomena. That is the nature of interdependent relative truth. For example, when one talks about *shunyata*, one can only do so by bringing up phenomena, because without bringing up phenomena, one cannot say anything about *shunyata*. Even spiritual practice is engaging material phenomena by using body, speech, and dualistic mind's conceptions with immaterial experience. So, it is not a mistake to learn about and discuss other religions in order to have a clear view of their theories and to be able to deal effectively with the followers of those religions, even for political reasons.

In some ways, the West's ideas about freedom and the rights of the individual are very thoughtful, and people can select from many alternatives in life, but they often do not know how to use their freedom and it can become twisted into something else. In the West there is an overemphasis on individual rights and freedom within the functioning of human society. I like the ideas of the American founding fathers on freedom of speech, freedom of religion, and preserving the rights of the individual, and I myself have been able to use that freedom independently in a positive way for some years, so I am very grateful to the founding fathers and the Constitution for this. Democratic freedom can cause very meaningful conditions, including for Dharma, if it is used in a proper way. Many others also have the opportunity to use these positive conditions, yet even though the writers of the Constitution tried to ensure freedom and equality for all people, the experiences of individuals are different. Beings' karma is not equal, and the way in which freedom and equality are understood and used by people is karmic. If one does not really recognize how to use freedom and equality, due to individual karma, these positive words can be turned into negative situations. Even though the founding fathers were great people, they did not have experience with Buddha's speech or consider Buddhist theory about the karmic system of cause and effect, and how different phenomena are caused within relative truth. So, long-term consequences were not foreseen, such as the ways in which interpretations of democratic ideas, which are supposed to cause social benefit, could eventually become a cause of social problems. Giving great importance to the freedom of the individual can also cause people to misinterpret the surrender of ego, perceiving it as a loss of individual freedom, even though giving up ego is the only way to attain actual freedom.

Buddha's teachings are like stainless sky, and sky is impenetrable and cannot be made false, yet there are some people writing books on Buddhism who not only pervert actual Buddhist teachings, but look for faults and contradiction in Buddhist teachings to criticize. Of course, if one wishes to live in the world, one has to deal with everything in ordinary reality being false, but if one truly cares about others and is wise, one should consider how to help connect people's minds to Buddhism through teachings and a correct point of view so they can go beyond the faults of ordinary reality. These non-Buddhist, nonspiritual, non-believing writers are doing the opposite of this. No matter where they are from, they sound like a pack of coyotes raising their noses up to the sky and howling. The sounds of each of them may have slightly different tones and rhythms, but the basic unpleasantness of the sound is the same since they follow the same pack leaders. The problem is that although these writers seem to be engaged with Buddhism, they are not. They are not even allowing their own people to re-light Buddha nature by letting them learn in a proper way about how Dharma works in the mind; how Dharma brings peace, happiness, and positive energy through prayer and meditation; and how to let Dharma flourish. In order to benefit beings, Buddhist teachings should be undistorted so that the transmission of genuine Buddhism can occur, but these writers are interrupting this transmission by altering Buddhism with misapplied ideals of egalitarianism and individual freedom, and teaching their alterations to others. This problem comes from their loyalty to self-righteous ego, which they try to preserve through exalting the personal power of the individual. This power is unrelated to the natural potential of each individual to reveal limitless spiritual power through egoless wisdom.

As an example, attachment to the ideals of egalitarianism and individual freedom make many people in the West unreceptive or even antagonistic to the idea of a Guru. (*Guru* is a Sanskrit term that means spiritual teacher.) Westerners are not accustomed to having pure phenomena toward spiritual teachers. Instead of having faith in them, they are paranoid, thinking that if they were to have a spiritual teacher, they would have to give up their personal independence. Because of their belief in the freedom of the individual, they negate the importance of teachers and de-spiritualize Buddhism, which makes them incapable of inspiring themselves. This is a great obstacle for Westerners. Instead of teaching the true Buddhist view that spiritual teachers are essential, some Western writers have objected to this.

If there is any spirituality in the West, that spirituality is eternalist, and gods are accepted in eternalism. Of course, without believing in something, religions cannot function, but it is strange that gods are considered acceptable while there is paranoia about spiritual teachers. Because of being worried about their individual rights, Westerners have the idea that a spiritual teacher could try to control them, but whether a teacher is controlling or not controlling students depends on the teacher, since individual qualities of teachers are different. It is unnecessary to generalize and oversimplify this by thinking that teachers only control others and stop others from being able to enjoy their individual rights, which is an extremely materialistic idea. I am not saying this because I am concerned that anyone will think this about me, and even if someone did think this about me, it is obvious that I am over the hill and do not have any reason to try to control anyone for anything. I am simply pointing out the misunderstandings that cause obstacles for receiving blessings from spiritual teachers, since I have been asked to talk about Buddhism in the West.

It can be difficult for Westerners to recognize spiritual qualities due to being overly conceptualizing and materialistic. Of course, racism is everywhere in the East and the West, and Westerners can also be occupied by racist attitudes about foreign teachers or traditions. The basic idea behind the Western rejection of spiritual teachers, however, is the egalitarian premise that there is not supposed to be any hierarchy, so no one is supposed to be above anyone else or greater than others.

It is hard to imagine a ballet company in which all dancers have to be equal, so that there is no prima ballerina, or in which no one can be a choreographer or instructor because those positions would be authoritarian or oppressive, but Westerners are so attracted to egalitarianism that they are willing to let their arts and culture decay for it. There is an orchestra that became popular after it did away with having a conductor, which was considered an egalitarian statement, even though someone must still be designated to set the tempo and signal the musicians to begin to play or they will not be able to synchronize with each other. Actually, anyone can become a conductor if they have the capacity, and if someone guides an orchestra with gestures to make more pleasing sounds, it can be beautiful. If no one could be unequal or above anyone else, rabbis, ministers, and priests could not stand behind their elevated pulpits to teach religions, and chancellors, prime ministers, and presidents could not be elected to their hierarchically superior positions to operate governments. Excessive egalitarianism is impractical and causes disorder. Even if people do not want someone else to be better than they are, as a result of karma it is inevitable that there will be some who are better than others at any endeavor, whether sports, academics, the arts, or gardening.

Just as it is obvious that people on a journey in an unfamiliar place must have someone guiding them who can help them go in the right direction, it is necessary for people to have teachers to guide them spiritually. Of course, there are many different spiritual teachers, but almost without differentiating between or analyzing their individual qualities, some Westerners reject all spiritual teachers with unreasonable suspicion and distrust just because they are teachers. Since Westerners like to regard all human beings as equals, it is typical for Westerners to react to spiritual teachers by refusing to have faith in anyone who appears in a human body or to accept that enlightened beings appear in this world as wisdom manifestations. Even when Westerners are fortunate enough to meet the right teachers, they cannot see their qualities or have faith in them. All teachers are seen in the same way, which is as a threat to individual independence, and there is no acknowledgment that many different kinds of qualities can exist among teachers just as they can among politicians, scientists, philosophers, scholars, or individuals in any category.

If individuals do not have experience in their field, they have to listen to those who do, and in a simple way, those who do are called teachers. In Buddhism, a teacher is imperative, unless one only wants to practice the Hinayana as a *rang-gyel*,[18] or Pratyekabuddha. These practitioners first listen to teachings from their abbots, and then at the end of their personal phenomena of existence after the purification of many eons, they can be self-enlightened according to their three prayers,[19] which include that without relying on a teacher, they can realize actual absolute truth. Even Pratyekabuddhas, however, have to rely on Buddha's teachings to finally become self-enlightened. Perhaps the Westerners who do not want to rely on teachers think their ideas are similar to the prayers of Pratyekabuddhas to attain enlightenment where there is no Buddha. Pratyekabuddhas, however, have already relied on teachers previously, and as the result of their prayer, they are then self-enlightened where there is no Buddha. I did not hear that these Westerners have prayed in this way, either previously or in this life. Furthermore, according to the Vajrayana, unless they are actual emanations of Buddhas, even after Pratyekabuddhas achieve the purification of the passions and attain nirvana, they will still have to return to existence to purify cognitive obscurations in order to attain the fully enlightened state. Without a teacher, one can miss the target by being unable to find the correct path within the time of this precious human life, which is a great waste. Particularly in Vajrayana Buddhism, one must rely on the teacher with faith to receive blessings in order to recognize wisdom. As Patrul Rinpoche said:

> Relying on the Lama is faith; it is not just a superficial manner.
> The method of accomplishment is Guru Yoga, which actually needs faith; it is not just saying prayers.
> For those who have faith, no matter what they do, they receive blessing.
> For those who have no faith, no matter what they do, there is no benefit.

Of course, teachers can be bad or good, but some nonbelievers masquerading as Buddhists have not been able to deal with their negative perceptions of teachers. They have extracted what they perceive as negative qualities and become obsessed with them. For any compounded phenomena, what seems to be negative or positive does not exist continuously and is changeable, yet these nonbelievers have fixated on making a big issue out of their perceptions of teachers' faults. Then they have applied this negativity to all teachers, which causes obstacles to developing their own pure phenomena and can also influence others to become overly cautious and judgmental toward teachers, which disturbs the flourishing of Buddha's teachings. One can see how this has happened by watching a film of Western Buddhist teachers at a meeting they held in Dharamsala, India, in 1993, which is still available, showing the Westerners' lack of connection with actual Dharma. They were completely preoccupied with their negative conceptions about the faults of Asian teachers, whether Japanese Zen Roshis, Asian Gurus, or Tibetan Lamas. It is so sad that they had no idea about the infinite qualities and activities that sublime beings can manifest for the benefit of sentient beings according to their various phenomena, or even a thought of their holiness. As if these Westerners were a pious, moralistic team of special purifiers sent from the pureland of Buddha Shakyamuni to reveal the faults of other teachers, they used this issue of faults and their own ideas about the purification of these faults to promote themselves as teachers of a revised Western Buddhism. This behavior exposed their assumption of their own superiority in comparison to the teachers they criticized, their savage inability to perceive spiritual qualities in teachers, and their lack of faith and belief in Buddhism while creating fear, suspicion, and distrust among other Westerners. An answer to the ideas expressed in this film can be read in *The Dakini Letters*.[20]

I gave an interview in *Tricycle*[21] many years ago in which I talked about the need for pure lineage and pure tradition in order for the Buddha nature of Western people to flourish, considering with good intentions how actual Buddhist lineage could be held in the West, which so far has not flourished in a proper way from lack of belief. If, with good intentions, people check what happened, they can see that instead of acknowledging the importance of lineage and Buddhist tradition, the ringleader of the magazine and her supporters attacked me. Revolution is a favorite convention in Western culture, and many Westerners enjoy revolting against any traditions. Of course, revolution against political injustice, dictators, or other forms of oppression can be appropriate and reasonable, but through a misinterpretation of the idea of freedom and individual rights, people can think that one must revolt against everything, and they can choose the wrong object and place to revolt against without reason.

To synthesize everything about the problems in the attitudes of Westerners toward Dharma, there is no belief in the next life, enlightenment, or karma, so no one wants to think about anything beyond the immediate reality perceived by their senses, and people are just like hungry dogs gulping down food until they are satisfied. If this approach is taken, instead of having a spiritual view, they only consider how to take advantage of others. Instead of following traditions and receiving spiritual lineage, they want to produce their own innovations, but these innovations can only be materializations that do not carry the spiritual energy of lineage. If one can receive the spiritual energy of lineage, which is always fresh and enlivening no matter how one studies or practices, one's energy can prosper from one experience to another experience, going up and up, so there is no need for materialized innovations. How can there be Dharma in the West when people do not believe in receiving the blessing of spiritual energy from Buddhas and sublime beings, the accumulation of virtue, or even positive conceptions that excel beyond the ordinary? These beliefs are the basis for engaging in the study and practice of Dharma. In any religion, one is supposed to believe in something, but in the West no one believes in anything except instant material answers. If something cannot be seen, it is thought of as fabricated, even when it is not fabricated but true. That is why Western Dharma students often have no commitment, conviction, or experience. Of course, this is a general problem in the West, and there are exceptions, including some Westerners who are practicing Buddhism with deep faith.

The problem in the West is that Buddhism is new and its spiritual traditions are not yet established in a proper way. For example, there were no lineages of nuns who held the full vows of *gelongma*[22] in Tibet, but there have been many generations of Tibetan women who have kept vows of refuge, *upasaka*, and morality, the same as nuns would, while simultaneously practicing according to the traditions of Vajrayana. There have also been many generations of Tibetan women who have followed the Vajrayana tradition of yoginis, and there have been many great yoginis throughout the history of Buddhism, including Yeshe Tsogyal, Machik Labdrön, and other sublime priestesses. Western women, however, do not know about these traditions, and when they start to learn about Buddhism, they often assume they should find a way to reconcile their feminist ideas with Buddhism. The ideas of feminism, however, are based on the history of women within worldly existence and are concerned with power and equality at a social, political, and economic level, and these should not be mixed or equated with a spiritual level. Even when Western women become nuns or yoginis, if they adapt Buddhist spirituality to feminist conceptions, they materialize and commercialize Buddhism, incorrectly thinking that this develops more feminine power.

Many Western women want the two sexes to be treated as if they were of an unspecified gender in order to ensure equal rights and freedom, but this is a political matter. From a spiritual view, women have Buddha nature the same as men do. Also, according to Buddhist theory, women are not always women, just as men are not always men, since the gender of one's present life's compounded karmic body is one of the many conditions in existence that are not permanent and constantly changing between lives. Beyond any ordinary conception of women, Vajrayana introduces the Dakinis of the Three Kayas, who are worshiped as enlightened manifestations since they are female Buddhas, such as Yeshe Tsogyal, Tara, and many more who appear from the state of Nirmanakaya to benefit many different beings. Nirmanakaya Dakinis can appear as anything, but Western feminism contradicts this by limiting the aspects that females are supposed to assume according to a social perspective in order to make them powerful among human beings. This just materializes women's bodies in an ordinary way, which contradicts a spiritual view because it is trying to materialize superior qualities, and makes women more ordinary by concretizing ordinary women's characteristics. By dictating that women should be a certain way, feminism actually tries to cancel or reduce the potential of the infinite qualities of Nirmanakaya Dakinis, which all women contain. Trying to make women more powerful in this way actually denigrates women and leaves their inherent wisdom Dakini unnoticed and unacknowledged.

Women naturally have their own power, including an ability to attract and control men unintentionally, but men run away from women who want to be of an unspecified gender. By ignoring their natural characteristics, even if women wish to be powerful, they lose their power instead. According to Vajrayana tradition, women are said to hold unique wisdom qualities and special powers, including those of ecstasy and the wisdom power to attract. This power can naturally subdue men, like bees attracted to the nectar of fragrant flowers, but strong, extreme feminist ideas can cause unattractiveness that makes men disperse, like the smell of a skunk. Then, when these women age, even though they scavenge for companions, it is very hard for them to find anyone, so they become miserable due to the residual energy they created from their way of thinking. If women really believe in the state of enlightenment and practice to rekindle their inherent Dakini's energy, it does not matter if the compounded energy of the *skandhas* decays, because their flawless wisdom ecstasy increases. Women can use Buddhist teachings temporarily to become great yoginis in this life, and ultimately to attain the state of fully enlightened great wisdom Dakinis indivisible with the state of the Dakas of the Three Kayas. If they are mainly concerned with attaching a conceptual structure of feminism to Buddhism, however, these holy teachings can become twisted into political or sociological ideas related to ordinary power and passions only for this momentary life.

Of course, Dharma is beneficial for beings, and among beings, human beings are especially capable of practicing Dharma, but Western ideas about freedom are such a strong, exclusively material influence that they can become an obstacle to practice. For example, in any kind of monastic vows, the support of a flawless and specific gender is necessary because these vows must be held physically, such as in controlling one's libido. Even though one has good physical conditions and mental characteristics that one is capable of using, one does not use them for worldly pleasure but for enlightenment, and one takes and keeps these vows to cause virtue, believing in karma up to the state of enlightenment. That is the meaning of vows. From an orientation of insisting on freedom, women's rights, and unspecified gender, however, these vows can be seen as interfering with individual freedom, while the idea of individual freedom is also used to defend the right to change one's gender. Lately, although medical science has made it possible to change the physical characteristics of the body from female to male and from male to female, this change in gender is obviously artificial and dangerous, and takes so much effort that is wasted because the result is not natural, but like a mannequin animated with electricity. Even if the physical body is changed, the energy of the body and mind can never become the same as the energy of natural gender. Likewise, although animals cannot be made into human beings, someday scientists can try to make human beings into ignorant animals just to boast about their abilities, but what is the benefit for human society? From a Buddhist view, this is horrible. One prays never to fall to the lower realm of animals, but to be reborn as a precious human being, and one prays for those in the lower realms to be guided to the higher realms.

Practice has to deal with phenomena, and the view of phenomena has to be established and used in a correct way. One cannot erase the differences between the phenomena of male and female energy, as synthesized in the Chinese terms *yin* and *yang*, and in the Tibetan terms *tab*[23] and *sherab*.[24] Of course, in the Mahayana there is freedom from fabrication, such as in the Madhyamaka, that goes beyond the state of duality in order to liberate. Also, in the Dharmapalas of the Vajrayana, there is the deity Maning, who is neither male nor female and beyond a particular gender, which has the meaning of union. And also, there are ordinary beings who are hermaphrodites. Generally, though, the phenomena of ordinary beings up to the appearances of sublime beings go through both *tab* and *sherab*, phenomena and emptiness, which naturally are always indivisible, and are reflected in the differences between the genders. Even in the material energy of substance within ordinary existence, the opposites of positive and negative charges naturally come together and are always related. In Buddhism, recognizing the state of the inseparability of phenomena and emptiness, establishing the view, and accumulating merit continue until the essence of wisdom emptiness and phenomena become indivisible and the state of enlightenment is attained. In the vows of monks and nuns and of yogis and yoginis, which are actually connected with Dharma, the distinctions of the genders are not invalidated, but are attributes of phenomena that are used in practice. Practice goes with phenomena and emptiness together; otherwise, one cannot re-light spiritual qualities.

While one has a precious human being's birth, it is extremely important to use one's mind to attain fully enlightened Buddhahood through believing with faith, practicing, and meditating. Even though one cannot catch it or hold it, mind exists intangibly within the five skandhas of form, feeling, perception, intention, and consciousness. It is absurd if one does not use the mind for practice but believes only in this momentary life, because no one exists who will never die. Although death is actually just the habit of mind, from the habit of living and dying, the elements will diminish and the body will become disposable because it is compounded, and whatever is compounded is impossible to keep, no matter how much one suffers by trying to make one's life as long as possible. Even though people want their lives to be long-lasting and try with so much effort to arrange this, their lives will not be long-lasting but will finish. Even then, they stubbornly keep repeating their habit of being nonbelievers from one life to the next with the misguided stamina that comes from enormous attachment to ego. One can occasionally hear about someone who has lived to be a hundred years old, but if there is no Dharma, that long life is wasted. When one has a precious human being's birth, it is so sad if one throws it away by not using this chance and being a nonbeliever attached to this momentary life. Wisdom is within one's own mind, so it is important right now, while one has a human body with precious Buddha nature, to use this opportunity to at least be a believer, abstain from negativity, create positive phenomena, and do spiritual practice, trying to let the uncompounded flourish to attain the deathless state through believing.

Instead of following precious Buddhist teachings, it is strange when someone only believes in the material and, as a nonbeliever in pure spirituality, uses Buddhist spirituality in a reverse way with a perverse view, such as measuring neurological or biochemical activity in the brain with modern technology to physically analyze the practice of *shamatha* or *vipashyana* meditation. This is very illogical and harmful, since it de-spiritualizes meditation. All of the equipment used to do this is totally compounded material, and any expert who conducts this analysis is collecting totally compounded ordinary conceptions. Both the measurements and the one who makes the measurements are equally materialistic and not in wisdom, so whatever is found is only coming from the influence of ordinary, worldly materialism.

In the context of the modern world, explaining spiritual states with conceptions about physiological processes and checking for physical evidence of immaterial states of mind are easy for nonbelievers to accept, without faith and without any experience of contemplation. Furthermore, in capitalistic countries where the importance of the individual is emphasized, everything can be used to create something to sell for personal profit, including even meditation. The idea of checking for material evidence does not support spiritual practice for enlightenment, but just adjusts to the geneal conceptions of nonbelievers, who like science. Liberation means to be free from any trap, and it is extremely dangerous to become trapped by scientizing meditation using machinery instead of learning a spiritual way of practicing properly. Even if all the scholars and philosophers of this existent world were to agree on the result of this kind of research, it actually makes human beings ignorant and prevents the flourishing of wisdom through encouraging belief in the continuity of mind in past and future lives, the purification of negative habit and karma and the accumulation of merit and wisdom to create positive karma and for enlightenment, and the opening of Buddha nature, to finally attain fully enlightened uncompounded wisdom body and mind, indivisibly. Those who examine a materialization of meditation should already know that their own bodies are material and that they are suffering because of material, so there is no point in finding more material. There are many people with reverse views who are destroying the lives of innocent beings, but more than that, people of this degenerate time who are destroying faith and belief are a hundred times worse. This is because they are preventing others from letting their Buddha nature blossom by believing in sublime beings' blessings and wisdom mind, distracting them with ordinary materializations and creating disbelief in spiritual phenomena. If there is belief in the Mahayana teachings of Buddha Shakyamuni, each being has Buddha nature that must open by having faith and believing in the accumulation of merit and wisdom to connect with Buddha nature and fully enlightened Buddha through the interdependence of beneficial intentions and bodhichitta for beings. "Beings" means those with mind, and the benefiters, or Buddhas and Bodhisattvas, are also mind. Then, someday, fully enlightened Buddhahood can be attained from the accumulation of merit and wisdom through being a believer.

Normal medical doctors easily deal with monitoring and measuring the physical processes of patients' bodies, such as telling people whether their blood pressure is high, low, or normal, with the intention of making people healthy by checking them and instructing them about their health, as in what foods to abandon and accept to influence the physical condition of their bodies. Making material measurements for material reasons with material energy in this way is much more pure than research on meditation, since there is no misinterpretation being made, because these doctors are not trying to associate what they do with enlightenment. They are not making up a connection between the physical and the spiritual, causing more unreliable, compounded, conflicting conceptions that endlessly circle in confusion instead of causing uncompounded wisdom body.

I totally have faith in uncompounded wisdom body, even though I am not a good practitioner. According to Old School (Nyingma) tantric teachings, the dharmachakra of peaceful wisdom deities abides in the heart, and the dharmachakra of wrathful wisdom deities abides in the palace of the skull of the jewel head. This does not mean materially. These wrathful deities in the palace of the skull are the manifestation of peaceful deities, and this connection is indivisible during the life of the practitioner. Whenever the practitioner separates from the karmic body at death, as a result of previous practice, these peaceful and wrathful deities fill the sky.

Naturally, view and meditation are connected with mind, and this is not creating more compounded conception. This connection is completely different from looking for something to be found using the nonspiritual science of nonbelievers. One can just ask oneself whether scientists are finding the state of enlightenment. Even momentarily, if an individual's mind becomes very turbulent and emotional, how can science make it calm? An individual can be given a pill, an injection, or anesthesia, but this is temporary. If a practitioner goes into a room to have his meditation evaluated by someone who examines it with electrodes or imaging equipment, when exactly will the one who is examining it see his meditation? When the practitioner has indefinite emotions or distress, what is experienced will not be the same as what is seen by the examiner. There is no way to use material measurements of spiritual experience to change the mind from being spiritually inert to developing it in a Buddhist way. At least Buddhism has the methods of prayers, visualization, and abiding in stillness, and if one believes in the teachings of Buddhism with faith, one can freely know how to do these so the mind can be used in a spiritual way. Those who transform spirituality into materialism are using ideas originating from nonbelief in spirituality, and from that, they try to invent something new to sell out of Buddhism's precious teachings. There are many examples of this in the degenerate age, and they should not be copied.

The essence and result of Buddhist practice are always Buddha, so it is always positive. In one way, practice can seem to be very difficult when one has to learn many methods, but in another way, practice can be very easy if one is a believer and has faith in Buddha and one's own Buddha nature because one has been introduced to one's own Buddha nature by a sublime being and has prayed. The experience of difficulty or easiness depends on the individual's capacity, the teachings received, the path that is taken, and the practice one does. As Mipham Rinpoche said in this Mahasandhi prayer:

By being so easy, no one believes in the secret of the nature of mind. From the power of the *upadesha* teaching of my Root Guru, may I see it.

Especially if one has faith without doubt in Mahamudra or Maha-sandhi, one can attain enlightenment in this life or the next, as is known by those who have a reliable wisdom teacher showing the correct view and who are familiar with the histories of previous sublime beings. If there is no Dharma, no positive habit, and no belief in the next life or enlightenment, the meaning of having a human life is completely lost, and mind stays in a nonbeliever's static state of dullness. Even though the mind stays this way, the habit of phenomena will not be quiet; the mind will move, be busy, and search for happiness, but it will be difficult to find happiness because of nonbelief, and there will be no way to find long-lasting, positive phenomena. One cannot deny that mind exists within tangible and intangible phenomena; one can prove this through dreaming, which shows that mind exists intangibly, one's habits exist intangibly, and these habits disturb the tangible nerves, veins, and vital energy. Whenever there is habit, one will be born somewhere through that habit, and it is uncertain where that will be and in which kind of realm. So the most precious use of one's human mind and skandhas while having a human birth and hearing the teachings of Buddhas is to believe in those teachings. Whether one is able to practice less or more, at least one can try to be a believer and pray, believing in cause and effect and in increasing virtue through accumulation according to relative truth until cause and effect become indivisible through medita-tion in the sole oneness of flawless ecstasy, which is absolute truth. For those who believe in the pure phenomena of enlightenment, deities, and wisdom, wisdom never dies. Death belongs to the delusion of the com-pounded reality habit of ordinary mind. Even though death itself does not exist, it exists for sentient beings because of the strong habit of sub-stance, and that is why one suffers again and again by circling between birth and death. Within that circling, even when there is happiness, it is short-lived and does not last.

Because they see all truth, all Buddhas who are abiding in the death-less state of enlightenment have taught sentient beings, from unob-structed compassion, that the nature of the mind is deathless Buddha. It is only that this nature is dormant, so one has to revive it through faith, purification, prayer, and meditation without grasping and without pressuring oneself with the expectation of reviving it until attaining the fully enlightened state, which does not need effort or reviving. If one can meditate, one does not lose anything. Actually, if one does not meditate, one loses everything, since whatever one possesses is lost because it is compounded, and whenever these possessions are lost, it causes suffering. Even though one does not want to lose whatever one has, one is losing it continuously until it all vanishes. When everything vanishes, there is no certainty about how it will come back or if it will be according to one's wishes. The only hope is to be a believer and practice. If one has no belief or practice, one will not have any confidence about where to stay or what to do. So it is very important to be a believer, however much one is able to practice. This belief is not in something mistaken, but in positive phenomena.

Of course, everyone has to survive in this life, and one can choose which way to do so, but it is necessary to believe. That is the key to practice. If one is not a believer, it is impossible to practice. Actually, one can still enjoy a good life in this world even according to ordinary life's phenomena with the practices of Mahayana and Vajrayana, because it is not necessary to give up desirable qualities for those who have faith in these yanas, if one can use them with skill to benefit oneself and other beings. That is why the Great Vehicle is called great.

If one's mind is occupied only by worldly concerns, one becomes too impatient to sit, watch one's mind, and relax. One does not relax because one is thinking about worldly phenomena, which are not real, although one thinks they are real because of reality habit. What is actual and true, which is believing in Buddha, practicing, and meditating, one thinks is unreal because of one's habit, and one feels they are a waste of time, and so one does something else that one thinks is not a waste of time. By doing this, one totally lures and discourages oneself because one ignores faith, practice, and meditation, even though one has to leave one's body someday. Impermanence is not only the death of the body. Although death is the most terrifying form of impermanence to ordinary human beings, everything is impermanent. Whatever is gathered must fall apart, and there is no power for anything to always be together, because of karma or circumstances. All circumstances change, and that is why

one cannot have any certainty about circumstances, since good circumstances can turn to bad and bad can turn to good, because they are all
only momentary and totally unreliable, because they are all whirling in
alaya. People in the West are generally scared to think about impermanence. They can see impermanence everywhere, but they do not like to
see it and will say, "We don't want to hear about those bad things." The
consequence of thinking about impermanence, however, is to reduce
one's attachment to reality and to increase belief, faith, and eternity's
wisdom body. Shantideva said:

> Suffering is not only negative; it has positive qualities.
> From being unhappy and sad, arrogance is purified
> And compassion increases toward samsaric beings,
> So therefore one will abstain from sin and become happy to
>   make virtue.

The ideas presented in some favorite Western Dharma books, such
as *Buddhism without Beliefs* and *The Faith to Doubt*, are in disagreement
with Buddhist views about belief and faith. These ideas do not exist in
any kind of Buddhism, and they are unbelievably dangerous because
they prevent faith and pure spirituality with ideas that are one-sidedly
materialistic. What can replace faith and belief? If people have something better, they should explain it. It is not necessary to teach others not
to have faith but to have doubt, because sentient beings already believe
in doubt even though they do not say so, and that is why they are wan-
dering in samsara. The faith to doubt is everywhere; it is not an exotic
or valuable teaching, and it does not need to be emphasized. Even when
human beings do not know anything about Buddhism, they have doubt.

Regarding doubt, the Buddhist scholar Aryadeva once said satirically
in a Madhyamaka text:

> This profound teaching of wisdom is so precious,
> One is not even going to have one doubt.
> If someone doubts this,
> All samsaric suffering is going to end.

This does not mean one should not have faith; it means Buddha's teachings are so powerful that even if one can connect to them by doubting, one can become convinced of their truth and eradicate samsaric suffering. It means that someone who has no faith can become completely full of faith and even enlightened. It does not mean that doubt is positive, as though lack of certainty were somehow intelligent. In these books, Buddhism is presented as historically devoid of faith. Obviously, however, Buddha Shakyamuni says in many sutras, including a sutra about the recitation of mantra in the practice of Amitayus (Buddha of Infinite Life):

> Whoever reads this sutra even temporarily will have the positive phenomena of human life and ultimately will achieve enlightenment, but whoever has doubt is not included among those who will achieve this result.

To teach people not to have faith and belief, and to prevent them from learning what Buddha actually taught about faith and belief by encouraging them to have doubt, is showing them how to be ignorant, cause suffering, and totally throw away the opportunities of human life. Also, it is impossible to try to prevent people's minds from having faith and belief. Phenomena mean everything that is happening in one's mind. Through believing, one can reduce negative phenomena and expand positive phenomena with the guidance of a correct teacher. Buddhist practices use the phenomena of mind by cleansing and transforming all negative phenomena into positive phenomena through engaging with Buddhas and, through meditation, abiding in the continuity of stainless wisdom without grasping or imagining it to be special in a certain way. Even though the nature of mind itself cannot be found anywhere, it can manifest everything, anywhere, at any time, and these manifestations cannot be prevented. If one does not deny the ceaseless continuity of mind's phenomena, including one's own personal phenomena and the general phenomena of others, one has to accept spiritual phenomena and especially Buddhist theory and logic about phenomena and the source of phenomena. Even if positive manifestations of spiritual phenomena are suppressed, there will be negative phenomena, because the nature of mind is unobstructed; but to allow negative phenomena and prevent positive phenomena is awful. Instead of trying to prevent the positive phenomena of mind, it is better to accept the continuity of mind, which causes negative and positive energy, and try to reduce or purify the influence of negative energy and develop positive energy, with mindfulness. As Nagarjuna said:

If there is no mindfulness, all phenomena are going to be ruined.

If one does not want any phenomena, one has to abide in stainless emptiness wisdom forever. That is the best choice, because that is the natural indivisibility of phenomena and wisdom emptiness. Otherwise, unless there is total unconsciousness, there are phenomena. Even if there is unconsciousness, whether it is for a long time or a short time according to personal karma, whenever consciousness is restored, phenomena will reoccur. Phenomena have already occurred, are still occurring, and will continue to occur, and it is only beings' habit from previous karma that determines how long these phenomena last. If someone does not believe in cause and effect with mindfulness, so that there is no conception of the antidote of positive karma, how can negative karma cease?

Instead of trying to cancel belief in the continuity of mind and to present one's individual thoughts, such as those expressed in *Buddhism without Beliefs* and *The Faith to Doubt*, as though they were ideas that apply to everyone else, personal negativity toward Buddhism should only be represented as one's own opinions and not applied to the general phenomena of others. Even if one unwisely perceives Buddhism as doubtful, without any reasoning or basis for this perception, and without analyzing that this comes out of one's resentment and hatred resulting from one's particular personal circumstances, to then project this onto others and expand it to include them is not nice. It is inappropriate to behave like a mad dog in this way, jumping and biting everywhere without disciplining oneself. One must acknowledge that beings have an unlimited diversity of phenomena and karma, so one cannot force others to share one's personal view or prevent their faith. If one wants to make personal statements about one's own lack of belief, one has to say, "I have faith in doubting Buddhism," or "I do not have belief in Buddhism," without trying to prevent others from having faith, since there are countless beings, and if they have the karmic connection to have faith, it cannot be stopped. Even if one can prevent it for one moment, one cannot prevent it in the next moment. It is not just illogical and extremely sinful to try to prevent faith and belief; it is impossible. This is because the nature of mind is infinite, intangible, and cannot be restricted or concretized; beings are infinite, time and place are infinite, and Buddha's teachings are unobstructedly infinite. Also, one cannot make doubt or lack of belief permanent, because these phenomena do not exist continuously according to the times, places, and circumstances of beings. It is also unwise to try to cancel all the spirituality of Buddhism, which can never be achieved, as a way to express the personal negative attitude of one finite person. As everyone knows, there have been many leaders who have tried to cancel all spiritual ideas in their countries, yet now that those leaders are gone, spiritual ideas, including those of Buddhism, are again flourishing in those countries.

As Patrul Rinpoche said:

Existence or non-existence, eternalism or nihilism, going or coming, and so on, all these phenomena
Are created by the continuity of dualistic mind, so how could they be prevented?
Even if one says something is beyond mind, saying that is still contrived.
Is it not as deluded as trying to block water with a dam made of water?
Some doctrinaires say there is existence, aiming at relative truth.
Some doctrinaires say there is non-existence, aiming at absolute truth.
Aiming at either of these or both is spreading the contagion of poison,
So how could the state of aimlessness of stainless Dharmakaya be seen?

In Buddhism, according to the Hinayana, the ending of the continuity of the phenomena of mind can occur through practice or meditation in *samadhi*, just before the state of nirvana is reached. Until that, mind is continuous. The cessation of phenomena, in which everything is cleansed so there is nothing left, is like the example of everything being burned by fire so there is not any remaining residue of passions or karma from the habit of mind. That is the truth of cessation. According to the Mahayana, the phenomena of mind exist until the obscurations of the passions and cognition are totally purified. For one's own benefit one never remains in samsara, and for the benefit of others one does not remain in the attachment to enlightenment, and this is the attainment of the state of full enlightenment, beyond the two extremes. According to the Vajrayana, the phenomena of mind exist until all ordinary phenomena of dualistic habit are transformed through practice to fully enlightened Buddhahood, by carrying the qualities of the state of all fully enlightened Buddhas into the path with sadhana practice through using the karmic body and passions, to attain only stainless wisdom mandala.

So, unless one attains the result of one's practice, Buddhism teaches that one cannot make the phenomena of mind cease because there is no other method for doing so. Even if a naive nonbeliever who is unfamiliar with spiritual logic tries to make the spiritual qualities of mind cease, the natural spiritual potential of beings will exist within tangible and intangible phenomena. It is a disaster to try to erase Buddha nature through illogical nihilist materialism rather than letting Buddha nature be rekindled and blossom through the many different methods for purifying obscurations and accumulating merit and wisdom that have been revealed by the omniscient Buddha. If one holds a nonbelieving attitude and uses that attitude to develop nihilist ideas that mislead others to disbelieve in and prevent spirituality, causing them to erase or deny the accumulation of virtue and the rekindling of Buddha nature, it is harmful to beings, especially human beings.

There have also been lectures available on the Internet about "the secular Buddha."[25] This kind of negative characterization cannot be given for the origin of all positive qualities. Buddha is ceaseless, everywhere and in every time, unaffected by anything. *Buddha* means that all obscurations are purified, including the reality phenomena of human beings who think they are either secular or nonsecular, and that all immeasurable wisdom has expanded. Although Buddha can appear in any aspect, Buddha cannot be put in the tiniest category of secularism. Buddha is fully enlightened with wisdom body, wisdom speech, wisdom mind, wisdom qualities, and wisdom activities, which are indivisibly pervasive and inconceivable, and at the same time manifest in an immeasurable way, so one cannot say that Buddha is either secular or nonsecular. It is ridiculous to try to expel Buddha from Buddhism, which was named after Buddha, and make even Buddha into a nonspiritual conception that can fit into the materialism of ordinary society with its different theories, groups, cultures, laws, and everything that belongs to the worldly phenomena of samsaric beings. A secular Buddha does not exist, since secularism belongs to society and ordinary beings and is not even connected with religion. More than religion, Buddha is wisdom, beyond belief or disbelief, neither aligned nor unaligned with anything, with the power to emanate as anything. So, Buddha cannot be put within one small nonreligious category. *Secularism* is not a term for fully enlightened Buddhas who are beyond all conception, including conceptions of society and religion or the rejection of religion. Buddhas are beyond all samsara and enlightenment, and also at the same time emanate toward all samsaric beings, not only secular beings, and pervade throughout all of the enlightened state, so they are forever stainless and beyond all thought. Buddha cannot be made to belong to this world, other worlds, or even this universe. Buddha is nowhere because Buddha is forever like stainless sky. One cannot catch or make stainless sky, but at the same time it pervades everywhere. Just like stainless sky, Buddha is everywhere because Buddha manifests effortlessly and unobstructedly within any realm, place, and time. It is absurd to try to limit this manifestation, like trying to hold all of the immeasurable sky in one small pot. Even if people cannot practice formally or traditionally, they still need to believe in a simple way, and no one should be trying to stop this.

Both the nonacceptance and acceptance of religions or gods come from different interpretations of manifestation while remaining within dualistic phenomena. Within dualistic phenomena, limitless ideas can emerge that can be rejected or accepted, so anything can be said about them, but manifestations of phenomena can never, never be prevented

or canceled, because the unobstructed state from which these phenomena arise cannot be prevented. Any view that tries to prevent the unobstructedness of phenomena is therefore illogical and disproves itself.

It is necessary to recognize that mind can cause all the suffering of
samsara and also immeasurable happiness, although one cannot touch,
grab, or see the mind, because it is intangible. As Sarahapa said:

> Sole mind is the seed of all immeasurable phenomena.
> It can manifest samsara and also enlightenment.

Therefore, as Mipham Rinpoche said in *The Prayer of the Meaning
of the Indivisible Basis, Path, and Result, the Empty Awareness Vajra Self-
Melody:*[26]

> Sugatas and Bodhisattvas of the ten directions and four times
> Holding indivisible wisdom body,
> Youthful Manjushri in the nature of evenness,
> May the meaning of not doing anything be self-accomplished.
>
> By faith in the beginningless primordial Lord, the glorious Lama,
> Seeing incomparable Dharmakaya,
> May actual wisdom lineage blessing transform my heart.
> May I receive the great empowerment of awareness.

When consciousness is engaged with the senses, according to Buddhist terms, it is called awareness, although this ordinary awareness
cannot be compared to wisdom awareness, which belongs to enlightenment. When there is no awareness, the basis of mind is in the undiscern-
ing dullness of indifferent stupor.

The Buddhist explanation of consciousness and the senses is not like
the beliefs of any form of nihilism. In nihilism, it is thought that consciousness and the five senses gradually develop in living beings and then
disappear at death; that mind depends on the physical body and finishes
when the body dies; and that there is nothing beyond the momentary
existence of the present life, such as a next life. According to Buddhist
theory, consciousness can become dormant at the time of death if the
being faints, but after death, consciousness will again occur somewhere

else. The senses, as well as the objects perceived by the senses, arise from consciousness, and when the physical body is left, the mind continues, whether there is consciousness or dullness. This is true whether one believes this or not.

In the Hinayana, the six gatherings of consciousness, called *namshe tsok druk*[27] in Tibetan, are the conjunction of the senses, which are the eyes, ears, nose, tongue, feeling, and mind; the objects of these senses, which are form, sound, smell, taste, touch, and phenomena; and the consciousness that corresponds to each of the senses. When the six gatherings of consciousness are believed to be reality because of grasping, they cause the passions of attachment and aversion, the emotions that are the activity of the passions, karma, and samsara. In Mahayana theory, there are eight categories, so that along with these six gatherings of consciousness, there are the gatherings of the consciousness of the mind of the passions, called *nyönyi*[28] in Tibetan, and *alayavijnana*, called *kunzhi namshe*[29] in Tibetan, which is the basis of consciousness, or the basis of all that can be perceived or analyzed. In alayavijnana, from the gatherings of consciousness, sentient beings create all the myriad aspects of phenomena. There are many ways of understanding the meaning of this, including:

> It is said that the meaning of alaya is the basis of all,
> So it is also the basis of enlightenment.

As Kunkhyen Rongzompa[30] said in *Entering the Way of the Great Vehicle:*[31]

> In general, in the lower yanas, the characteristic of alaya is that it is where the root and the effect of all false phenomena recede, occur, and remain, like the ripening place of fruit, and it is also the basis of all phenomena of flawlessness, like medicine in a vessel of poison. In the view of the Mahayana, the characteristic of alaya is that from the beginning, it is abiding in the pure essence of enlightenment, so it is called the basis of enlightened mind. The passions and all habits, including those of the lower realms, are just sudden temporary stains, like gold obscured by stains or jewels remaining in mud. The natural quality is temporarily not conspicuous, but the nature is never lost.

It is said in *The Vajra Ornament:*[32]

> A sparkling precious jewel,
> Although temporarily sunk in the mud of a defiled place,
> Is not going to lose its natural quality of self-radiance
> That can illuminate the sky.
> Likewise, the precious jewel of the nature of enlightened mind,
> Although temporarily obscured in a defiled body,
> Has the natural radiance of wisdom,
> So its light is always in the sky of Dharmata.

All ordinary negative and positive phenomena are occurring in the alaya of consciousness, created by the phenomena of perception. Thus, whatever ordinary phenomena arise do not exist. It is just that from the lack of recognition of wisdom, ignorance arises and causes delusion and the mind's grasping at reality. Then, from habits sown in alaya with the subject of ego and its object of reality, beings follow after their passions and intentions and produce karma according to interdependent relative truth. Actually, an essence of alaya cannot be found anywhere in a material way, since its nature is insubstantial and baseless; it is just that cause and effect are made in it from interdependence, or in Tibetan, *tendrel.*[33] All phenomena are naturally enlightened for those who can realize this; it is unnecessary to find the path of enlightenment from somewhere else. For all immeasurable Buddhas, from beginninglessness, there is no alaya, because immeasurable Buddhas' truth is stainless wisdom, which means there is no basis of ignorance.

As Kunkhyen Longchenpa explained according to Mahasandhi teachings, the alaya of consciousness that creates all habit can be described with the example of the ocean, which is the basis that supports all kinds of beings, including many sea animals, and also boats and any other material objects that can remain, abide, and travel upon it. The alaya of actual truth from the beginningless beginning can be described with the example of sky, because it is the same as Dharmakaya, excelling beyond any material cause or condition. It cannot seed any cause, effect, or conditions, but at the same time, its quality of stainlessness is the basis of all pure phenomena. Dharmakaya is indivisible with wisdom, so there is no basis of samsaric phenomena or dullness of indifferent stupor, and wisdom is continuously abiding and effortlessly manifesting. From beginninglessness, it is the nonsubstantial, inexpressible, unchangeable basis of absolute truth. It is where all immeasurable Buddhas abide, manifest, and recede, and is the beginningless origin of unobstructed manifestations, unintentionally only beneficial, that appear and recede according to conditioned beings' phenomena. This is the mandala of wisdom of all the Buddhas of the Three Kayas. Just as sky is unobstructed—and one is not supposed to think sky is only empty—from characteristicless, stainless, unobscured wisdom emptiness, infinite characteristics of manifestations pervade tangibly and intangibly, with characteristics or characteristiclessly, and throughout beings' phenomena within the limitation of time and place. The quality of the openness of unobscured sky is not numbness or nothingness; it can appear as rays of light or emanate as sun, moon, or stars. Likewise, the unobstructed qualities of Sambhogakaya can appear as the infinity of Buddhas and purelands [Buddhafields], which are intangible according to tangible phenomena, and beyond the grasping of beings with obscured, tangible phenomena who cannot see that state. Only immeasurable wisdom Buddhas are sustaining in that pureland state, from which unobstructed compassion manifests according to the reality of the phenomena of beings, with a performance of activity that is seemingly within reality. This is Nirmanakaya, which itself has no actual reality or material karmic birth because Nirmanakaya is free from interdependent relative truth, but according to beings' phenomena of relative truth, Nirmanakaya emanates in whatever form is suitable to beings' faculties. It is said:

> Some beings are born from karma.
> Some beings are born from prayer.
> Buddhas manifest from the power of wisdom.

Even if one does not recognize the original state of the basis of samsaric phenomena and enlightenment, it cannot be erased, because it is continuous and has no limitation of time and place. Wherever beings stay or go, there are time and place, and time and place are only beings' momentary compounded phenomena of habit. Since the manifestation of Dharmakaya is unobstructed and cannot be prevented, the best choice is not to remain continuously in alaya or in dullness, but to follow and believe in the prayers and teachings of Buddhas, recognizing that all manifestation is coming from Dharmakaya, and that all manifestation is actually pure awareness and ecstasy. No matter what the forms of manifestation seem to be, their essence is flawless ecstasy because they come from the state of stainlessness. Beings may think ecstasy is only within compounded material experience, but it actually comes from Dharmakaya. The flawless emptiness of Dharmakaya is substanceless and immaterial, so it is forever naturally evenness, and evenness is flawless ecstasy because it is not causing the disturbance of contradiction that comes from two things. From Dharmakaya come the wisdom manifestations of Buddhas. Whatever appearances arise are manifesting from the flawless ecstasy of Dharmakaya, so these manifestations are naturally flawless ecstasy, and that is why they give the blessing of ecstasy to beings within compounded material body and mind.

When there is no cause of a reality of samsaric phenomena, it is called Dharmadhatu or Dharmakaya. Wherever there is Dharmakaya, that is Dharmadhatu, and wherever there is Dharmadhatu, that is Dharmakaya, so even though Dharmadhatu and Dharmakaya are discerned with different terms explaining the aspects of their qualities, their essence is indivisible. Dharmadhatu's quality is immeasurable space. The manifestations of immeasurable female and male Buddhas and Bodhisattvas are emanating from, receding to, and abiding in Dharmadhatu. *Dhatu* means the great expanse, and is the quality of stainless space. It is the immeasurable speechless state and the quality of emptiness. Dharmakaya's quality is pervasiveness throughout all form. *Kaya* means form, and all kinds of pure phenomena. Although Dharmakaya has no particular discerned form itself, there are infinite aspects of Dharmakaya, so it is kaya. Dharmakaya's quality of form is Rupakaya, which is the immeasurable Sambhogakaya and Nirmanakaya, so Dharmakaya perfectly pervades all existence and even non-existence, within the material and immaterial, as all pure phenomena. That is why there are limitless phenomena of kaya. There is no form, or kaya, that is not pervaded by Dharmakaya, from which all forms are manifesting and to which they

are receding. The kaya of Dharmakaya is not nil, because the manifestation of form and sound are immeasurable. According to Mahayana
and Vajrayana teachings, the most pure form is Sambhogakaya and the
manifestations of the five Buddha families, which are indivisible from
Dharmakaya. From Sambhogakaya comes Nirmanakaya, which is indivisible from Sambhogakaya and Dharmakaya, but manifests according
to beings' faculties, time, and place as the pure appearances and retinues
of Nirmanakaya that can occur in impure and pure aspects throughout
the realms of existence, reflecting beings' impure and pure phenomena
within *tendrel*, or interdependence, to connect to them and guide them
to the ultimate purity of enlightenment. Although there are histories
of the forms of Nirmanakaya that have appeared in this existent world
according to different beings' faculties, actual Nirmanakaya is wisdom
body, which is indivisible from Dharmakaya, and is the unobstructed
qualities of the manifestation of Dharmakaya, which is indestructible
forever, even if these qualities manifest as destructible or changeable as
the aspects of Nirmanakaya. Just as all of the other elements of earth,
water, fire, and air have the seal of sky, no matter what color, shape, form,
sound, or quality exists, there is nothing that is not pervaded by Dharmakaya. Although beings are remaining in alaya, from prayer, faith, the
blessings of Buddhas, and the introduction to wisdom by great teachers,
they can recognize Buddha nature and simultaneously excel in Dharmakaya. Then there is no name of alaya. It is said in *The Tantra of the
Expanse*:[34]

> Not the basis of conception,
> Natural non-existence is the basis of absolute truth.
> It is called the space of phenomena, Dharmadhatu.
> That is wisdom as it is.

Dharmadhatu is not the basis of conception; whatever causes conception causes passions, which cause karma and karmic form because
of not excelling in Dharmadhatu. First, a self causes passions because
it has not been cleansed, and since there is a self, there is other. Then,
between self and other, there are negative and positive phenomena,
with attachment to what is positive and trying to get it, and aversion

to what is negative and trying to run away from it or attack it, which are all caused by passions that make a nest of karma. That is called samsara. Although phenomena cannot be denied, one can misuse phenomena and cause samsara, or one can use phenomena correctly and cause virtue. By praying, relying on holy teachers, and recognizing Buddha nature or wisdom deity, if one truly re-enlivens wisdom, the basis of the phenomena of consciousness and habit is cleansed in Dharmakaya. Whenever it is cleansed, there is no cause of suffering because there is no ordinary grasping ego, which causes conception and karma. If one listens to the instructions of one's teacher, is introduced to the nature of mind, and abides in stainless mind, as Buddha said, all suffering will cease because conception is purified. The reason it is important to meditate is that it frees one from death and birth, because the nature of mind is Dharmata, the deathless continuity of wisdom. If one can stay for one moment in that state, there is nothing born, so what is there to die? This is not like a nonbeliever's view of denying phenomena without logic. Learning is precious, but abiding for one moment in stainless mind is a million times more powerful because it makes all suffering cease. If one can abide in that state as Buddha taught, whatever previous negative or positive thoughts or habits one had cannot be found. Likewise, one cannot find a next life because there is no karma, but this is not like a nonbeliever's idea of denying karma. Through recognizing and abiding in that stainless state, cleansing karma, one abides in the deathless state.

In a brief way, we all have mind. Even if one cannot see the next life's mind, it is necessary to believe in the mind's continuity. Because of the seeding of habit in alaya, beings must be born again and again with attachment or self, and from animals to human beings, one can see the difference between what is created by negative and positive habit. By believing in the continuity of mind, one can create the accumulation of only positive virtue by believing in and worshiping the Triple Gems, and at the same time one can meditate in stainless emptiness in order not to cause karma with attachment. The positive phenomena of virtue cause the form of Rupakaya, and meditation causes the formlessness of Dharmakaya, which are the indivisible basis and path, so one can attain the indivisibility of full enlightenment forever.

The phenomena of ordinary mind are continually changing, causing compounded phenomena that bring frustration because one is reluctant for them to change. Dharmakaya does not cause unreliable changing phenomena, because there is no self. It is stainless, so the body, speech, mind, and purelands of Buddhas never cease to manifest. These manifestations are always changing, but this is not like deluded phenomena that change from grasping mind. It is the unobstructed quality of wisdom. If one has faith in this continuity of wisdom, according to interdependent relative truth, someday one can receive blessings and naturally recognize one's own awareness mind. If one can stay in that immaculate state, it is wonderful. When meditating, one does not need to search for anything, trying to find either alaya or Dharmakaya. Whenever conceptions arise, one can transform them into virtue. Wisdom is a continuity, so one must just come back to that continuous state. As Patrul Rinpoche says:

> By seeing all, then aiming is lost.
> How can the path of liberation be found later?
> Whatever you do, it becomes the path of liberation.
> Whatever you meditate, it naturally expands in the continuity
>   of Dharmakaya.

For this to occur, as Kunkhyen Longchenpa said:

> Even though one recognizes one's own stainless wisdom mind, if one
>   does not become familiar with being in that state,
> One will be captured by the enemy, conception, like a little boy in
>   battle.

Even though wisdom is within one's own mind, it is dormant, and that is why one suffers in samsara. If wisdom is opened and one meditates, one can naturally be released from suffering. That is the great meaning of meditation. The essence of any teaching of Buddha is to meditate, because it liberates from suffering. If one has faith and belief, without grasping, one can recognize this someday because of being a believer, so naturally one's mind comes into that inexpressible state. If one grasps, even if one is meditating, it can make it dissipate. If one has faith in Buddha, one can definitely re-light wisdom because of the inter-dependent connection of receiving blessings.

When alaya has not excelled in stainless Dharmakaya so that beings' minds are in alaya, various causes and effects can come according to beings' attachment, like the examples of the phenomena of nightmares or pleasant dreams, and the phenomena of the suffering of hell realms or the exaltation of heavens. The conspicuous phenomena of reality that are apparent to ordinary senses come from compounded phenomena that are unreal and eventually will become inconspicuous due to remaining in alaya continuously and due to the inevitable disintegration of all that is compounded. This characteristic of compounded phenomena is not like a general nonbelieving view that everything must finish. Even when the compounded skandhas seem to finish, they are not finished; only the material forms of the skandhas are finished, but the habits of ordinary dualistic mind remain in alaya and re-cause samsara. Again, because of not recognizing and abiding in Dharmakaya, whenever circumstances or the phenomena of previous habit arise, samsaric phenomena that have temporarily subsided will again occur.

According to different beings' intentions with passions, since anything can appear from or recede back to alaya, in this movement of samsara, karmic phenomena increase and decrease like seeds that are sown and develop into plants, and then later fade and return into the ground, leaving seeds that will again begin to grow. Although samsaric phenomena always circle between being born, remaining, and ceasing, many people think that whatever has faded or receded is finished. For example, people have asked why Buddhism continually repeats its discussion about nihilism and eternalism, and say this issue is based on a historical context that no longer exists, so it is not relevant anymore. This is because they think that if something recedes, it has ceased, since they believe in material reality and do not think anything that recedes from this reality can still recur or be revived. This way of thinking is actually based on a nihilist view, and shows that it is dangerous to study spiritual ideas when they are misinterpreted from having nihilist habits. Those who hold a nonbeliever's view only accept what is conspicuous, but as long as beings' minds are not enlightened, they always have to circle in duality where phenomena appear and recede.

The time and place when dormant phenomena will be revived or restored by appearing from alaya depends on beings' karmic phenomena within time and place. For example, in the last century, conspicuously and unforgettably, fanatical doctrinaires arose who changed their countries by reintroducing earlier forms of beliefs that previously seemed to have receded, causing the increase of political disturbances and violence among beings. Obviously, ordinary beings cannot know what will result from circumstances because of their cognitive obscurations, so even when they try to influence circumstances according to their capacity, they cannot determine what will be ultimately harmful or beneficial within appearing and receding phenomena, because they misunderstand and misinterpret how the immaterial affects the material. Only the omniscient Buddha knows the way in which beings come into existence within time and place, and the way that all dualistic phenomena are created. Even though there is Buddha nature in each being's mind, ordinary beings do not know this. Because ordinary beings are in a state of unknowing from not excelling beyond alaya, they have nihilist habits and eternalist habits, so there are beings who are nonbelievers in a spiritual view and beings who are believers in a spiritual view.

Whether those who are not connected with Buddhist teachings are nonbelievers or believers, when they equally do not believe in karma, they can equally kill other beings. Not only nonbelievers have killed other beings; spiritual leaders have killed others for supposedly spiritual reasons. Being a nonbeliever from a lack of being spiritual does not need to be explained, because almost all beings are like that, including human beings. Even though their phenomena are temporary and only endure for a little while, some of these temporary phenomena seem very long, and some seem very short, which depends on the personal habits of the individual or the noncomplementary disagreement and complementary agreement of group habits.

It has only been a little while, within the last few generations, since many beings were killed by infamous nihilist leaders such as Hitler, Stalin, Mao Zedong, Pol Pot, and the leaders of many African countries. This terrible killing is a sign of the way in which circumstances are seeded by the conditions of intentions and aspirations. As it is said in the sutra *Entering into Langka*:[35]

Consciousness came from mind.
Mind is coming from alaya.
From alaya, all kinds of thoughts will come,
Just waves of the river.

Anything can occur from alaya, and from the misinterpretation of the manifestation of Buddha nature, even though negativity does not exist, negativity can be caused from this basis of habit, due to not excelling in Dharmakaya. Those dark leaders brought so much suffering by not having any hesitation to kill many beings, even though there was no benefit to them. They are now gone, but their names still remain. From that, negative karma could be reproduced. While they were living, they lived with fear and frustration, and when they died, they had nothing to carry with them from all the effort they had made except the habit of hatred, anger, violence, and fear that is following their minds through future rebirths after leaving their negative legacy in this world. Through the nonbeliever habit of lack of belief in the karmic system and only seeing what was in front of them, they did whatever was possible to materially obliterate others with hatred, including their own countrymen.

Nonbelievers are extremely absurd. Although they know and believe that the actions of these harmful leaders have occurred, they have no way to explain them except as temporary circumstances between human beings. Since nonbelievers do not believe in anything, they think everything just happens by itself, like mushrooms appearing overnight after a rainfall in the forest. If one believes that beings have continuous mind, and that habits are created by previous intentions, the genocide of all the millions of people who were killed by these harmful leaders is understood to have had the power to occur from intention. Even if the specific causes cannot be seen, it is obvious that these leaders were more powerfully harmful than other beings, and this mental power was based on habits that were seeded in alaya. From these habits, their thoughts became reality, and from their karmic debts to each other, all of these killers and all of those they killed were caught in the winds of their karma, acting out the habits they had seeded from their thoughts.

Although these leaders killed millions to acquire power for themselves, as quickly as one moment passed into another moment, they had no power left to use and they died. Even if these leaders thought they were acting to benefit others with similarly twisted ideas, these others also had to die, since anything that exists materially cannot be continuous but will change, so whatever they could have imagined to be beneficial was only very, very temporary.

Of course, in the last few generations, there have also been some special leaders who have given positive examples showing the way to cause the result of peace. To create peace in this world, it is so meaningful to have a spiritual view and to believe in cause and effect, which prevents negative karma and causes positive karma, as many histories of Bodhisattvas from ancient times reveal according to causal Mahayana theory. These histories show why intention and prayer are so important: in order not to cause continuous essenceless samsaric phenomena in alaya, but to excel beyond it.

Even though circumstances may seem to be negative or positive, it is uncertain what their result will be, which depends on the habits, intentions, and prayers that are created. Some beings live their lives with negative habits, such as Alexander the Great, Genghis Khan, Tamerlane, and Atilla the Hun, who killed many beings for conquest until they died. Some beings transform negative habits into positive habits, as in the history of King Ashoka, who was first an ignoble prince, but became a Dharma king by listening to the history of Buddha. Also, in an Indian account from the time of Buddha Shakyamuni, a murderer named Finger Rosary[36] who killed ninety-nine people and wore a necklace made of their fingers finally regretted what he had done, took refuge from Buddha, attained the state of seeing truth, and found liberation. Some beings go from a positive state to a more positive state, such as Mahatma Gandhi, who always acted with positive intentions and accomplished the activity of virtue with compassion, which brings peace. Some beings go from a positive state to gaining pure spiritual confidence, such as in the histories of many Bodhisattvas.

If the basis of mind (alaya) has not excelled in Dharmakaya, anything within the different realms of existence can occur within the phenomena of reality, which includes not only the phenomena of existence experienced by ordinary beings, but the phenomena of spirituality that are not connected with the stainless state of wisdom, including the phenomena of any kind of eternalism. From a Buddhist view, it cannot be ultimately liberating to hold an eternalist belief in a god who does not go beyond selfhood. If one reads each of the eternalist religions' theories about gods carefully and keenly, it is seen that the gods of eternalism, and therefore the followers of eternalist religions, never let go of ego. If they do have a selfless view, it is not eternalist but Buddhist, even though it appears to be in an eternalist form. A sign that eternalist gods have not given up self is that their followers, who worship and pray to these gods, create more self. People can examine this aggressive selfness.

Tantric teachings about wisdom deity may seem to be similar to eternalist teachings about gods, whether formless or with form, but the view of wisdom deity is entirely different because deity is selfless. In tantric teachings, according to the path, the ordinary self has to be cleansed through stainless wisdom, which as mentioned is called vajra pride, although there is no self that is proud, because there is only wisdom. Then, from that stainlessness, manifestations of wisdom arise, which have no self. It can be said in Buddhism that deity has wisdom ego, but this vajra ego or the vajra pride of deity is selfless. It does not have to fit anything anywhere, because there is no object that challenges and no subject that defends, competes, or compares. The characteristic of ordinary pride or arrogance is that there is object and subject, because it comes from a strong self, and whatever object is perceived as other than the self cannot fit with the self, due to the lack of recognition of one's own reflection. Then, by seriously separating a subject of a self from an object of what is other than a self, one cannot accommodate any other qualities.

Of course, enlightened manifestations can appear in the aspect of worldly gods, so I cannot say whether or not eternalist gods are manifestations of Buddhas; but when a self is retained with grasping and without pure selfless wisdom vajra pride, one cannot go beyond eternalism. The problem is that every kind of problem comes from a self. If a god retains a self, self cannot be reduced, because a self is concretized, and

followers must follow this with re-concretizing a self, so a self develops
further and causes conflict with other beings. Eternalists are suffering
because they are occupied by a self, since their god has a self, and so they
keep feeding, retaining, and developing selfness. The reason they cannot
go beyond a self is that their main heritage and practice are to reaffirm a
self. Eternalist religions can never go beyond Buddhism, which is unsur-
passable and beyond all of whatever is said in eternalist religions about
heavens, gods, or deities, because Buddhism goes beyond the self. As
mentioned, the main practice of the Hinayana to attain the Arhat's state
is to annihilate the self into selflessness, which is the total destruction
of the enemy ego and its passions and karma. In the Mahayana, by only
thinking of the vast intention of benefiting all beings through bodhichitta, which is selfless compassion, and making the effort to benefit
others, the result is unintentionally to become fully enlightened Buddha. In the Vajrayana, through faith and nonhardship, by believing in
the selfless beginningless purity of Buddha, which is the state of Vajradhara, the result is carried into the path up to reaching the indivisible
path and result.

Since eternalist gods have a firmly permanent ego, there is no way
to surpass ego within the eternalist perspective, so eternalist teachings
always build ego no matter what is taught. As Kunkhyen Rongzompa
and Kunkhyen Longchenpa have said, when the object of refuge is not
released from ego, the followers of that object of refuge cannot know
how to be released from ordinary ego. Also, people like ordinary ego
because they feel secure with it, even though as long as they have ego,
they are continuously losing whatever they are and whatever they have
because these are occupied by the compounded phenomena of duality.
When there are gods but there is no mention of I-lessness, it means
these gods are worldly gods who must protect ego, because if there is
ego, there always must be an object, and objects cause fear. That is why
Westerners are afraid to prostrate before Buddha's statues.

Aside from the basic problem of keeping a self, many eternalists
actually hold a nihilist view of disbelief in spiritual phenomena beyond
ordinary perception and only accept obviously existing appearances, not
actually acknowledging the immaterial but just believing in what occurs

in front of them. The details of the extensive explanations and philo-sophical analyses of eternalism and nihilism from the time of Buddha cannot be given here, but in brief, nihilism is easily understood as dis-believing in anything beyond the five senses and only accepting what is here and now, and eternalism is the belief in a permanent god. Eternal-ism often seems to be like nihilism, however, because there is no consid-eration of consequences or belief in what is beyond the perception of the five ordinary senses. If one checks the history of the religions of the world, one can see how the misinterpretation of phenomena through attachment to reality has affected the followers of eternalist religions. The obvious evidence for this is that the followers of these religions are always fighting and killing for material power with material weapons. The starting point of spirituality is thinking about what is beyond mate-rialism, so this fighting has nothing to do with spirituality even if it is identified as the defense of a religion. The fact that eternalists are fight-ing indicates that they are actually pure nihilists, because whatever they want to accomplish is motivated by seeking this life's power and control, which is why they want to defeat and subjugate enemies. This happens because they conceive of an enemy as a true enemy of a true "I." The power that they try to build is only for their own race and their own religion, which is not religion.

Killing enemies for power or for revenge is physical; it is not mental. It is not killing ego. Therefore, it is very simple to understand that the people who are fighting do not believe in what is beyond physical reality. The delusion of sentient beings is so amazing, since they can think they are religious and yet hold a totally nihilist view. Even though eternalists are supposed to at least consider immaterial phenomena beyond ordi-nary existence, including an immaterial or formless god, they have con-tinually fought with each other for material power in this world. Their delusion is that they are not seeing the nature of stainlessness, so they are fighting and killing for a material result with stained minds, taking reality seriously so that it becomes substantialized in only a material way, and without knowing how to be relieved from that state. According to Buddhism, this is not really spiritual. Even though some eternalists will say that God is light and God is love, why have they fought? That fighting is heavy and dark, not light, and it is full of hatred, not love.

This world does not have peace, because people believe only in material reality, and they fight because they are thinking only of ordinary power within material reality. That is why there is continuously war. This is not new. All the eternalists throughout history who only believed in acquiring material power have held the same belief in a nihilist view. This is also so for those who thought of themselves as Buddhists but were only fighting for material power, although if they did so, it was not Buddhist, but nihilist, no matter what they seemed to be or to think. As reported in the media, purported Buddhist fanatics barbarically killed a respected scholar and his two attendants.[37]

In Hinayana, one has to purify self in I-lessness; in Mahayana, instead of harming, one is supposed to benefit other beings with bodhichitta; and in Vajrayana, others are seen as the emanation or reflection of wisdom deity. So there is no cause for violence for whoever is truly Buddhist.

It is important to distinguish between negative and positive fanaticism. It is possible for fanaticism to be reasonable, with faith, so that one is determined about what one believes with pure intentions. Therefore, it does not matter if others think one's beliefs are illogical or if others do not agree with one's ideas. This kind of fanaticism that comes from deep faith is positive, because even though it may appear stupid to others at a worldly level, it actually causes morality, stability, and loyalty, and it increases faith, so it can cause stable, stainless *samadhi* and enlightenment. This kind of reasonable fanaticism, in which one is determined about what one believes with pure intentions and a correct view, is only positive, so it can only cause a positive result. Negative fanaticism is based on a stubbornly wrong point of view, including the bullying mistreatment of others, belief in wrong gods, or a misinterpretation of virtue, such as by sacrificing the blood of other beings.

From the circumstance of the delusion of excessive attachment to power, Westerners are susceptible to another new form of terrorism arising in the West. When violent activity is disguised as a spiritual path, and a supposedly spiritual path is turned into its reverse, it can cause an even more dangerous form of violence than ordinary nihilism because it is concealed by religion. Even though it is covered with the appearance of spirituality, it is terrorism when human life is sacrificed from aggressiveness for material power without compassion, faith, or belief in karmic cause and result. This problem has already existed for many generations in Tibet in the form of sectarianism, as everyone knows, and now that Tibet has been lost, these terrorists who wear a mask of Buddhism are attempting to attract spiritually hungry Westerners. This can really seed the development of another form of sacrifice in the West, in which Westerners will be the victims. This has already started, and there are people being schooled in and studying these ideas in Europe, North America, South America, Australia, and even some countries in Asia. If they follow this worst kind of dogmatism out of their excitement about anything that seems new, there is no question that they have already lost the value of their precious human lives, which will be wasted on a negation of actual spirituality. In this degenerate time, beings with bad karma can listen to the misinterpretation of spirituality by excessively doctrinaire leaders aggressively recruiting Westerners, so religion is twisted to evil energy instead of being beneficial even in this life, ruining the lives of other beings. This kind of terrible disease can be caused in the West from the circumstance of being attracted to a materialization of spiritual power. The basic Western problem is excessive attachment to material power, which is not only in this matter.

If eternalists really believe in God, since they think God is supposed to be immaterial and cannot be seen but is there, they are not supposed to materialize God. The believer in God is the mind, and the mind is immaterial, whether one recognizes this or not, so the mind needs to believe with faith, and to unite with God. It is not necessary to fight for material to attain the immaterial state of God. One has to believe and keep an immaterial view so that one does not cause material killing. Believing that God is immaterial and believing in this immaterial God with faith will not cause disconnection.

The Tony Blair Faith Foundation is in accord with this. Blair encourages those who believe in peaceful coexistence for people of all faiths to voice their ideas instead of allowing the message of terrorist extremists to predominate. Among eternalists, Blair's words are like liquid ambrosia dripping from a dry rock mountain, and I so appreciate his pure, logical speech, which is very precious in this degenerate time. It is also very positive for Blair to be a believer in spiritual lineage, which can be assumed since he converted to Roman Catholicism with its tradition of apostolic succession, and as a believer to want to have peace in this world. I also like Blair's comment that he is concerned about extremists of all religions. As he mentions, the terrorist message already publicly exists. Terrorists are already publicly sacrificing human beings, and terrorist guides are publicly teaching others that the sacrifice of human life is virtuous, not sinful. As it is taught by extremists, sacrifice is considered to be a very easy way to get to heaven, and many beings have been born with the karmic connection to believe this and to train in becoming extremists. If there could be a miraculous manifestation of compassion among those extremists, such as Buddha Shakyamuni or even Mahatma Gandhi or Martin Luther King Jr., it could be helpful. If the people of other religions just keep their own beliefs, however, trying not to interfere with anyone else's religion, it is logically very hard for them to bargain with any kind of religious extremists. So, it is unlikely for peaceful coexistence to happen because, whether for reasons of religion or politics, people are always racing against each other for power. Even religious leaders can be power-hungry from lack of actual faith and can use religion for power. The leaders of all religions have to reduce their attachment to being their religion's leaders. Eternalist leaders have to be careful about what is taught in their religions, because if the essence of what is taught is only concerned with material power, even what seems to be the performance of religion is really concretizing a nihilist view and can cause violence if there is no actual spiritual influence. Often, from allegedly spiritual teachings, the strong habit of nihilist reality is re-created, and from misusing religion, violence is caused. Eternalist doctrinaires should be careful not to cause this kind of misinterpretation, which happens from extreme materialistic intentions that lead to violence against others for material power, with material weapons and physical reactions.

From lack of spirituality, eternalists who are attached to their own religion and try to create an imitation of purity through their extremist position will misconstrue spirituality, with the actual result of causing nihilism. It becomes dangerous to think one's own religion is pure or

ultimate when taking an extremist position that concretizes a nonspiritual view, since whatever is concretized becomes nihilist. By aggressively concretizing one's own view, whatever extremist position is taken,
whether nihilist, eternalist, or even Buddhist, one can think one is acting
in the interest of one's beliefs when one has totally lost an actual pure
view. When there is no authentically spiritual view, there is no benefit,
and one can even choose violence against others and think that this violence is a religious act. Many people have obviously liked a religion even
though its acts of sacrificing living beings have been seen by everyone,
and despite the fact that the benefit of its beliefs cannot be proven. It
does not mean that beliefs are positive if a majority of people like them,
because in a spiritual way, the agreement of a majority is not significant,
no matter how many people are involved. Whether people are old or
young, they are not necessarily wise, and if one accepts the beliefs of others in order to be in agreement, it is disastrous. That is what is happening in the world. If one does not make peace forever, there is no peace.
That is why Buddha Shakyamuni always says to pray not to be born in
a savage country, or to be born with great compassion.

There are many conceptions of prayers and belief among eternalists
that are truly positive and not negative at all. Prayer means there is a
connection with sublime beings, and sublime beings are supposed to
be positive and bring positive energy, so there is nothing wrong with
praying. Even so, there are many nihilists devoid of beliefs who disparage prayer. Those who are nihilists do not have to be strongly against
religion or against others' being spiritual or against belief in prayer and
having faith, but some Western nihilists do not like these at all. Generally, Westerners do not believe in the continuity of mind and karmic
cause and effect, so in the West there is no belief in Buddha's speech
about continuous mind causing karma unless one believes positively in
attaining enlightenment by believing in karma, and by abstaining from
negative karma and creating positive karma to go beyond karma. If there
were no karma, how could some beings be born as terrorists and some
be born as their victims? I have never heard that there was a place in this
existent world where it is discussed who will become victims and who
will become sacrificers, yet beings are born to become victims and sacri-

ficers. If human beings believe in karma, they can understand the causes of consequences, not only for this life but for all subsequent lives up to attaining enlightenment. Then they can be in peaceful coexistence by believing in Buddha's teachings while they are living, and when they die, they can be reborn in purelands or at least in circumstances of peaceful coexistence instead of violence.

In Buddhism, there are wrathful activities in sadhanas, but the view of these activities is entirely different from ordinary physical violence. The object of these wrathful activities is one's own ego, which has caused suffering for oneself and others for many lives. That is the demon being annihilated. If one annihilates "I," then all other enemies or evils are naturally defeated, because where are they coming from? They come from "I." That is why, when one begins the visualization in all outer and inner Vajrayana sadhanas of deities, one first has to cleanse all ordinary dualistic ego, which is the source of all demons, in wisdom, saying OM MAHA SHUNYATA JNANA BENZAR SOBHAWA ATMA KO HAM. This is actually the annihilation of all material habit of reality. Also, in the Mahayana, there are histories of the wrathful activities of Bodhisattvas, but these are enacted out of compassion for other beings, not to defeat them with hatred or anger. In the Vajrayana, wrathful activities of deities that are revealed in sadhanas are the way that all the self-absorption of material ego that is the cause of suffering is annihilated by the view of I-less wisdom.

There are many tantric explanations of wrathful activity, but for practitioners, wrathful deity is coming from one's own mind, and *rudra,* or demon, is coming from one's own mind. This is unlike the view of eternalists who actually fight against each other with material weapons and material conceptions with a nihilist view. Especially in the theory of inner Vajrayana, in the annihilation with a wrathful aspect of any obstructing demonic influence, the view is totally different from the views of eternalist religions in the way that one practices and in relation to oneself. The meaning of the visualization of wrathful deities is actually not to harm at all but to gain the power of nondualistic wisdom. This is according to the path of practice, because the practitioner has "I," and so there are objects that come from that "I." If there is a harmful object, so that the practitioner has the conception that the object is evil, and also has the subjective conception of being deity, the view of deity annihilates the conception of evil. So, in practice, conception is subdued by conception. In sadhanas, a representation of *rudra* is made objectively, and subjectively one has to visualize oneself as wrathful deity with vajra pride, which is selflessly being deity. Through compassion and with wrathful activities and gestures, one conceptualizes the destruction of those who harm other beings and cause hell realms due to misinterpretations of annihilation. According to actual relative truth, even in this life, this momentarily brings peace, and it prevents beings from going to the lower realms through one's intention of compassion. Ultimately, according to the result, it is the destruction of duality in indestructible wisdom through the power of noncontradictory wisdom mind. This is the general idea of these vajra activities, but it depends on individual intention, capacity, and practice; it is possible that someone could have negative intentions due to bad karma, but this would be against Vajrayana *samaya*. Sometimes, although rarely, it could be heard that there was conflict among extremists in Tibet, but generally, the Mahayana theory of always having compassion for other beings was taught and practiced in Tibetan Buddhism.

These ideas about eternalism and how they are different from Buddhism are mentioned because Westerners generally have an eternalist heritage. Although eternalist religions are accepted by the majority in the West, as mentioned, whatever is believed by the majority is not necessarily true. As said in *Magic Dance*, there was once a king whose subjects had become crazy from poisons in rainwater that had contaminated their wells. The king had protected his own well, thanks to the prediction by an astrologer who had warned him that this poisonous rain would occur in one week; thus, he did not go crazy himself. But when everyone else's phenomena became so different from his own by drinking this water, the king decided to drink the poisoned rainwater too, in order to become complementary with his subjects. After that, they were all in agreement with each other, but all of their phenomena were equally hallucinated.

Of course, nihilists are nonbelievers, so there is no expectation for them to be receptive to spirituality, but I have heard many times that Western eternalists have been against Buddhism and have attempted to prevent Buddhism from flourishing. Also, I know that people with eternalist backgrounds have voluntarily become Buddhist from their incisiveness, and not from any effort made to convert them to Buddhism. As one can read in the amazing original histories of Buddhism, many of Buddha Shakyamuni's students had previously been eternalist; also, Buddha's emanation was predicted by great Hindu sages.

Sometimes eternalist ideas are compared to Buddhism, but Buddhism cannot be said to be comparable or not comparable to eternalist religions, because no limitation can be placed upon it. Buddhism is forever openness because there is no partiality of self-phenomena. Although the aspects of the histories of eternalist religions are different, according to Buddhism all of their views are the same, whether considering Hinduism, Islam, Judaism, Christianity, or any other form of eternalism, and they are distinguished from Buddhism by their belief in permanent gods.

All eternalist religions refer to heaven, whether this is conceptualized as being located somewhere in the universe, in another dimension of existence, as a heaven that will appear on earth or as a state of mind, and whether it is described as the realm of God or as an everlasting state of communion or union with God, and eternalists generally pray that they can go to heaven after death. Even though believing in heaven and God is positive, eternalist views about what to believe, the object of belief, and the special, sublime qualities of the object of belief can be ambiguous, depending on the group or individual view. Eternalism is much more hopeful than nihilism, however, because those who are believers can become pure Buddhists through their belief. This still cannot definitely be decided, because it depends on individual karma and faith or belief. Since mind is continuous, nihilists can become eternalists, nihilists can become Buddhist, eternalists can become nihilists, and eternalists can become Buddhists. Some eternalists are not really connecting with actual spirituality and are only named eternalists while they have transformed into nihilists, and some nihilists can rekindle actual spiritual qualities since they have Buddha nature. No one knows except the omniscient Buddha, who sees the karma of sentient beings transparently.

From a Buddhist view, the place where sentient beings will stay or go or come depends on their view and practice. The six realms of sentient beings already exist everywhere through beings' karmic habit, whether one believes it or not. One requests and prays for fully enlightened Buddhas to manifest in order to guide sentient beings to go beyond these six realms, according to relative truth, and reach enlightenment. According to the Mahayana view of the Three Kayas, all Buddhas manifest from stainless Dharmakaya, the purelands of Sambhogakaya, and the compassion of Nirmanakaya. It is not that one tries to go anywhere within the realms of existence or to keep one's place within existence and ask God to come and stay there. The manifestation of Buddhas is unobstructed, and because sentient beings are infinite, there are infinite manifestations that can appear. Whenever the benefit of manifestations is complete, these manifestations recede. Whatever manifestations occur are coming, going, appearing, and receding in correspondence to the karmic phenomena of sentient beings.

According to the Buddhist view, there can be completely positive characteristics of the pure phenomena of purelands, which benefit through these positive characteristics, or there can be a completely characteristicless state, which benefits by being totally characteristicless. Pureland is pure form, as in Sambhogakaya and Nirmanakaya, which are pure because they are coming from stainless Dharmakaya. All of these are not easy to put into words, because of their inconceivable qualities, and it is also not enough to say a few words about them, unless someone is gifted and a special practitioner and can catch the meaning. The main key is that purelands are connected with the subject of believers, faith, and an object of a blesser. Through a correct view, practicing on the path, and achieving the result, there is ultimate union. This is dealing not only with the material but with the connection between the material and the immaterial. The way to reach the limitless state beyond duality forever depends on the believer, the method of the path, and a correct view.

In order to reach the purelands of the stainless wisdom body, speech, and mind of Sambhogakaya, the reacher needs to establish the path and have the decisive commitment to be born in pureland, and then the reacher can be reborn there. In the Mahamudra and Mahasandhi teachings of Buddhism, *yargyi zangtel*[38] means the transparency above, which is the view that there is nothing above this, and that there is no blockage between anything. This is like the example of the pureland of Akanishtha, which means there is nothing beneath, because wherever there are Buddhas, there is no separation. After death, one can reach the state of pureland with the confidence of the transformation of transparency, seeing unobstructedly because there is nothing in between. There is no outer or inner, and there is no border. In order to reach that state in this life, one needs meditation with a correct stainless view to be in the state of nonduality, which depends on the practitioner's realization. If someone is in the transparency above, without anything that is inner or outer, there is no practitioner.

It is said in the tantras of inner Vajrayana that by making immeasurable offerings to deities, one receives siddhi, or spiritual accomplishment.

> Among merit, *ganachakra*[39] is the supreme accumulation
>   [of merit].[40]
> In this life, whatever is wished will be fulfilled,
> And in the next life, one will be reborn in the state of the pureland
>   of Vidyadhara.

If one makes *ganachakra puja* in a proper way according to the instructions of one's sadhana with faith, it is said that this will be the result. One is supposed to establish this within the present life, and this connects with the next life, pureland, and the state of Vidyadhara and becomes the indivisible state. There are many different religious views of offering substances. For example, Christians have wine and bread, thinking it is the blood and flesh of Jesus. In Buddhist *ganachakra*, or offerings of *tsok*,[41] there are samaya substances of meat and alcohol, but animals whose bodies are offered are never killed or ordered to be killed. This non-slaughtered meat is used to connect with beings with compassion. Also, the use of alcohol as nectars is according to samaya, and it does not mean to drink until satisfied or to become drunk. When practitioners eat and drink the substances of the ganachakra that have been blessed by mantra, visualization, and immaterial *amrita* wisdom, it is different from ordinary drinking and eating; it brings the ecstasy that can liberate by taste. It is using these substances, from wisdom to wisdom, with the joy of detachment from ordinary substance, without ordinary desire or aversion. One is already using this joy on the path, and from one's own spirit, one continuously bring this on the path. From doing that, one who passes this compounded life in this way of enjoyment is unsurpassed, from becoming oneness. Then, between this life and the next life, there is no separation, and when the compounded body is left, uncompounded enlightened body expands, which is called pureland. Visualizing deities and performing ganachakra are using the result of enlightenment as the path, so when the practitioner passes, whenever the body has been left, there is nothing left. There are no phenomena of passing away; there is not even anything transcended. The result reappears, which is enlightenment and pureland. According to a Buddhist view, it depends on the individual's determination and insightfulness whether to be reborn in pureland after death, or whether to carry pureland on the path as a method for attaining this state within one's life.

In some extremist materializations of eternalism, there are beliefs that forbid representations in form of what is thought to be formless, and beliefs that images are idolatrous. These reactions to holy images led to statues of Buddhas being destroyed in Afghanistan. Actually, Buddha's wisdom body is indestructible, so no one can destroy it. Since those images appeared from the blessings of manifestation, at least they made some connections to beings. In Buddhism, whenever images are consecrated by invoking and requesting blessings with the prayers of sadhanas, they are also blessed with the power to return those blessings to their purelands when harmful elements arise such as earthquakes, floods, or fire, or when beings' reversed karmic results are unavoidable. And, as Nagarjuna said:

> Whoever harms Buddha has still made a connection to Buddha,
> Which benefits harmful beings, so I bow to you, Buddha.

Buddha's speech is inconceivable. Although Buddhist consecration is asking Buddhas to come to stay in images, temples, and land until for some reason they should return to their purelands, it has its own logic. *Buddha* means fully enlightened, which means never remaining in samsara, never having grasping mind, and so never having to hold a personal place or land. Vajrayana Buddhist teachings, and especially Mahasandhi teachings, mention that whatever realms exist, if one realizes one's own mind is stainless Buddha and believes in and recognizes that state correctly through a great guide, all habits of the samsaric defilement of the six realms are naturally cleansed. Then, no matter where one stays or goes or comes with the previous residue of a body, one is already sustaining in Buddha's pureland. Buddhafields[42] naturally occur from the guidance and introduction of precious teachers, since Buddha's purelands are contained within one's wisdom mind, so the state of sustaining always in Buddhafields can happen.

Even though eternalism seems to be a different view, according to a Buddhist view one has to be careful about considering what to reject or accept. A Buddhist scholar has said:

> For whoever insults eternalism too much,
> All the immeasurable varieties of aspects of Buddha Vairochana
>   become distant.

Vairochana in Sanskrit, or *Namparnangdze*[43] in Tibetan, is the name of one of the five Buddha families.[44] *Nampar* means "in the aspect of," and *nangdze* means "to appear"; *Namparnangdze* means to appear in any aspect unobstructedly, including not only as living beings but in seemingly inert forms such as trees, mountains, bridges, or rivers that benefit beings as Nirmanakaya manifestations. Therefore, because Buddhas can appear in any aspect for the benefit of beings, temporarily to make them happy and ultimately for them to attain enlightenment, Buddhism actually does not reject any kind of positive ideas from eternalism, such as calling Jesus the son of God, since one can think of them as manifestations having the qualities of Namparnangdze. Discerning wisdom means that any aspect of appearances is pristinely clear. Whatever forms or sounds are differentiated, their essence is forever equal, which is the wisdom of evenness that has no contradiction of dualistic habit, so that all manifestations are evenly pure.

God is often described as formless in eternalist religions, as well as being the creator of the universe; yet other than identifying phenomena as being created by God, phenomena are not explained, and it is difficult to know what to believe or not to believe. Although the Muslim idea of going to heaven by killing beings for sacrifice is only harmful, as long as beings have attachment to ego and materialism, even though enlightenment cannot be reached from eternalist views, eternalist religions can temporarily be comforting to some beings. While the eternalist view of going to heaven by being good encourages virtue, which is positive and creates positive results, this idea cannot be compared to the profound Buddhist explanation of phenomena and the immeasurably vast explanations of the pure phenomena of the Buddhas of the Three Kayas. In Buddhism, there are so many different methods of practice to attain the enlightened state, which is beyond practice. Among these are the five supreme paths of Dharma without practice, which include *powa*,[45] the practice of sending one's consciousness to pureland; receiving the blessing of a wisdom Dakini to bring the attainment of siddhi; having *dutsi*[46] made with the flesh or hair of a Bodhisattva in the last life before attaining the state of no more rebirth, which has been made and blessed with the sadhana of deity; liberation by tying, such as through touching precious mantras that have been tied to one's body; and liberation by hearing. Buddhism reveals inconceivability, beyond anything that can be imagined with ordinary mind's materialism.

Even though it is said that eternalist gods cannot be imagined and are immaterial and formless, they are still originating from what can be imagined, because all of the different theories and doctrines of eternalism began with the individual phenomena of beings in different times and places within form, through messages that were received according to beings' phenomena. For example, Allah was first identified by Muhammad, who sometimes practiced in a cave where he saw Allah as real to him in his vision, and who then brought Allah's message to others, which later became the eternalist doctrine of Islam. This doctrine began as personal phenomena and then became general phenomena as other beings became followers of this doctrine through their karmic connection. It is actually originally phenomena coming from alaya, but by materialization, it became a doctrine whose followers have to worship in particular ways, including with the sacrifice of living beings. Even though followers say their god is immaterial, this god brought the creation of the material habit of bloodshed for virtue.

Karma is so true and so powerful. If one does not have positive karma, one cannot control the ability of one's mind to determine what is wrong and what is right, so one can be thinking that something is right while going in the wrong direction. From the lack of prayer to Buddha, or recognition and mindfulness of inherent I-less wisdom, one can become susceptible to inherent evil. Without recognizing stainlessness, one can be born from one's karmic air in an uncivilized country when personal negative karma ripens, and then be trapped into following barbaric phenomena that are named a religion.

Other eternalist religions also consider their gods to be formless. Although there are differences between their theories, such as whether Jesus is accepted as the Messiah who has already come, or not accepted due to the belief that another Messiah will come in the future, each of the different eternalist theories originated from the phenomena of individuals. Even though these theories seem to endure for thousands of years or eons, they are still temporary phenomena, and that means they are compounded.

According to Buddhism, the uncompounded is beyond eternalism and nihilism. There is nothing certain that can be decided about the uncompounded, and that is why it is inconceivable and always unobstructed. Eternalist gods are not beyond eternalism and nihilism, and therefore they are compounded. These gods can be perceived, but only by someone who is able to perceive them, and then from that one person, many followers are created. There is no explanation of an uncompounded state from which manifestations appear, nor any explanation that all sublime beings are within awareness mind. It is only taught that there is a formless god who must be accepted, or that gods and devas exist within form, although these forms are generally imperceptible to human beings, and that they must be accepted; and although there is no proof, some sentient beings are born to believe that it is necessary to have a connection with these gods. All of the different theories of eternalism within various times and places—whether there is a single formless god or multiple gods within form, and whether they are associated with the performances of negative or positive appearances—are still coming from the stained phenomena of the beings who found them, and are actually individual phenomena that became general. Therefore, all of these aspects of eternalism are coming and going from alaya.

As Kunkhyen Longchenpa explained,[47] according to Mahasandhi teaching, the basis of mind is always stainless. From that stainless space, whatever unobstructed manifestations arise naturally become wisdom body, speech, mind, qualities, and activities, because stainless Dharmakaya is forever stainless, so whatever manifests from that state is always stainless. But beings cannot sustain that stainless state, so they have stained phenomena. If the clean water of a river runs over stones for a long time, even though the water is clean and pristine, the stones can become covered with mold. Like the pristine basis of mind, the pristine itself can seem to become stained. If there is no recognition of stainlessness, and no sustaining in that state unwaveringly, stainlessness seems stained. That, too, is the quality of stainlessness, just as a stainless mirror can reflect many stained qualities and shapes because of its stainlessness. It is the luckiest person who can hear of the quality of stainless space. By believing in the evenness of space, anything can be invoked as positive manifestations, and what individuals can believe is very versatile. This is unlike eternalist religions, which do not have explanations of profoundly inexhaustible emanations from the immaterial. For example, in the sadhana of Vajrasattva, it says:

> In Dharmakaya where all Buddhas evenly abide
> With all victorious Bodhisattvas and Bhumisattvas,
> Please may you arise as Rupakaya in Vajrasattva's form
> And come to bestow blessings to me.

Also,

> Your wisdom body is measureless and cannot be counted;
> Its pervasive evenness is just like sky.

The power of your various manifestations of wisdom body is
indestructible,
So I praise your vajra body.

All Buddhas are manifesting from stainless Dharmakaya, so these manifestations are always stainless.

According to the explanation of Dharmakaya or Dharmadhatu, no
matter whether an interval of time is short or long, it is a manifestation
from Dharmakaya, so it will always manifest positively. The origin of
manifestation is stainless, so there is no definite duration in stainless
Dharmakaya. Whatever negative phenomena arise are based on the
alaya of indifferent stupor, so its manifestations are stained. If eternalist gods were stainless, since stainlessness is the basis of peace, their
manifestations would have to be the ecstasy of peacefulness; yet the
manifestations of eternalism can become the awful negative phenomena of samsara, even though when beings' negative karma is ripening,
they think these phenomena are wonderful. This is because when evil
arises from one's own inherent evil habit of many lives, which awakens according to time, it can be misinterpreted as the manifestations of
gods, which is how beings can come to believe they can even worship
by sacrificing the lives of other beings. The duration of whatever manifests depends on beings' habit. For example, the individual phenomena
of someone who believes in sacrifice can affect others within general
phenomena for a while, and the bloodshed of beings can be called worshiping, but according to the general karmic phenomena of beings, the
influence of that doctrine can again be reduced. When the phenomena
of beings again change, evil beings can appear as guides with negative
habits who reinstate bloodshed as worship, or some powerful beings
can again reduce negative phenomena and restore the phenomena of
peace. If someone has a human body but has no faith, and doubts the
path of Bodhisattvas or the path of enlightenment's state, awful consequences can follow when they remain in phenomena derived from the
unreliable appearances of individual manifestations and influence others to hold doctrines that resulted from them. From the nature of beings'
unobstructed mind, when evil conception occurs and leads to grasping

and developing an evil view, actual evil activities can occur. Then attachment to negative misinterpretations of manifestation can become a very strong habit. Through not recognizing the actual divine Buddha, this negative habit of misinterpreting manifestation can turn everything into an egregious distortion of the divine. One must at least have faith in Buddha. For any thoughtful human being, the highway for entering the noble path to enlightenment is having faith in Buddha.

Also, the nature of manifestation is uncertain. The manifestation of Buddhas can even occur in the aspect of evil forms. Although the essence is Buddha, these manifestations of Buddhas can appear in the form of evil, due to the nature of compassion, in order to annihilate actual evil. Also, evil can manifest in the disguise of the divine to mislead beings in the wrong direction. It is beyond ordinary beings' capacity to decipher the unrecognizable nature of these manifestations, which can only be known by omniscient Buddhas and sublime beings. The only solution is to believe in omniscient, all-powerful Buddhas and pray for their guidance, protection, and blessing to purify and dispel all obstacles.

The manifestation of Buddha's reflection has unlimited power. According to Hinayana Buddhism, before attaining Buddhahood, Buddha took birth in this world as a human being in the form of Prince Gautama in the Shakya kingdom. By abandoning the passions with hardship, Buddha finally attained nirvana. According to Mahayana theory, for beings of Mahayana faculties, Buddha developed bodhichitta in front of Dezhin Shekpa Rinchen Nyingpo, Essence of Jewels.[48] After the purification of obscurations and accumulation of merit over many eons, Buddha first was enlightened in Akanishtha Heaven and then emanated in this existent world as Buddha Shakyamuni and turned the Wheel of Dharma for beings to attain the state of the Three Kayas, which is the fully enlightened state, the same as all Buddhas. According to the doctrine of the Vajrayana, the fully enlightened state is the beginningless, unchangeable state of Vajradhara. So the Three Kayas are the state of full enlightenment. The reason all fully enlightened Buddhas are always abiding in the state of Buddha is that there is not even an iota of alaya. They are always abiding in Dharmakaya, but natural unobstructed qualities manifest according to the faculties of many different beings. All of these beneficial phenomena are the unobstructed qualities of manifestation, which is self-sustaining, so there are no phenomena of dualistic contradiction, because they have manifested from stainless Dharmakaya.

The nature of mind is actually Buddha. As it says in the sadhana of Vajrasattva, the body of Vajrasattva sustains the glorious qualities of samsara and enlightenment simultaneously. Vajrasattva has no karmic body, but Vajrasattva's wisdom manifestation is always pervading in unobstructed manifestations. Of course, without question, the manifestations of the fully enlightened state of Buddhahood are pure, but the body of Vajrasattva can even manifest samsara's glorious qualities in infinite reflections of ecstasy, which is the untarnished mirroring quality of stainlessness.

Dharmakaya is the basis of all wisdom manifestations because it is always the stainless state of openness. So, in that state, all Buddhas are abiding, which is forever manifesting peaceful deities and wrathful deities, effortlessly, and without any conception of basis, path, and result, always in nondiscrimination. From lack of recognition of that nondiscriminating basis mandala, sentient beings misinterpret pure manifestation so that phenomena become samsaric phenomena. Whoever has the fortunate karma to transform samsaric phenomena through practice by recognizing wisdom mandala, which is inherent in each being, can practice with sadhanas to open inherent wisdom deity.

Even some of those with Hinayana faculties who do not accept Buddha nature according to Mahayana theory, and of course do not accept Vajrayana theory, nonetheless do accept that human beings who have minds with keen faculties as a result of accumulation can attain enlightenment through the recognition of selflessness. They do not like to hear themselves called the followers of the Hinayana, or the inferior doctrine. They think the ultimate attainment of Buddhahood is the state of Arhat, which is the state of having vanquished the passions of ego. Those who follow the Mahayana and Vajrayana doctrines believe that one has to excel beyond the Hinayana view by not just purifying the personal obscurations of ego, but also purifying cognitive obscurations; purifying both these obscurations causes fully enlightened Buddha. According to

Vajrayana theory, wisdom deities inherently exist within each individual's mind, even though they are temporarily dormant from lack of faith and belief. Simply using ordinary logic, one can infer this by seeing the qualities of wrathfulness and peacefulness within ordinary existence. For example, ordinary anger, jealousy, hatred, and all the passions of ferocious emotions with reality attachment are signs of wrathfulness. Through misinterpreting these emotions with reality attachment, some people who are full of attachment to their own mind's passions hold the arising of these passions as a reality, and from that reality, wrathful emotion is caused. In the behavior and activity of some religious eternalists, violence can occur because what is called a religion, but is actually the worst aspect of nihilism, causes a misinterpretation of phenomena as a reality that does not exist. Buddhas have no reality object, so they do not have a reality object of hatred or a reality object of sacrifice that could lead to killing beings everywhere. Also, some beings have very attractive mental characteristics, such as joyfulness and peace that they impart to others, and physical bodies with pleasing energy, which are also signs of a connection with the manifestation of sublime qualities of Buddhas or wisdom deities.

In the tantric tradition, one brings the basis of wisdom mandala to the path in practice, in order for wisdom mandala to occur as the path, and then finally achieves the result, which means that the basis of Buddha, the path to Buddha, and the result of Buddha become indivisible. The qualities of wrathfulness and peacefulness are signs that each being has inherent wisdom deity. When beings are happy, even though it is momentary, that happiness is connected with the peacefulness and desirable qualities of deities, so that even the faces of human beings with karmic bodies change to express joyfulness and serenity when appropriate circumstances occur. Their complexions become appealingly reddened and flushed, their physical bodies can exude blissfully sensual energy, the sounds they express become attractive and soothing, and their mental characteristics can draw others to them as a sign of their connection with the manifestation of sublime qualities of Buddhas or wisdom deities. Also, when beings are disturbed with signs of wrathfulness, such as anger, jealousy, hatred, and all the passions with ferocious emotions that are misinterpreted from reality attachment, their physical attributes, including their complexions, the expressions on their faces, the sounds they make, and the energy of their mental characteristics, are not pleasantly flourishing but can become horrifying, with agitated nerves, veins, and channels.

All these ordinary peaceful and wrathful passions can be used by bringing them into the practice of sadhanas with the correct view, visualization, and meditation, to recognize and abide in the always beginningless enlightened state, like Samantabhadra, who is always abiding in changeless, fully enlightened Buddhahood. Until the basis, path, and result become indivisible, the same as all flawless Buddhas, the way of bringing the result of deity, which is sublime body, speech, and mind, onto the path is the special method of Vajrayana, or tantra, which is the continuity of inherent wisdom. The purpose of the sadhanas of deities is to excel in sublime phenomena. The ordinary uneven phenomena of sentient beings are not even because the basis of inherent enlightened deity has not become equal with abiding in the result of enlightenment. The uneven basis and result of ordinary duality are made into the evenness of the sublime through practice and precious teachings. By bringing the unevenness of ordinary phenomena into practice, the evenness of the sublime state of Buddha occurs. As it says in *The Noble Shoulder Tantra*:[49]

> Buddha, even though your nature is naturally free from attachment
>   and aversion,
> You manifest desirable qualities for those who have desire,
> And you manifest wrath for those who are wrathful.
> By skillful means, you always guide beings. I bow to you.

Buddhas have already ripened peacefulness and wrathfulness. Human beings have the nature of these qualities inherently, and they can practice to attain the state of the immaculate peacefulness and wrathfulness of Buddhas. It is because beings misinterpret the nature of these stainless qualities that they experience them as reality peace and wrath, but for Buddhas, these qualities are stainless.

According to Buddhist theory, until reaching fully enlightened

Buddhahood, which is the complete purification of dualistic habit, one has to believe in the continuity of mind as a support for developing on the path of enlightenment, throughout life. It is especially important to believe this so that one will use one's precious human life for virtue through believing that suffering is caused by the influence of previous negative habit, and happiness is caused by the influence of virtue. There is nothing wrong with being a believer. It is only beneficial, because those who are believers will abstain from holding nonvirtuous intentions, try to purify negative karma, and develop virtuous intentions and create positive karmic results. As Dipamkara said:

> Until conception is exhausted, there will be karmic cause and effect,
> So one must believe in cause and effect.

At least those who believe in Buddhism will believe in consequences. By being believers, at least they will believe in peace and happiness, so at least there will not be a cause of terrorism. If one just thinks about the Buddhist beliefs in bodhichitta and karma, it is obvious that Buddhism is always harmless and beneficial. If one is Buddhist, one has to think about karma, so one believes in the next life and does not want to cause negative karma. Other religions do not consider the importance of not harming others in the same way. Buddhist compassion is not like the compassion of eternalist religions, which is to help and be kind to those in one's own group, but to harm other beings if necessary; it is to be kind impartially, with the vast idea of benefiting all beings.

So, in comparing Buddhism in the West with Buddhism in my early years in Tibet, there are basic differences in beliefs and ways of understanding and thinking. In the West, people predominantly believe in and protect reality rather than considering spirituality. Actually, practicing Dharma is much more beneficial than is generally acknowledged, even in its effect on the reality of society; of course, the aim of Buddhist practice is fully enlightened Buddhahood, but Buddhist beliefs also cause harmonious energy within ordinary existence. As an example of this, practicing makes the mind tranquil and creates positive energy, such as that of faith and compassion, if one uses immaterial ideas wisely. As said before, even if one just considers the Buddhist belief in karma, the result of this belief is to prevent negative causes and effects. The basis for the explanation of karma is the Buddhist belief that this present mind is continuous up to enlightenment. Since mind is continuous, it always causes effects unless one creates great virtue, meditates, and attains full enlightenment.

Many Westerners are not interested in spirituality, because they think it is not useful for this life but concerns the unreal and imaginary. They always want only reality. Even some Western Buddhists have this attitude, yet these Westerners are using Asian Buddhism however they can, disrespectfully. Also, some Westerners think all Buddhism is Hinayana, not recognizing that Buddha is omniscient and can teach according to beings' various phenomena and faculties. Naturally, those who like the Hinayana teach their own view and behavior, and Westerners who are searching for something pure and learn about the Hinayana think it is necessary to abandon desirable qualities and that it is the actual teaching of Buddha to do so. This is taught by Hinayana doctrinaires, and it is also a Western concept among those who have difficulty believing in the Mahayana and Vajrayana, but it creates misunderstandings about the expanse of Buddhism. This also happened in Asia after Buddha took *parinirvana*. So Westerners who have only heard Hinayana teachings on abandoning the passions and think this view represents all Buddhism believe that they will have to give up desirable qualities in life if they practice Buddhism. They actually do not need to be afraid that if they have faith and practice, they will have to deny the material world, lose everything they have, and damage their worldly life. The accumulation of merit, which ultimately leads to fully enlightened Buddhahood forever, occurs through using the phenomena of this life, and if one practices, one does not lose the luck and prosperity of this life, but increases them. There are two kinds of merit: one is the accumulation of merit of all positive phenomena with faith and compassion, which temporarily causes positive results such as wealth, long life, and happiness, and ultimately causes Rupakaya. The other kind of merit is the accumulation of wisdom, from visualizing, meditating, and abiding in stainless mind, which temporarily transforms the turbulence of ordinary mind to serenity and ultimately results in the attainment of Dharmakaya, which is the fully enlightened state of Buddha.

The purpose of any Dharma practice is to change phenomena. The phenomena of sentient beings must change into the phenomena of Buddhas, which is called the quality of the changing of phenomena. The view of the accumulation of merit in the Mahayana and Vajrayana traditions is always related to phenomena and using phenomena in the correct way. One can use anything, anytime and anywhere, without attachment, for accumulation; in this way, one develops spiritual qualities by using phenomena. Buddhism is very vast, and there are many choices for how to practice, which is very suitable for Western life. According to the Mahayana, one sees any phenomena like magic: they exist but at the same time do not exist. Therefore, one accumulates merit within phenomena while seeing everything as magically unreal. Furthermore, whoever has faith in the Vajrayana can practice within reality phenomena using desirable qualities, which become deity phenomena. So it is not necessary to think that in Buddhism one is always supposed to totally abandon the material world. With a correct point of view, material phenomena can be used to accomplish one's practice. Westerners are not supposed to gasp with fear at the thought of having to give up material phenomena in order to develop immaterial phenomena. Within relative truth, one uses material phenomena to increase spiritual appearances with faith and belief. Then, until attaining the ultimate result of enlightenment, wherever one is born and wherever one stays, one can always have positive phenomena. One needs to both think this and make it happen, so that one creates complementary circumstances with material phenomena and meditates in immaterial *samadhi*, which temporarily reduces dualistic conflict and ultimately expands stainless wisdom Dharmakaya, which is fully enlightened.

As said, although mind's Buddha nature is temporarily dormant from karmic circumstances, its potential to open is continuous. When this mind opens, there is the path of enlightenment until fully enlightened Buddhahood is reached. Until one reduces and totally purifies obscurations, there is virtue and nonvirtue, so one accumulates virtue; and in order not to be attached even to virtue so that one does not cause karmic attachment again, there is formless meditation to attain fully enlightened Buddhahood, the same as all Buddhas.

Many Westerners have been interested in Zen Buddhism, which is very honorable and cannot be disrespected; Zen and the sublime beings of Zen were predicted by Buddha Shakyamuni in the Mahayana sutras. Zen always mentions formless meditation, the same as in the Madhyamaka explanation in Tibetan Buddhism of the term "abiding in evenness." The idea in Zen is to stop causing more material phenomena, but whether this is able to be accomplished depends on the individual and the recognition of wisdom.

Many previous Indian and Tibetan scholars have had a different way of considering emptiness and phenomena, however, and have taught that the nature of mind is both emptiness and clarity, which are indivisible. Emptiness is not nil, and as already mentioned, the cessation of conception depends on the capacity of the individual. According to the path, it is taught in Tibetan Buddhism that practitioners can misinterpret the cessation of conception and may remain in a state of dullness but think it is emptiness. This prevents the accumulation of virtue, because virtue comes from conception, and there is nothing to use for accumulation if conceptions are supposed to be stopped. If one cuts conception—although one cannot cut it, but if one tries—there is no support for the accumulation of virtue, so one can remain in inert nothingness. Therefore, Tibetan Buddhism has taught that instead of trying to make conceptions totally or suddenly cease, from the beginning, phenomena should just be allowed to be turned into the accumulation of virtue, until nonvirtue is transformed into virtue. Finally, even the conception of virtue is transformed in nondualistic wisdom mind, without causing any material conception that can become the object of attachment. Until then, one must use phenomena for accumulation, which temporarily causes the accumulation of positive phenomena and ultimately causes Rupakaya, the wisdom body of Buddha. The problem is not conception; the problem is attachment and grasping. Phenomena cannot cease because they are unobstructed, so one should just let them flow as the quality of unobstructedness and use them by temporarily accumulating virtue with these phenomena instead of trying to prevent them or make them suddenly cease. In this way, phenomena are used in the accumulation of virtue and meditation until conception is naturally exhausted in stainless emptiness with unobstructed manifestation, which is Rupakaya, which means Sambhogakaya and Nirmanakaya, the pure form of Buddha, and until Dharmakaya and Rupakaya become indivisible.

For whoever recognizes the nature of wisdom mind, one cannot only say that phenomena cease and are not used. If there is realization, there is not only emptiness. There is light. Buddha Shakyamuni said:

Profound peace, free from fabrication,
Uncompounded light, I found Dharma precious like nectar.
Even if I show it to others, they are not going to understand,
So I had better be silent in the forest.

Wisdom is light. Light is phenomena and not just nothingness. Of course, what is recognized and believed depends on the individual's practice. Also, one cannot decide that there is always light in a material way, because the essence of the nature of light is empty.

In Tibetan, ja,[50] or rainbow, means immaterial. Also, mind is immaterial. Whatever is immaterial does not have any of the ordinary five skandhas, so it is liberation. The actual rainbow teaching is tögal.[51] Some people think rainbows are only connected to tögal teachings, and it is true that they are naturally connected to tögal, even though tögal is not practiced, because the nature of mind is immaterial light. Even if one cannot practice tögal owing to lack of diligence, it is still possible to attain immaterial enlightenment, since mind is immaterial. Even though momentarily this quality of mind is not occurring, it is naturally rainbow. Whenever one leaves the compounded, disposable ordinary five skandhas, there will definitely be rainbow body, because of being released from the karmic body. From prayer and practice, immaterial wisdom rainbow body will occur. Rigdzin Jigme Lingpa said in Hymn of the Vajra: Fulfillment and Confession:[52]

From the state of the basis, due to the manifestation of the
    movement of karmic air,
The mind of habit is trapped in the womb of the mother,
And from that come the elements of earth, water, fire, and air corre-
    sponding to flesh, blood, warmth, and breath. All these skandhas
    that come,
I offer to you. May I receive rainbow body.

Of course, this is all an answer to your question about Buddhism in the West. When Buddha was asked a question about whether there was an end to existence, Buddha never answered, and that not answering is called an excellent answer because it reveals how ordinary mind is always circling since it is occupied by dualistic habit and is never going to end. Since I am answering your question about Buddhism in the West, however, and the West is a land of human beings living on this earth, I have to answer with human beings' examples. Giving great importance to ideals of individual freedom without a spiritual point of view can affect many Westerners in their ability to understand and practice Buddhism, influencing their capacity to give up egoism and to truly rely on spiritual teachers and sublime beings for guidance and blessings. As mentioned, Westerners temporarily lack a mental attitude of being accustomed to discerning the results of their actions through an understanding of the karmic system, or of considering how to go beyond the appearances of ordinary existence, and are focused one-sidedly on the power of the material, which is the cause of conflict and trouble. Also, because their immaterial spirituality is not blossoming, it is very hard according to relative truth for them to engage in Buddhist practice. The reason Western mind is often not deep enough is that it is not connected with the inconceivability of spiritual qualities.

That is why many books written on Buddhism by Western Buddhist teachers are not actually Buddhist books and do not have even a taste of a spiritual point of view. The quality of mind is to manifest anything, including deities, but even when these Western teachers are well educated in an ordinary way, they misinterpret mind's manifestations from their extreme habit of materialism and cannot discern mind's spiritual qualities. Without opening these qualities of mind, they cannot even function wisely in a material way in writing, speaking, theorizing, or the arts. Whatever they express or produce becomes fragmented and shallow and then becomes worthless because these expressions cannot go deeper or farther, but run out. Then the students of these Western teachers read their books, which mislead them into more shallowness. That is why bookstores have to change the books on their shelves so frequently. If books really have value, this value is long-lasting and one book can be read by many generations. Every year, books change with the arrival of new material conceptions, and since whatever is conceptualized is not connected with actual spirituality, readers become bored and sellers have to change their inventory. This lack of worth is not harmless; it is extremely harmful, because it means the writers are not catching inexhaustible qualities since they are not connecting to inexhaustible mind. Because they are disconnected from the source of versatility and expansiveness, which is fully discerning and incisively pristine wisdom mind, their minds cannot accommodate inconceivability.

The circumstances of democracy, free enterprise, freedom of religion, and the protection of individual rights in the West give people many opportunities, which are wonderful for creating material prosperity, but at the same time can cause so much corruption of the legacy of previous sublime beings by trying to adapt it to these aspects of Western culture. If this legacy diminishes, what is really true and not true about Buddhism will not be understood by new generations due to Western influences. For example, the movie *Little Buddha* was not accurate in its portrayal of Buddha. Although Buddhas traditionally have not been referred to as being little, in general whether Buddhas are seen as little or huge depends on the individual perceiver and the manifestation of Buddhas according to time and place. Buddha can be the size of one atom, or within one atom there can be countless Buddhas or one huge, immeasurable Buddha. So the use of the word *little* is fine. In this movie, however, Buddha was born crying behind a curtain, and his mother, Mayadevi, was expressing sounds of pain while in labor. According to old texts of Buddha's history, from the time that Buddha entered his mother's womb, Mayadevi was totally filled with ecstasy and Buddha blessed her womb so that it became a wisdom palace. While Mayadevi was pregnant with Buddha in her womb and while she was giving birth, she was in bliss. Buddha had no pain and Mayadevi had no pain.

By trying to fit everything into the ordinary, any unusual, special qualities are twisted into usual Western phenomena. How can anyone excel beyond the ordinary without belief, faith, and reverence for what is beyond the ordinary? The sublime histories of Buddhas and the teachings of Buddhism are full of meaning and are all connected with the Buddhist view, which is beyond any cultural limitation, and they should be purely transmitted so that Westerners can receive the authentic Buddhist lineage of blessings, which can cause their Buddha nature to rekindle through faith and belief so that Buddhism can flourish in the West. Whoever saw this film, especially young people, should read actual Buddhist history. Instead of learning about Buddha's actual history, if the next generation has only seen these kinds of films and thinks the history in them is accurate, how will anyone be able to benefit from Buddha's actual sublime history? What can be beneficial about being afraid to express authentic sublime histories, or about changing Buddha and Buddha's history by converting them into what seems suitable to social phenomena? I would like to request that this film be fixed to show the actual history accurately and not to accommodate nihilist taste, before the history shown there becomes like "yak butter."*

Since each being has Buddha nature, why can't Buddha nature blossom in Westerners? Of course it can. In order for Buddha nature to blossom, however, one has to believe in the intangible phenomena of Buddhas. It makes it difficult for this to happen if even Western Buddhist teachers are suppressing mind's Buddha nature by not believing and not having faith in Buddhas, and are indirectly and directly passing their disbelief on to others, preventing them from letting their Buddha nature blossom. This happens because many Western Buddhist teachers actually have nihilist ideas and a need to be acknowledged by society, and most of society is nihilist. If one talks about the idea of enlightenment or the genuine view of Buddhism, they cannot fit it in their minds. That is why they are willing to compromise Buddhist teachings by adapting them to Western disbelief.

Some Westerners say that they do not believe in statues or prayers, and that they do not believe in an outer Buddha but have Buddha in their own mind. Actually, this shows that their inherent Buddha is sleeping and demons are appearing, since these people have no way to connect to Buddha's qualities because they have invalidated Buddha through their inability to perceive holiness and understand manifestation. The

---

* Since *yak* refers to a male animal in Tibetan and only the female (*dri*) can produce butter, this phrase expresses an impossibility or something incorrect.

rejection of an outer Buddha and misinterpretation of an inner Buddha
come from ego, not realization. Buddha said that each being has Buddha
nature, but it must be rekindled through faith. Although each being has
Buddha nature, including dogs, horses, and cows, the problem is that
from lack of recognition and faith, mind becomes obscured, deluded,
and lost in the habits of ordinary beings, so Buddha nature becomes
dormant and must be enlivened. It is very important to remember Buddha with faith, because it naturally awakens awareness.

If Westerners recognize that Buddhism is important for others,
they are supposed to help Buddhism flourish with good intentions and
inspire people to have faith, but this is very unlikely. So far, in Europe
and America, there are Western Buddhists who are instead causing
a mistrust of Buddhist traditions of faith and belief in Buddhas and
deities, and are bending, changing, and modifying Buddhism into what
can be accepted by nihilist society and is suitable to a materialistic
orientation.

When a sublime state is reached beyond the two truths, there is no
conception of mind, the material, or the immaterial. Even in high levels
of realization, individual phenomena change between the material and
immaterial because the positive immaterial power of mind is developing.
If we talk according to relative truth, however, in which there is always
manipulation between subject and object, beings with dualistic mind
generally have many different material phenomena. In the West, as was
said earlier, material ideas naturally predominate due to a lack of belief
in immaterial spiritual phenomena. If one has faith in the immaterial,
however, one does not need to worry that this will endanger anything in
life at a material level. Clearly, all Buddhas and sublime beings, whether
living previously or now, have the continuous power of blessings, so they
unintentionally thrive and flourish in every way. As the great Tibetan
scholar Sakya Pandita Kunga Gyaltsen, Victorious Banner of All Joy,
said:

Even if those who are intelligent want to be successful in this material
life, it is much more powerful to accomplish this through Dharma.
What is the difference in perfection between the lives of sublime

beings and thieves? Sublime beings are not making an effort to gain wealth, power, or anything, but they can naturally accomplish them comfortably through their spiritual power. For those who are faithful and practice, letting Buddha nature bloom through faith, this life will not fail.

Whatever I have explained here I thought would be a useful frame for understanding how phenomena start and how general and individual phenomena occur. As said, Westerners are very new to actual Dharma, and because of a cultural basis of nonbelief, they only consider what is useful for the present temporary life. From this cultural influence, parents and teachers advise, train, and educate children to believe that everything has to be tied to reality phenomena, which is silently accepted by everyone, so that even people who study Buddhism are not really sincere, but are naturally attracted and attached to this life's ambitions for their own self-importance within society. Unless someone is gifted and has unusually good karma, it is very hard to engage in actual Dharma due to the overpowering effect of nihilist culture, which is the opposite of a Dharma influence; people would rather choose what they feel is reality, while faith, reverence, merit, accumulation, karma, and meditation, which are all basic to Buddhist teachings, are very unfamiliar or foreign to them. This is true for both the young and the old in the West. Even for older Westerners who have had some experience of samsaric suffering and the way that everything in their lives is always changing, it is still very hard for their minds to connect to pure Buddhism because their attachment to ordinary reality is so strong. Even when they have had many experiences about the futility of chasing after ordinary reality, and even when they have been introduced to Buddha's teachings, they are still disinterested, hesitant, reluctant, or afraid to be involved in pure Dharma even in a simple way.

This is why it is really very awkward to answer your question about Buddhism in the West truthfully. One sadness in the West is that when Eastern teachers adjust to Western ideas based on materialism, disbelief, and democratic principles, they actually cannot deliver any sublime qualities. Even though they teach from the Mahayana up to Dzogchen, they are not going to have an effect according to pure Buddhist tradition if they are just excited about being nonsectarian and egalitarian in order to be accommodating to people with Western values. Dharma is for all sentient beings. Buddha Shakyamuni taught the four boundless wishes, which are to be kind impartially to all sentient beings according to relative truth, and according to absolute truth, the wish that each being's Buddha nature can flourish and all beings can evenly realize it. What more do they need than that? This kind of teaching is missing, and nihilist ideas are replacing them. Teachers, students, and sponsors are responsible for creating obscurations. In the West, there are both students who are not engaging in practice according to pure tradition and teachers who are not adjusting according to pure tradition, but who are only living within this world's existence with the same wishes as general nihilists. Of course, the teachings of Buddha are to liberate all beings, including nihilist beings, but one needs teachings, practice, and engagement in Dharma to be liberated. This is not what Western students and teachers are thinking. Without any faith, devotion, practice, and meditation, they just reconfirm the samsaric stained habits they already have, and if they keep these habits, they will die with them. That is not Buddha Shakyamuni's teaching. It does not matter whether students or sponsors dislike it or like it. Teachers have to take the speech of Buddha seriously, without thinking about their own personal power or material income.

Generally, nonsectarianism means to respect any kind of religion. According to Buddhism, as it is taught in the Kagyupa Mahamudra teaching of the four yogas, everything is seen as one taste. In the Kadampa school, the teachings of all different sects must be realized as noncontradictory. According to Mahasandhi's teaching, *rangnang ri-me*[53] means that all different phenomena are recognized as one's own manifestation, and since they are one's own manifestation, there is no reason for bias. It is not right for Dharma centers to always advertise that they are nonsectarian, yet to actually be otherwise beneath the advertising and to disregard all these pure teachings. Since enlightenment is so precious, there are obstacles, but even if one could not practice thoroughly, one is still supposed to try at least a little bit to actually practice instead of turning everything to politics, economics, and manipulation. All of this is true, but it is hard to discuss because people can hear it as complaints and become offended. Then they become defensive and attack back, even though it is only said to help change these circumstances so that Dharma can flourish.

Although there is a big difference between a Dharma orientation and Western life, I believe, as Buddha Shakyamuni revealed in the Mahayana, that each being has mind, and mind's essence is Buddha nature. According to general phenomena, within all compounded existence, sometimes phenomena can disperse and sometimes phenomena can appear. As it says in Buddhist texts, from the waves of the ocean pushing sand, an island can appear that did not exist before, or sometimes land can disappear into the ocean. This is because these phenomena are compounded elements, and compounded phenomena always change and are going to continue to change, following beings' karma. Beings' karma is infinite because beings are infinite, so we cannot cause beings' karma to be a certain way, but since each being has Buddha nature, I hope it can someday be beneficial for this to be written in your magazine even though temporarily it is very hard for Western nonbelievers to believe these ideas.

I hope and pray that even though Westerners lack a previous sublime history of Buddhism, since they have the basis of Buddha nature, they can realize their potential for it to open. For this to occur, though, it is very important to be a believer. Even if one can be a believer for at least an hour or a day, developing faith so that one can become aware of one's own Buddha nature, one's experience can grow by using passions and circumstances. If one has experience with practice, faith will naturally expand and one will engage in practice more and more. That is how Buddhism can flourish in the West.

What does immaterial spiritual reality mean?

Your question is a good one. In the nonbelief of nihilism, there is no immaterial spiritual reality. There can only be said to be immaterial reality, which is blank without wisdom, and anything found within that reality cannot be considered ultimate. Even if something is thought to be ultimate, such as an ultimate particle, another ultimate particle can be found later that replaces it, since each compounded conception is canceled by the next compounded conception. Nihilists believe in a reality that does not exist, but they think that it does. As Longchenpa said:

> Whatever is appearing, whenever it is appearing,
> It does not exist. It is just instantaneous.

The meaning of spiritual reality is the appearances that occur according to the different phenomena of beings as different manifestations. It is not static material; it is the manifestation of unobstructed wisdom within material and immaterial conception, according to beings' phenomena.

There is nothing in all existence that is not permeated by immaterial wisdom. As Minling Trichen Rinpoche said in *Emanation of a Rosary of Prayers:*[54]

> The all-pervasive changeless eternal wisdom of vajra,
> Essence of all endless existence,
> Magic dance of the nature, luminosity, and wisdom manifestation,
> Anything can be emanated. I bow to you, glorious Guru.

Wherever there is material, there is the immaterial. Any form is naturally formless. One does not need to make this up; it is. Wherever there is form, there is wisdom. As it says in *The Hevajra Tantra:*

> Great wisdom is abiding in form.
> All conception is completely abandoned.
> The pervasive ruler of all material existence
> Is abiding in form but is never born from a form.

Not believing in wisdom deities only comes from thinking deities are conceptualized, made up, or not real. If a believer believes in wisdom deity, even though the believer cannot immediately see wisdom deity, the believer can receive blessings from the truth of immaterial spiritual reality.

Immaterial spiritual reality, which is within relative truth because it is connected with reality,[55] can be said to be the influence of the immaterial on the reality conception of practitioners. According to the phenomena of practice, the practitioner's mind develops within material compounded energy through faith, belief, worship, prayers, and meditation, corresponding to each individual's capacity. As practice progresses, the influence of the immaterial spiritual energy of practice permeates material reality until they become one taste. This is like the example of gold that has the stains of impurities being refined more and more, until there are no longer both gold and impurities but only the pure metal of gold, which becomes totally stainless. Also, if one sharpens a knife with a whetstone, the knife and the whetstone simultaneously become lighter and thinner as dullness becomes keen. This is like the quality of the immaterial occurring when the material diminishes, so spiritual power becomes more and more immaculate as obscurations are cleansed.

When I was in Tibet, there were ideas of science and technology, since wherever material phenomena exist, there are always material explanations and results; science exists everywhere, not only in the West, although there are differences in how much the material ideas of science are developed. Previously, in many countries in the East, spiritual ideas were more developed than material ideas, whereas in the West, material ideas have flourished more, because Westerners have developed material phenomena more than immaterial spirituality. This makes it is harder for them to be involved with immaterial ideas. Of course, material technology can be very useful. In ancient times, one either had to walk or use horses to travel. With ships crossing oceans and trains running below and above ground, distances that had taken many months to cross on foot could take only days or even hours, and beyond these, airplanes can now fly these distances within hours or minutes. Information can be known easily by telephone, radio and television channels, or computers. Through misusing technology, however, catastrophes can happen, including the explosions of nuclear weapons. I am not denying the advantages of the development of material phenomena, and I am using these developments, including coming and going on airplanes and relying on technology, since I have this body, but an independent material solution can never be found. If whatever was found were ultimate, it would not change. The point of this is that when beings are attached to reality, they can only think about reality and cannot think beyond it, so their spirituality becomes shy and incognito. If one is extremely attached to only the material, it is very hard to have faith and believe in Buddha, Dharma, Sangha, the state of inconceivability, and especially practice. Also, from an emphasis on individual rights and freedom, there is a fear of having faith in sublime beings such as Buddhas, Bodhisattvas, or deities, because people are afraid of losing their ego if someone is seen as more powerful than they are.

As Buddha Shakyamuni said:

> If one measures according to the general phenomena of beings,
>   samsara is endless because the phenomena of beings are endless.
> If one measures according to the personal phenomena of an
>   individual, samsara is endable.

This is because if an individual has a karmic connection to meet the precious path of enlightenment and practice, fully enlightened Buddhahood can be attained, and so samsara ends.

Until samsara ends, its phenomena are continuous, and anything can exist, including science. Whether considering the general or individual phenomena of samsara, according to Buddhist tradition, all human knowledge is contained in the categories of the ten sciences. These ten sciences can be synthesized into the five sciences of art, medicine, language, logic and philosophy, and inner awareness. Inner awareness is taught in the Tripitaka, which are the teachings of the three categories of the Vinaya, the Sutras, and the Abhidharma that are all upwardly contained in the samaya of the developing and completion stages, and great uncompounded self-occurring wisdom of the Vajrayana. This fifth category of inner awareness is for the development of immaterial spirituality for enlightenment. Also, the knowledge of any of the five sciences can be used to increase the influence of immaterial spiritual reality within material phenomena for accumulation according to the individual's wishes. For example, while living within this existent world with ordinary human beings' phenomena, one can use the science of art, which includes not only painting, drawing, sculpture, architecture, and design, but also technology, mechanics, physics, and anything that can be made within material substance. In the Buddhist tradition, these outer arts can be used in many ways for creating holy substances to develop inner spiritual qualities. By doing this, whatever positive qualities are increased become merit, which is positive, not negative. Since the accumulation of merit occurs through material, the material cannot be considered only negative, because it is used in this way for practice. In the sutras and in the Mantrayana, immeasurable merit is the cause of the result of Rupakaya, and wisdom merit is the cause of the result of Dharmakaya. According to the path of enlightenment, the accumulation of merit and the accumulation of wisdom go together until fully enlightened Buddhahood is attained, which means the Two Kayas[56] become indivisible. This occurs from using material phenomena. If momentary material phenomena are not used for practice, however, spiritual phenomena will be dormant, so material phenomena will not be able to cause lasting happiness in the world of existence, but will be an obstacle to attaining immaterial wisdom phenomena.

In Western culture, which is predominantly engaged with materialism, immaterial spiritual reality is weak or dormant and everyone is occupied with their attachment to instant, compounded phenomena and unable to find peace. Material is just material, and it is used only for material purposes. People cannot make themselves ultimately happy because they have missed the solution of immaterial spirituality and have no way to prevent the unavoidable disturbance of samsara. If people really believe in immaterial spiritual reality, such as believing in the next life, previous lives, increasing positive karma, preventing negative karma, being compassionate, and having faith in Buddha, the consequence will be less influence from nonspiritual reality and more influence from spirituality, which temporarily causes peace and ultimately results in Buddhahood. In this degenerate time, however, it is very hard for people to turn from material reality toward immaterial spirituality, especially when materialism is highly developed. People are totally occupied with the mindlessness of highly developed materialism, and there is no way to affect their minds, which are like electronic brains controlled only by material phenomena. In countries with highly developed technology, young children, the middle-aged, and the elderly in their eighties are all infantile and cannot even actually communicate about anything other than material phenomena, causing a realm of babies. That is the characteristic of existence and the way of life for those in materialistic cultures, until the last breath is taken. Even though Buddha nature is actually present, no one believes in developing it or in abiding forever in uncompounded wisdom body, speech, and mind.

In Tibet, people who had faith in the omniscient Buddha could be very noble, loyal, and trustworthy. If people do not have faith, they can be the opposite of this. Those who do not have a spiritual connection can be dishonest, disloyal, uncompassionate, and negative, which all come from being under the power of materialism and trying to take advantage of others with a fear of losing the chance to obtain satisfaction within each instant. Because the material seems real and obvious, and immaterial spirituality seems unreal and mysterious, they use their lives to try to grab material phenomena whenever they have the opportunity. The immaterial can be misinterpreted. When spirituality becomes too dogmatic, inflexible, and extreme through materialization, its misinterpretation can become the reverse of spirituality. Those who have supposedly spiritual ideas, yet are attached to these ideas with aggressiveness, can cause nonspiritual violence. This is what happens if spirituality is only materialized, as occurred in Afghanistan in the previously mentioned destruction of the statues of Buddhas in Bamiyan. Eternalists who have done this are not connected to their own spirit or spiritual doctrines of belief in a formless god as an ultimate refuge. The sign of this is that they think Buddhas exist within tangible material, and that they can affect this material. Even in an ordinary way, spirit is connected with mind. Even the idea of using the word *spirits* for alcohol implies that if one drinks, the mind is affected, such as by becoming happy, and that happiness is coming from mind, not from liquid alcohol. Spirituality means not ordinary, temporary happiness but what is beyond the ordinary.

According to relative truth, even though eternalists can sacrifice their own lives and the lives of others for their gods, they can never destroy Buddha, and trying to do so shows they cannot imagine Buddha's inconceivability. If these eternalists believe their god is formless, why did they have to think of the forms of those statues of Buddha? It was actually through nihilist habit that they tried to break or destroy the indestructible body of Buddha, thinking of Buddha's statues as real. They can think of these statues with faith in order to receive blessings, but they cannot destroy Buddhas with a nihilist view, because they cannot destroy the immeasurable Three Kayas.

Many nihilists, eternalists, and even Buddhists who do not understand this have destroyed images of Buddhas from hatred and sectarianism, armed with their theories and doctrines. As Patrul Rinpoche said:

> If examined, all can be found to be true, but at the same time all are false.
> Whether true or false, they are only momentary phenomena. What do you want to do?
> However much effort is made to accomplish a doctrine, it can never be accomplished.
> Everything is true according to one's own phenomena,
> So debating about other theories and who is right and wrong is just the water of a mirage.
> For this harmless water, why is it necessary to build a dam?

In Tibetan history, there have been people who have destroyed images of Buddhas and holy writings of sublime beings who would have been considered Buddhists by foreigners, but whose extremist sectarian habits and intentions were actually caused by nihilism, which itself caused negative karma. Also, in Bhutan, previously wise sublime beings who were founders of Buddhism in Bhutan had established the practice of rituals of Padmasambhava to be performed every year in monasteries and retreat places. In this *kaliyuga*'s degenerate time, however, some Bhutanese in charge of monasteries have purged these rituals for worshiping Padmasambhava in their own Buddhist country because of sectarian extremism, even though the founder of their own sect of Buddhism and many generations that followed had practiced these rituals, which came from the time of the golden age of Padmasambhava when Buddhism flourished. Also, in Tibet in another century, one high teacher threw statues of Guru Rinpoche in water. These are examples of totally nonspiritual misinterpretations of spirituality, with no understanding of incorporeal, indestructible wisdom body. Everywhere and in every time, there are nonsubstantial manifestations of Buddhas, which cannot be affected by perceptions and intentions with a substantial reality of hatred. Even if people feel they have destroyed something, no one can ever destroy the manifestations of Buddhas. When spirituality is overly materialized, it becomes nonspiritual, and those who act destructively because of materializations of spirituality are actually just destroying their own spirit.

Even without belief in manifestation, if one believes in conception and mind just in an ordinary way, one has to acknowledge that one cannot make conception cease. Therefore, many deluded, negative phenomena can arise. Instead of only allowing that to happen, if one can turn one's mind to all immeasurable Buddhas and their unobstructed qualities, their manifestations are there, whether one believes this or not. Whether manifestations appear to be impure or pure corresponds to the negative or positive karma of beings, but manifestations, which cannot cease, are always pure, and the negativity of beings' delusion cannot prevent this. So, even if some beings have chosen their own negative paranoia and have created more and more negative phenomena about holy manifestations instead of choosing to increase positive appearances of enlightened phenomena, these holy manifestations are continuous.

For animals, human beings, and, beyond them, for superior beings, there is compounded immaterial spiritual reality. Whether or not that reality is occurring within a particular time and place only depends on the individual's habits, but it cannot be denied that it is possible for the existence of spiritual reality to appear anytime and anywhere. When nonspiritual compounded reality becomes apparent, nonbelieving beings do not recognize that uncompounded reality always simultaneously exists, inconspicuously and indivisibly. They only believe in compounded reality while it appears, which is the phenomena of ordinary beings; and then, when that compounded material reality recedes into uncompounded space, they decide there is nothing. But whenever compounded material circumstances arise, immaterial reality inherently and simultaneously exists along with it, each appearing and receding in the circling of samsara.

Immaterial spiritual reality is occurring to believers' minds within compounded material phenomena, with uncompounded immaterial spiritual qualities, and developing up to immaterial spiritual power, so spiritual qualities expand until the divisible phenomena of contradiction are transformed and phenomena become oneness in the indivisible state. Even when existence is apparent, it is indivisible from non-existence. As Shantideva said:

> Whenever phenomena do not exist,
> Whenever they will exist,
> And until their existence occurs,
> The existence of phenomena is never separate from non-existence.

When wisdom develops, since immaterial spiritual reality is within material conception, at that time it cannot be said that there is what is called spiritual reality. Spiritual reality is positive reality conception. Through faith, prayer, and meditation, karmic obscurations and ordinary defilements become less and less because the power of immaterial spiritual reality is expanding within the material. Obscurations become less and less, because clarity becomes greater and greater. That clarity is immaterial spiritual reality.

Immaterial spiritual reality sounds like a contradiction because the immaterial cannot be called real. But within practice, when the practitioner is still dealing with reality, immaterial spirituality can begin to influence the reality of the practitioner with actual immaterial spiritual energy. It is said:

> The impure, the impurely pure,
> And the extremely pure
> Are the stages of sentient beings, Bodhisattvas,
> And Buddhas.

The immaterial has tremendous power to reduce material conception and karma. Immaterial spiritual reality can therefore be used for practitioners and even for the stages of realization of Bodhisattvas from the first stage onward, which are not always sequential but always excel beyond material reality from the influence of immaterial spirituality.

When immaterial spirituality becomes more powerful, and material energy and reality conception become less and less, as practice progresses through spiritual levels and experience develops, it can be said that immaterial spirituality is influencing the reality of the practitioner. When attaining the fully enlightened state, which is absolute truth, there is no reality, so this term cannot be used. There is only oneness, as Buddha said:

The unborn is the sole truth.

Reality is not actually real, but beings think it is real. Whatever anyone finds that is real cannot be found to have any ultimate reality. Beings caught in their reality cause their own suffering by making everything real, trusting in that reality, leaving that reality as it is, dying in that reality, and again being born in that reality. Mind does not exist anywhere within the material or immaterial, but beings think mind is always inseparable from a self, and they think a self exists until they die. According to Buddhism, although a self is just a delusion of the mind, until the delusion of mind is cleansed, there is always the conception of delusion and nondelusion. Mind is continuous, and all its phenomena of being born, remaining, and ceasing are ordinary mind's reality and not actually the nature of mind. Whatever previous reality habit arises in this life's phenomena, this habit is not real. Habit is only habit, but from habit, beings think it is real. Any kind of samsaric reality, which is the reality of inverted relative truth, is actually unreal. As everybody knows even if they do not acknowledge it, all beings' compounded energy and conception always change and will keep changing, yet beings do not believe it, even though these are changing continuously before their eyes. This is because of their reality habit, even though a continuous reality does not exist. Since everything in reality is created by grasping conception, and conception is created by a self, which makes many countless habits, one manipulates oneself by one's own habit.

The essence of mind, which is Buddha nature or Dharmata itself, is always pure, but it is misinterpreted from not recognizing the pure nature of its unobstructed manifestation, which causes the delusion of ordinary dualistic mind and its reality of passions, emotions, and karma.

So the pure essential nature becomes dormant, and many, many conflicting samsaric phenomena are created. Then, although the essence of mind, pure Dharmata, is continuous, from lack of belief and ignorance, beings do not use it but waste it by letting it remain dormant, just like a noble tree that is rotting inside its bark.

Depending on one's personal positive connection, Buddha nature according to Mahayana, or inherent wisdom deity according to Vajrayana, can blossom through having faith and with fortunate circumstances such as meeting holy teachers and accumulating virtue, which occur within immaterial spiritual reality. This state of immaterial spiritual reality does not occur for obscured minds, but occurs in faithful practitioners' minds. This is the reality of actual relative truth, because Buddha nature and inherent wisdom deity are appearing in their minds from their previous accumulation of merit and wisdom. For nonbelievers, it is unreal. For believers, it is real because it is actually occurring in their minds and it will continue to occur up to enlightenment. This immaterial spiritual reality never lures one in the wrong direction and only benefits by delivering continuous positive phenomena and positive energy through the recognition of the truth of one's own immaterial Buddha nature or inherent wisdom deity, so one's realization can develop up to the fully enlightened state of Buddhahood. Buddhahood is absolute truth, beyond any reality or unreality.

Material reality belongs to dualistic habit. Believing in the immaterial, and not believing in reality, is spiritual. Reality comes from the compounded material of heavy stained habit, and whatever is compounded is not immaterial. Although the pure wisdom body, speech, and mind of sublime beings undeniably exist, they are not an actual material reality, although they can manifest in reality to reality beings.

The problem people have is that they have strong nihilist habits and do not even believe in Buddha nature, but they need to believe in it and rekindle it. As I quoted from *The Uttara Tantra* in *A Cascading Waterfall of Nectar*,[57] there are three reasons that beings always have Buddha nature:

> The body of Buddha is manifesting in the minds of all sentient beings.

There is no difference between the nature of Buddha's wisdom mind
and sentient beings' minds.
All beings hold the lineage of enlightenment.
So therefore, beings are always the essence of Buddha for these three
reasons.

As this says, there is no basic difference among beings; the only difference is whether Buddha nature is obscured or unobscured. And since
it says in Nagarjuna's *Jewel Rosary*:[58]

If it is so important, you have to repeat it at least twice.

So, again, as it is also said in the *Uttara Tantra*, with logic that proves
Buddha nature:

If there were no Buddha nature in beings' minds,
There would never be the sadness of samsara.
Also, there would not be a desire for enlightenment,
And also, there would be no wish to accomplish anything.
Seeing the faults of samsara is sadness.
Seeing enlightenment's state is happiness.
Seeing this suffering and happiness clearly is seen by the mind,
And it is a sign of Buddha nature.
If there were no Buddha nature, all these negative faults and all
these positive qualities would not be seen.
They are the manifestation of the lineage of Buddha nature.
Wherever there is no lineage,
There is no awareness to discern anything.

In Tibet, there were many practitioners with positive energy from
their practice. That positive energy is actually the quality of the immaterial. Mind is immaterial because the source of mind is immaterial wisdom, and wisdom is very powerful. From practice, wisdom permeates
the mind and changes negative phenomena to positive phenomena. That
is why practicing with faith and belief in Buddha affects one's mind and
energy; this happens because one is receiving the blessings of Buddha's
wisdom qualities. Buddha is fully enlightened, which means there is not
even an iota of material in Buddha's body, speech, and mind, because

Buddha is stainless emptiness. This is Dharmakaya. Dharmakaya is the evenness of stainless, immeasurable wisdom, so therefore it evenly pervades all material and immaterial phenomena. The nature of Dharmakaya is not made up from compounded phenomena or concepts, so the power of stainlessness pervades within the immaterial or the material, never causing the trap of suffering. By definition, the word *immaterial* does not go with reality, but one cannot deny that there are spiritual phenomena occurring within reality because spirituality has this quality of pervasiveness, which affects reality phenomena. Also, it evenly permeates the immaterial state.

So, to synthesize this, immaterial spiritual reality is the occurrences within reality of inexpressible, inconceivable manifestations of wisdom, which can never be concretized but always pervade the material. That is why it is wondrous forever. If we actually have faith, even if it cannot be seen, it has to be believed, without causing any limitation by trying to divide material reality phenomena from immaterial spirituality.

Empty sky is uncompounded, but if compared to wisdom emptiness, the emptiness of the sky is inert. Still, one cannot say sky is useless, because all other elements are occurring from space and receding in space, and without space, the other elements cannot function. But great wisdom emptiness is uncompounded. Inert empty sky is just an example to show this. Wisdom emptiness is never inert, because all immeasurable wisdom qualities are occurring and abiding and receding; it is the source of all manifestations and the result of all manifestations. The occurrence of these manifestations is immaterial spiritual reality. It is reality because it affects beings who have reality phenomena. That is actual spiritual reality, which temporarily brings all kinds of positive energy, enlivening phenomena within the material, and ultimately liberating beyond reality or a material or immaterial state, which is the flawless state of fully enlightened phenomena. This enlivening occurs through faith, practice, and worship according to phenomena, and through being indivisible according to meditation, for those who are believers. Even though there are nonbelievers, they have mind, and mind has Buddha nature, so even if they are temporarily caught in momentary compounded reality habit from being nonbelievers, Buddha nature will open when their fortunate karmic habit arises.

Immaterial spiritual phenomena occurring within reality are not made up by anyone. Even if their recognition relies on the temporary compounded phenomena of the five skandhas, they do not actually remain in compounded material phenomena that are diminishable and destroyable, and fall apart. Any immaterial spiritual phenomena come from and are permeated by nondualistic wisdom mind, so they are never lost and never fail. That is why they are immaterial, up to fully reaching the uncompounded inconceivable flawless state of Buddha, which never falls anywhere into an indifferent stupor, because there is always awareness. Awareness's manifestation occurs within the material and immaterial, yet this manifestation is itself free from the material and immaterial forever. Whoever enters the path to that state, accumulating merit and wisdom until all material or immaterial habit is cleansed through faith, prayer, worship, meditation, and experience, will go up and up, higher and higher. One will be happy without expectation, and one's positive energy will pervade and spread toward others in a beneficial way. All these are actual immaterial spiritual truth.

All fully enlightened Buddhas are abiding in nondualistic wisdom from the beginning, forever, so there is no dualistic habit of the phenomena of being born, the phenomena of remaining, or the phenomena of ceasing. Their nature is free from being born, ceasing, and remaining, so they are always in that unwavering state, with pure immaterial phenomena, which has no material that traps because it is the uncompounded state of uncompounded phenomena. Since it is always abiding in stainless Dharmadhatu, it can be called sublime, which means absolute truth, because it is never deceiving. From absolute truth, pure phenomena unintentionally emanate in many different forms, sounds, and aspects within the appearances of beings who have compounded reality attachment, including beings who like reality even though reality is unreal, just as even unreality's conception is unreal, to release beings from any compounded suffering.

As it is said in Patrul Rinpoche's *Praise to Mahasandhi, Liberated from the Beginning: The Speech of the Lord Sugata Called "The Stainless Sapphire Garland"*:[59]

Whatever exists is true just according to instantaneous phenomena.
Whatever exists is not true because the nature of mind cannot think
of or express its inconceivability.

Also, as Kunkhyen Longchenpa said:

All phenomena are the self-accomplished essence of enlightenment.
If there is familiarity with the essential point of effortlessness,
From the original Buddha, again Buddha manifests,
Which is the meaning of the supreme essence of Vajrayana.
The essence of the nine *yanas* is the great enlightened expanse.
Even though the mandala of the sun and moon is shining in the
center of the sky,
If the essence is completely obscured by dense clouds of
nonrecognition,
Enlightenment, which is self-abiding, is not manifesting.
Just as dense clouds disappear naturally by leaving them as they
are in space,
From effortlessness there is freedom from the clouds of karmic
cause and effect,
So the essence of enlightenment self-arises in stainless space.
Due to differences in faculties, there are various *yanas*,
In the expanse of Dharmadhatu the sunlike esence shines,
Illuminating all impartially by its power, like rays
Pervading the earth and water bodies with warmth.
So vapors arise, from which the manifestation of clouds appears,
Obscuring the essence itself and also its power.
Like that, by the impure self-manifestation of the essence
emanating,
Recognizing the essence itself is obscured.
In whatever exists as the phenomena of the outer universe and inner
beings, there are inconceivable deluded appearances.
Just as from the manifestation of sun rays comes the movement of
wind that clears away clouds,
By recognizing self-nature, its manifestation arises as an ornament.

Since delusion is liberated from beginninglessness, self-liberated in
    its natural state,
Without abandoning deluded phenomena or grasping at delusion,
    they are purified in stainless space.
Going nowhere in clear sky,
The sun of self-manifesting wisdom body and wisdom mind shines,
Not coming from anywhere else, just one's own pure self-
    phenomena.

So, Melvin, you and I both believe in that state, so we will not get lost
forever.

A Message for Young Bhutanese

According to Aum Neten Zangmo's insistent request.

The Honorable Aum Neten Zangmo first wrote to me by e-mail asking me to give some advice for a new organization called Druk Nangpai Zhoennu, the Young Buddhist Association of Bhutan, in whatever way would be the best for the country. Later, after she had attended a meeting in Washington, DC, as a representative of the Bhutanese government, she came to my residence in Palm Desert, California, to make this request again, with good intentions to benefit the young people of her country. I have heard that Aum Neten Zangmo is called "Dasho" now, but I have the habit from when I lived in Bhutan of using "Dasho" for males, and females always being called "Aum" or "Ashi." So, if I say "Dasho Neten Zangmo," the sign of male genitals instantly comes up from my old habit, and this becomes very uncomfortable for me.

Ever since I met Aum Neten Zangmo, she has normally been very incisive and intelligent. Of course, she is young and may not have studied Buddhist spiritual theory deeply, so she can be attracted to a few materialized words from Westerners. Recently, for example, she sent an article to my student saying that an organization of two hundred religious leaders in Switzerland, made up of Muslims, Christians, Jews, Hindus, and Buddhists, had voted that Buddhism is the world's best religion this year. Buddha Shakyamuni said:

Beings' minds cannot be judged, except by me and those like me.

So I cannot say that those who voted are wrong to have made this judgment. All Buddhas are omniscient, however, so they know there are countless sentient beings with countless different faculties, and Buddhas guide these beings according to time and place with suitable teachings, timelessly and directionlessly. Therefore, since Buddhist teachings are limitless, one cannot use a limited idea of Buddhism's being the best religion at this time, for this year. That is what is done in annual beauty pageants when one woman is chosen as the most beautiful, in musical contests when a musician is chosen as the most talented, or in the World Series when the Yankees win as the best baseball team for that year. All these judgments come from ordinary conception with ordinary phenomena. Buddhism cannot be judged or compared in this way forever, whether at this time or some other time.

The basic idea of a contest between religions comes from the materialism of Western capitalism, where everyone must compete. Of course, according to Buddhism, immaterial energy influences both the material and immaterial, and immaterial spiritual qualities flourish within beings with material phenomena, although whether spiritual power is decaying or flourishing depends on the karma of sentient beings. Even when Buddha's teachings are used within compounded body, speech, and mind, however, they are still connected with immaterial uncompounded mind, and immaterial uncompounded mind cannot be materialized by saying which year it is better. For any organization that uses changeable, compounded group conceptions to conclude that Buddhism is the best religion of the year is unreliable because it is based on materializing time and place with dualistic conceptions in an ordinary way. Buddhism is never ordinary. Whatever the members of this Swiss organization say, Buddha's blessings will be continuous, corresponding to sentient beings' faculties. Buddha's teachings cannot be materialized, and it is not right to try to put the incomparable, limitless qualities of Buddhist teachings into the limitation of a certain time or place with this kind of idea. Even phenomena within the limitation of time and place can occur in countless different ways, but especially Buddhist teachings are always limitless. According to the phenomena of sentient beings, there can seem to be a limitation, but this is only due to their obscurations. Buddha's teachings are always flawless and continuous until beings are liberated from suffering.

Material conceptions are always disprovable. For example, many millions of people can agree to vote for a particular person for president, thinking they are making the best choice. Whenever circumstances change and something goes wrong, however, even if it is only a few months or a year later, the same people who voted for that president may say they want to impeach him. So it is silly for Aum Neten Zangmo to accept this Swiss organization's decision, although she did so with sweet and positive thoughts. Even though for others Aum Neten Zangmo can be ferocious according to circumstances, for me she is a lovely lady, so I don't want to irritate her too much, but to answer her request for advice for young Buddhists in Bhutan.

In one way, I am glad to hear the name of this new organization of young Buddhists, but in another way, since no one knows what circumstances will bring, and this organization has been named before it has done anything, the name is also inappropriate. Wise sublime beings of ancient times have said:

Whatever you do that is positive is supposed to be done
    anonymously with discipline and good intentions.
Whatever is excessively exposed will cause more obstacles.

As this says, in order to create virtue, one must never boast but be inconspicuous, since showing off attracts the attention of demons. Unless one is encouraging or inspiring others to make virtue, one has to be disciplined and quiet about virtue, as Buddha Shakyamuni taught, without forgetting to dedicate it for enlightenment, without dedicating it for ordinary aims, and without having regret, all of which exhausts virtue.

Garab Dorje[1] has been spreading the teaching of Troma Nagmo[2] so that Troma is being practiced throughout Bhutan, and now the sounds of *damarus*[3] playing and bells ringing are everywhere, even disturbing the local dogs. So, Garab Dorje is not incognito these days. I heard that Garab Dorje had the good intention of honoring Buddha's birthday with a parade of the Young Buddhist Association of Bhutan, yet even though parades exist everywhere in the world and are generally accepted, when their parade arrived at the Memorial Chorten[4] in Thimphu, the caretakers turned them away and stopped them from entering. It is shocking that Bhutanese people prevented other Bhutanese people from entering a holy shrine, as though they were like dogs going to eat the *tormas* inside. But anyway, I will pray for the Young Buddhist Association of Bhutan to do whatever will be meaningful and beneficial for the country.

In writing this message for young Bhutanese Buddhists, I am also considering the entire country of Bhutan and the preservation of its Dharma heritage. The Protector of the degenerate time's beings, the Vajra Master Padmasambhava, blessed this world, including Tibet, Nepal, and Bhutan, and blessed many holy places in order for these holy places to bless future generations. Also, when my Holy Father, Dudjom Yeshe Dorje, was young, he traveled through India, Sikkim, Tibet, and Drukyul, the Dragonland of Bhutan. In Paro, he made a very spiritual connection with Paro Pönlop Tsering Paljor. Later, according to an invitation from Tashigang Dzongpön Dasho Dopola, my Holy Father attended in the district of Tashigang and gave Rinchen Terdzö དབང་ལུང་ [*wanglung*, empowerments and transmissions][5] of the holy teachings of Guru Rinpoche's Treasures.[6] After that, he again gave the Tersar[7] *wanglung* of Tragtung Düdjom Lingpa's Treasures from time to time in East Bhutan, and later the *wanglung* of Pema Lingpa's Treasures in Samtse, and so on. There is such a special connection with Guru Rinpoche's Treasures in Bhutan. Also, about myself, I stayed with my family in Kurtö, and then later in Tashigang District. So we have a positive connection with many Bhutanese people, although due to my health I stayed abroad for a while and could not go to Bhutan the same as before.

When the fourth king of the Dragonland kingdom of Drukyul, His Majesty Jigme Singye Wangchuck, asked all the people of Bhutan to make the country into a democracy, insisting on this, the people reluctantly accepted the democratization of the country according to his wishes and held elections. The Honorable Lyonchen Jigmi Yoezer Thinley, Light Rays of Fearless Activity, was victorious and became the Prime Minister. My Holy Precious Father's disciple, Lama Kuenzang Wangdue, was sent by the Prime Minister with his བཀའ་ཤོག་ [*kashok*, official decree][8] that I should come to Bhutan, with great intentions and great consideration for the Bhutanese people. He said that the Bhutanese people have faith in Guru Rinpoche and also have a connection with my Holy Father and with me, and since they were longing to see me, I should speak to them and remind them again about Dharma in order for Buddhist teachings to flower continuously and to refresh their positive energy. Of course, all of you know about Buddhism from the teachings of sublime beings, because Bhutan has been a Buddhist country for many centuries, so I do not need to explain anything about Dharma. There have been many previous scholars and good practitioners in Bhutan who have already taught Dharma, and there are also scholarly and saintly sublime beings and their followers who are there now, and whatever they have taught is more than enough if people keep these teachings in mind continuously.

Nevertheless, in order to honor the Prime Minister's command and to honor the people of Bhutan, I prayed to have the opportunity to restore my energy a little bit in order not to cause trouble for others. Even though I am aging and have health conditions, and even though I do not usually travel so much from place to place but stay quietly, I fulfilled the wish from my heart to return to Bhutan, which I had always wanted to do because of a positive connection with the Bhutanese people. Now, for auspiciousness, as a donation for the people of Bhutan, and especially for young Bhutanese, including those studying various aspects of Western culture, I will just say a few more words like fresh rain as an offering to the Triple Gems for the benefit of increasing the pure river of Dharma, as Aum Neten Zangmo asked.

According to Buddha's teachings, there are countless sentient beings, and each sentient being has mind. This mind is not inert like stone or mindless material, as nonbelievers decide. In general, the term *consciousness* is used to describe the mind that functions within the senses and occurs between the duality of subject and object. Nonbeliever beings think that whatever is experienced by this consciousness as momentary negative or positive phenomena will eventually finish when the body dies, and that there is nothing left of consciousness after death. Without question, the experience of the ordinary consciousness of nonbelievers does not support reaching enlightenment; even within this short life, this experience does not support being able to change states of unhappiness to happiness, either in a lasting way or even a temporary way. The general characteristic of nonbelievers is to be concerned only with whatever will benefit this momentary life and with how to take advantage of their immediate circumstances. They have no method to influence these circumstances, however, which are uncontrollably changing due to karma, although nonbelievers do not acknowledge this.

In order to try to create lasting happiness, there have been many different spiritual doctrines with historically different views and theories, such as Hinduism, Judaism, Islam, and Christianity, with many different human beings who have believed in them. Although those who follow other religions believe in the accumulation of merit and the purification of obscurations, only Buddhist teachings support the attainment of fully enlightened Buddhahood, beyond all habit.

According to Buddhist theory or logic, mind is unlike inert elements because there is a knower. Human beings especially have the capacity to know what is wrong and right, and what causes suffering and happiness. Even though one knows what causes suffering and what causes peace and happiness, if this is not connected with the teachings of Buddhism, one cannot cause happiness that endures for many other lives as well as this life, and there is no support for attaining the state of full enlightenment, which is forever flawless ecstasy wisdom body and mind, the same as all Buddhas.

Those who believe in Buddhist teachings with faith have a continuous support for the accumulation of merit, and especially for attaining fully enlightened Buddhahood. According to Buddhist teachings, mind is the basis of unhappiness and happiness forever, and even in this life, whatever previous habit or result is experienced can be changed by the mind with prayer and meditation. Also, according to the Mahayana, each sentient being has the potential to become Buddha, but it is dormant from obscurations or lack of recognition. It is only called a potential when it has not opened, but when it opens, it can completely expand as Buddha's wisdom, free from all obscurations and the same as all Buddhas.

Within the ordinary habit of ordinary beings, since there is mind, there are phenomena, even though these phenomena are seen as impure due to attachment to samsaric appearances. Whether phenomena are seen clearly or not seen clearly depends on the extent of the habits of obscuration, and whether mind is more or less obscured. Since phenomena are undeniable, why can these phenomena not be turned from negative phenomena to positive phenomena, and from positive phenomena up to enlightenment? If one is a nonbeliever, one will not abstain from nonvirtue's activity with intention, which becomes the cause of negative karma. This is a terrible misuse of human life because it delays the opening of Buddha nature, which occurs through belief with faith. Even though nonbelievers decide there is not a next life, there will still be a next life as long as the obscurations of mind have not been cleansed. Phenomena become what one creates, so by believing in Buddha with faith, developing positive appearances through prayers and the accumulation of virtue, and creating wisdom phenomena, wisdom opens. Without doing this, the ordinary phenomena of the six realms appear through the karmic movement of mind.

There are countless sentient beings, and if all these sentient beings are categorized according to Buddha's speech, they are contained within the six realms, which include the hell realm, the hungry ghost realm, the animal realm, the asura realm, the god realm, and the human realm. The way that all of these realms are created through cause and effect is all known from the speech of Buddha and the explanations of Buddha's speech in the commentaries, or shastras, of sublime beings. This can be learned by whoever studies cause and effect and analyzes the source of suffering and happiness wherever the six realms exist.

In a brief way, how are the six realms caused? They are caused by the lack of attaining the state of full enlightenment the same as all Buddhas, which results in cause and effect because of ignorance. In comparing the human realm to the beings of other realms, the characteristic of human beings is that they can talk and understand whatever they say to each other. From a previous lack of the accumulation of merit, however, although humans can communicate with language, they do not use their abilities meaningfully but rely on the temporary phenomena of their ordinary senses. Beings are born in the human realm with the five senses and their consciousnesses: eyes and the consciousness of the eyes, ears and the consciousness of the ears, a nose and the consciousness of the nose, a tongue and the consciousness of the tongue, a body and the consciousness of the body, and also mind and the consciousness of mind, and then they experience reality form, sound, smell, taste, touch, and phenomena. These are called the six gatherings of phenomena, or ཚོགས་དྲུག་ [tsokdruk].⁹ When humans use their senses in an ordinary way and only believe in the existence of this momentary life, whatever appears to them occurs within these six compounded gatherings of phenomena, which are temporary. When human beings do not believe in anything beyond this ordinary reality, including not believing in karma, previous lives and future lives, other realms, gods, deities, and the Triple Gems, which they think do not exist so that they are not even interested in hearing about them, they are called nonbelievers, or nihilists.

It is obvious, however, that disbelief in what is beyond the phenomena of one's immediate ordinary perception is illogical, since mind can create countless appearances that are beyond ordinary reality. For example, as said in *A Cascading Waterfall of Nectar*, "when the appearances of waking reality cease at the time one falls asleep at night, the body while dreaming still remains lying on a small bed that fits its size while the mind experiences countless appearances that are as vast as the universe, all based on fluctuating between happiness and suffering. These appearances are similar to daytime reality. Definitely, one's body did not get up from the bed and go outside in order to experience these countless phenomena of happiness and suffering, and neither are these countless varied aspects of phenomena coming from outside into one's small bed. It is impossible for them to fit. This experience is solely the result of the deluded phenomena of the habits of appearances of daytime reality or the magical deceptions of the habits of past and future lives, only occurring in one's own mind."¹⁰

It is a disaster if one is born as a human being but only believes in ordinary reality without recognizing the continuity of mind, because one will waste one's human life. Even though one has Buddha nature, it remains dormant by being nihilist, which prevents one from causing the positive phenomena of creating virtue that will create positive karma for future lives in high realms up to attaining enlightenment. In Dharma terms, this is called དགེ་རྩ་བཅད་པ་ [ge tsa chepa],¹¹ or cutting the root of virtue, which is why nihilism is a disaster. When there is no positive believer, there is no power to influence where to be reborn or not to be reborn, because there is no faith, virtue, or practice. When the karmic body is exhausted, there will have been no preparation for the next life by having created positive karma, so there is no support for positive karmic circumstances. Therefore, one will have to follow without choice whatever karma has been created in previous lives and accumulated in the basis of mind.

In the speech of Buddha, it is said that sentient beings have mind. Even though mind cannot be touched or seen because it is intangible, it is not like empty nothingness. Mind is immaterial, but it causes material and immaterial phenomena. Unless fully enlightened Buddhahood is attained, mind is continuous, and within that continuous mind, even though it is ordinary, Buddha nature pervades. As long as mind exists, there is Buddha nature, which is mind's essence, even though it is dormant from lack of belief. In Mahayana teachings, this essence of Buddha is called བདེ་བར་གཤེགས་པའི་སྙིང་པོ་ [dewar shekpe nyingpo][12] according to Chöke [classical Tibetan Dharma language], or Sugatagarbha in Sanskrit. All Buddhas are fully enlightened, which is སངས་རྒྱས་ [sang-gye][13] in Chöke, or Sugata in Sanskrit, which means "gone to the state of exaltation," as all Buddhas have gone. Even though beings have not gone to this state, Buddha introduced that beings have the potential to attain this state, and that is why this is called སྙིང་པོ་ [nyingpo],[14] which means the essence or pith of Buddha. This essence is still within dualistic mind, which is within cause and result. While according to Mahayana sutras this is called the essence of Buddha nature, in Vajrayana it is called inherent wisdom deity, ལྷན་གཅིག་སྐྱེས་པའི་ལྷ་ [lhen chik kyepe lha],[15] or the deity of Dharmata, ཆོས་ཉིད་ཀྱི་ལྷ་ [chönyi kyi lha],[16] until attaining fully enlightened wisdom mandala.

According to Buddhist theory in the Sutra tradition, in order to become fully enlightened Buddha, one accumulates virtue and purifies obscurations. First of all, in order to be a believer according to Buddhist theory, it is necessary to recognize that any kind of habit is created by dualistic mind. There are many different names for habit, but in order to understand it clearly, habit actually means addiction. Whatever addiction was previously seeded in the mind, as nonvirtue and the enjoyment of causing nonvirtue, is negative habit, or བག་ཆགས་ངན་པ་ [bak-chag ngenpa].[17] This negative habit again causes negative seeds in future lives, just as, when a poisonous seed is planted, it grows into a plant that produces poisonous fruit, and when this fruit ripens, it again causes poisonous seeds. The negative results of habit can occur in this life also, so that even though one has a human life, it is wasted because one likes to engage in nonvirtue due to previous habits, or addictions, which were placed in the continuity of one's mind. This can be seen in people who like to kill, to engage in war, to disturb other beings, and to be harmful, which are all the result of negative habit or addiction, or bakchag ngenpa, and also negative karma, or ལས་ངན་ [le-ngen].[18] Some human beings have previously accumulated merit that in this life has resulted in always naturally liking virtue, having a good heart, having the intention to benefit others, and having faith in the Triple Gems or deities. All of these are good habits, or in Dharma terms, བག་ཆགས་བཟང་པོ་ [bakchag zangpo].[19] Recognizing that this human life is precious and not wasting it but trying to transform old negative habit, or bakchag ngenpa, into positive habit, or bakchag zangpo, is the accumulation of virtue.

Finally, from virtue, one can reach the state of Sugata, or བདེ་བར་གཤེགས་པ་ [dewar shekpa],[20] "gone to exaltation." According to Mantrayana theory, all phenomena are the mandala of the great exaltation of wisdom deity, or ཡེ་ཤེས་ཀྱི་ལྷ་ [yeshe kyi lha].[21] Even though teachings such as these appear differently according to the different faculties of beings, with differences in the terms that are used, such as Sugata and wisdom mandala, the result is the same, which is forever abiding in stainless wisdom body, speech, mind, qualities, activities, and purelands, with no name of even an iota of suffering. Not wavering from that unwavering state, benefit manifests continuously for all beings. As Jowo Je, Glorious Atisha, said, however:

> Until all dualistic conception and its habit are exhausted in the stainless state, there is cause and effect.

So, cause and effect must be transformed into positive cause and effect through practice and meditation, until cleansed in the sole stainless state of fully enlightened Buddha.

Since Guru Rinpoche, Shabtrung Rinpoche,[22] and other sublime beings came to Bhutan and revealed precious Holy Dharma, the country of Bhutan is a precious holy place of Buddhism. The beings of the degenerate time are not like those of the golden age with keen spiritual faculties, however, so circumstances are changing and the culture, philosophy, and science of nonbelievers are invading. The way that the passions arise is increasingly gross, and beings are extremely engaged with the power of materialism and material life's habit. Actually, spirituality is beneficial even within the material because of its pure immaterial influence, but in this degenerate time, all human beings believe one-sidedly in material happiness and power, so therefore effort is made primarily to gain material phenomena. In this world, culture and education are also connected with extreme material power, so whatever is learned and studied is materialized. Desire is too excessive for materialistic gain within human life, and even though human life is short, human beings think it is long, using it for making the effort to cause material results. In Western countries where the power of materialism is highly accentuated, all existence seems to survive only from material phenomena. Even many Asian countries that have previously been Buddhist are becoming more attracted to material power. Ultimately, it does not bring any happiness to trust extreme material power. Whatever is material is compounded, including one's own body, so it must decay, fall apart, and diminish. According to the times, even though young people in Bhutan have to study the information of non-Buddhist cultures to adjust to other phenomena of the existent world and its modern developments, I hope and pray they will recognize the main key that they must never, never lose Buddhism, which is the original source of happiness for all beings. They can temporarily learn and use what is known in the world, but they must keep their Buddhist beliefs.

Since everything is interdependent, one has to see what is actually there to be able to see what causes circumstances. In order to see what is there, one first needs to look at what is nearer, or the root circumstance of oneself, the subject. It is necessary to look closely, like looking in a mirror, at what is wrong and right to see one's own faults so that one can correct them. Also, one needs to look at what is farther, at the projections of one's mind from previous lives or this life, using one's

mind like binoculars or a telescope to see the objects of perception that
are the reflection of the subject. By observing both subject and object,
and observing what will occur within cause and effect, one must see
and consider what is abandonable and what is acceptable, for one's own
country and for enlightenment, to be a pure Buddhist with a discerning
mind.

In this existent world where there are many different countries, the
karmic results of the happiness and unhappiness that human beings
experience are related to the circumstances of the places where they are
born and live. These karmic results are also connected with the influence
of each country's religious and worldly leaders, who affect the circumstances within their countries. Among the countries of human beings,
the country of Bhutan is one of the best so far because it has Dharma as
a result of people's previous fortunate karma. Religious leaders are most
important to their countries, and Bhutan's religious leaders have been
entrusted with sustaining this Holy Dharma country from virtue with
good intentions. By having good religious leaders in Bhutan who follow
the traditions of previous sublime beings, happiness will be maintained
and can be continuously increased.

It is very important for religious leaders to consider interdependent
relative truth's cause and effect. Otherwise, seemingly positive ideas
can be transformed into negative energy. According to interdependent
relative truth, it is not enough to think only of one's own momentary
interests and how to survive within one's own group by cultivating
one's power or position, since only thinking one-sidedly about one's
own immediate circumstances, group, or country can cause a negative
result. Even though circumstances may momentarily be all right, they
can change because the nature of existence is that it is compounded.
One has to think deeply about others, including those in neighboring
countries and the potential effect one's actions will have on them, by
considering the meaning of interdependent relative truth and thinking
in a vast way about what should be caused and what kind of effect will
occur from these causes. Those who have the most power have to be
even more careful than others not to overuse their power and twist it
into something else, but to benefit everyone.

Whenever someone becomes an important spiritual leader from previous good karma, this must be recognized as a blessing from the Triple Gems, and this blessing must be used as an opportunity to create more benefit for all beings, including the people of Bhutan, with a view of noncontradiction between Kagyu and Nyingma. No one should ever take advantage of being in a position of power by opportunistically trying to convert others, including Nyingmapas. Nyingma is the teaching of Guru Rinpoche, and there have been many generations of followers of Guru Rinpoche in Bhutan within the Nyingma tradition, and not only followers of Drukpa Kagyu. The heritage of the noble spiritual traditions of Bhutan and their previous leaders should be kept, without excessive sectarianism that leads to thinking only of temporarily gaining power, which will not help one's religious position. Instead, it can cause a negative result.

It is definitely logical and pure to object to the conversion of Nyingma retreat places, temples, and their leaders, placing them under the control of the central and local Dzong.[23] It unnecessarily seeds problems to colonize Nyingma retreat places with Drukpa Kagyu authorities, which will finally become like Britain colonizing America, causing America to revolt. If Dzong leaders are wise, they should recognize and accept that Nyingma followers still belong to the country of Bhutan, just as they have for many centuries in Bhutanese history. These Nyingma followers are from the same Bhutanese people with the same skin, from the same Bhutanese land, and hold the same Bhutanese religion of Mahayana and Vajrayana tantric Buddhism, even though due to time and place there is the differentiation of Sarma and Nyingma. For example, Longchenpa, Pema Lingpa, Dorje Lingpa, many manifestations of Guru Rinpoche, and many Tersar lineage holders are still very much a part of the traditions and culture of the Bhutanese people. When everything is already perfect, why is it necessary to try so hard to make it imperfect? It was said in ancient times that if one blows on a fire, the fire will react back and burn one's own mustache. Look at the world, where there is no peace but conflict, disturbance, war, and suffering, with the consequence of terrible energy.

There were many complaints in the past about human rights issues by misinformed international organizations, and there can also be many influences from outside the country that can affect Bhutan in the future, including in connection with the idea of religious freedom, as well as many others. Even when people intend to benefit others, sometimes they can benefit and sometimes they can cause confusion instead, so the wrong side is defended and the aggressors are protected instead of the victims. (Although international human rights organizations generally try to protect those who are victimized, in this case they protected people who were trying to take advantage of Bhutan's leniency and tolerance. Of course, if a human rights organization does what is right, it has to be respected, but if it uses the name of human rights while making the wrong people right and the right people wrong, that is not right. Although these misunderstandings were corrected, Bhutanese can remain aware of the potential for misinterpretation by people of other countries. It is not necessary for Bhutan to be afraid; Bhutan has its own human rights to protect. If Bhutan had followed the ideas of international human rights organizations at that time, that itself would not have been in support of human rights for Bhutanese.)

Bhutanese religious and political leaders must persevere in their own historical religious traditions without creating a new problem between the country's own religions. To cause infighting gives an excuse to others to intervene. It is important not to cause arguments that could undermine stability in Bhutan. The Bhutanese people have to be alert about protecting their own culture and religion from non-Bhutanese influences instead of creating disturbances between the followers of their own Bhutanese religions, which share the same root of being Buddhist. Bhutan has an extraordinary history from many sublime beings, including a history during the reigns of three kings that did not have this kind of serious contradiction between the Drukpa Kagyu and the Nyingma. There is no question that Bhutanese culture has been wonderful up to now, including its spiritual traditions of Dharma, which I thought were impeccable.

According to Mahayana Buddhist methods, Buddha taught that wherever there is disturbance, for spiritual reasons and with the selfless intention of bodhichitta, one may have to disturb others in order to make peace, harmony, and stability. This does not apply to actions performed in order to conquer, occupy, misuse, or overpower others for political reasons with selfish intentions, which disturb peace and tranquillity. If religious leaders provoke actions of discrimination and order conversion through being biased and overly attached to their own positions, it is especially dangerous for the future of the country of Bhutan. Although Bhutan is a tiny country, it is blessed by Guru Rinpoche to be a pure Dharma country, which was further established by many sublime beings, including Phajo Drugom Shigpo,[24] Omniscient Longchenpa, Pema Lingpa, and Shabtrung Rinpoche, all of whom did not discriminate between Old School (Nyingma) and New School (Sarma) traditions but taught to keep faith in Guru Rinpoche unshakably. From this great legacy, Bhutan is one of the most stable places in which pure Dharma traditions have been maintained. If religious leaders follow whatever traditions flourished previously in the same way, it will be very uncomplicated and much more beneficial for all. It will not cause contradiction between Nyingma and Drukpa Kagyu, but will continue the recognition of Guru Rinpoche as being not only for Bhutan, but the sole wisdom emanation of Buddha Shakyamuni and the protector of the entire world, including the people of Bhutan. I cannot say what the karma of the younger generation in Bhutan will be in the future, but it is certain that it is much better for Bhutanese to encourage Buddhism to flourish than to ignore it, for the benefit of all beings, including Bhutanese.

As everyone in Bhutan who is faithful and has a virtuous mind knows, Guru Rinpoche's holy places are everywhere, from Paro Taktsang, the holy place of wrathful Padmasambhava, to Drakar, through Bumthang Kuje, which has the imprint of Guru Rinpoche's wisdom body, up to Kurtö Seng-ge Dzong, the holy place of Vajrakilaya and also Guru Rinpoche and Yeshe Tsogyal. It is not that the Old School (Nyingma) is not Bhutan's own religion, and Bhutan's own religion is Drukpa Kagyu; whoever thinks in that way is making a big mistake that could cause dissension, polarization, and gradual political destabilization through problems invented among Kagyu, Drukpa Kagyu, and Nyingma. If the people of Bhutan keep their country's traditions according to Shabtrung

Rinpoche and those who have been wise in the past by trusting in Guru Rinpoche and recognizing, praying to, and worshiping Guru Rinpoche as the protector of all beings of the *kaliyuga*, including the people of the country of Bhutan, their country will be preserved. This is crucial, because Bhutan is a precious holy place.

We do not need to be negative about nations in Europe and America that have their own theories about human rights and democracy, but I hope and pray that the democracy of Bhutan will not feel that it has to follow the ideas of other nations when these ideas are not compatible with their own Buddhist culture, which is the most profound culture in this existent world and unsurpassed by any other nation. This precious Buddhist culture of Bhutan must be kept as it is by upholding the Nyingma and Drukpa Kagyu traditions that were brought to Bhutan by Guru Rinpoche and Shabtrung Rinpoche. If opposition is created between the practices of these two traditions, it will add to further difficulties caused by the introduction of foreign political ideas and eternalist religions. It is very weird and absurd to create contradiction between one's own complementary indigenous religions of Nyingma and Drukpa Kagyu through sectarianism inside the country, and at the same time to condone and bring in incompatible foreign political theories and eternalist cultures from outside the country.

In Jetsun Milarepa's hymns, he teaches:

When I fall sick, no one will ask how I am;
When I die, no one will lament or cry.
If I die alone in this hermitage,
I, a yogi, am satisfied.

Wherever I go, no one is asking after me;
There is no target for wherever I have gone.
If I die alone in this hermitage,
I, a yogi, am satisfied.

The flies will suck my nerves and veins,
And my rotten flesh will be devoured by maggots.

If I die alone in this hermitage,
I, a yogi, am satisfied.

Instead of practicing like this, these days there are followers who are
only practicing in order to build compounded power. That is why they
try to convert others and take away their freedom by sending them in a
perverted direction against pure Dharma.

Due to my health condition and age, Even though I could not stay
in Bhutan because of my age, health condition, medical treatment, and
many other reasons, I have faith in all Buddhas, including Guru Rinpoche and Shabtrung Rinpoche, because Shabtrung Rinpoche worships Guru Rinpoche. Shabtrung Rinpoche, who is most important
in the country of Bhutan, is not against Guru Rinpoche. If one reads
Shabtrung Rinpoche's history, one can know how he praised Guru Rinpoche and established the tradition of pujas to Guru Rinpoche, which
can be found in the shastras of Shabtrung Rinpoche and Drukpa *sadhana* practices, including སྐོང་བཤགས་ [*kongshag*].[25]

Among the Kagyu lineage, there are many sublime beings, both
scholarly and saintly. From the Karma Kagyu of Tibet, there are the
most saintly Karmapa Rangjung Dorje and Khakhyab Dorje, and from
those who are holders of the doctrine of Drukpa Kagyu, there are the
most scholarly Kunkhyen Pema Karpo and the most saintly Shabtrung
Rinpoche. All of these sublime beings worshiped, praised, and prayed to
Guru Rinpoche, and also continued the tradition of pujas to Guru Rinpoche. This precious tradition and the unforgettable kindness of Guru
Rinpoche have to be remembered and cherished. Guru Rinpoche's connection to the country of Bhutan is not something new; this history has
existed over many centuries. If young people do not know this because
they have not read this history in detail, they must now read it with
faith, pray, and practice the Buddhist traditions held by their ancestors,
visiting and receiving blessings from Guru Rinpoche's holy places in
their own country.

Ever since Shabtrung Rinpoche established practices of Guru Rinpoche's sadhanas, the Bhutanese majority has been practicing these sadhanas, including Guru Rinpoche's *drupchen*[26] every month or year, for

many generations up to now. This historical basis has to be acknowledged in Bhutan by spiritual practitioners and people with faith. If they
keep this faith for all Buddhas, including Guru Rinpoche, even if those
who are young cannot visualize or imagine Buddhas clearly because
they have been mainly studying in school or working in the world, they
can synthesize all immeasurable Buddhas within Guru Rinpoche and
Shabtrung Rinpoche with profound faith and pray to them for the benefit of all sentient beings, including the people of Bhutan. It must be
remembered that previously, many indisputably wise sublime beings
made predictions and also gave advice to pray to Guru Rinpoche in this
degenerate time.

Instead of practicing with pure intentions and increasing spiritual
energy that naturally benefits all beings, if religion is used to create conflict these days because of attachment to material power, it can be tragic
for the future of the people of Bhutan. Although there has been some
damage and injury, all is not totally lost, so the young people of Bhutan
have to consider carefully how to keep the Drukpa Kagyu and Nyingma
from falling apart.

When I was living in Bhutan, everything was ideal. For example, if
a Bhutanese family had two, three, or four offspring, according to the
wishes of the parents, some of them would stay in the home and work,
some of them would go to the castle, or Dzong, to become monks
and nuns, and some of them would become yogis and yoginis, or
སྒོམ་ཆེན་ [gomchen].[27] Of course, beings' minds are always in contradiction,
so there is always something wrong, but it is unnecessary to make up
more contradiction by creating conflict within the beautiful Buddhism
of Drukpa Kagyu and Nyingma, which has to be sustained impartially
so that it can flourish spiritually.

To do this, young Bhutanese have to be careful to keep Bhutan cleanly
and purely Bhutanese so that the country of Bhutan and its spiritual
heritage can be conserved. For the young people in Bhutan to have special qualities, since special qualities come from special minds, they have
to trust in the Triple Gems, including Guru Rinpoche, and let these
qualities open by putting first their Dharma activities of praying, worshiping, and practicing, and then doing whatever work they do.

So far, India is to the south, Nepal is to the west, Tibet is to the north, and China is to the east. We do not know the karmic effects of what will happen to the beings who live in those countries, but historically, most of the areas surrounding Bhutan were Buddhist. At least it is positive for Bhutan to be situated between all these countries with Buddhist connections. Especially, Nepal is the country where Buddha Shakyamuni's flawless wisdom body bloomed in Lumbini, and India is called the Land of the Sublime Ones[28] and is the country where Lord Buddha turned the Wheel of Dharma and blessed many, many holy places, including Bodh Gaya, Kushinagar, and Varanasi. These are the four great holy places of Buddha.[29] That is why all previous Asian Buddhist countries have called this area རྒྱལ་ཁབ་འཕགས་པའི་ཡུལ་ [gyalkhap pakpe yul, Land of the Sublime Ones].[30] All Buddhas, including Buddha Shakyamuni, and Bodhisattvas came to this place and revealed precious Dharma teachings. In Nalanda, Vikramashila, and many other universities, the Sutra and Mantrayana teachings flourished, as well as in Oddiyana, where Vajrayana teachings flourished. Later, this Land of the Sublime Ones was the home of the great saint Mahatma Gandhi, who remained in prison for many years and fought for *shanti*. Today in India, most people are Hindus worshiping many gods, but historically Buddha Shakyamuni and many Bodhisattvas have turned the Wheel of Dharma in this land. China, which is for a while communist, has historically been Mahayana Buddhist from the time that Buddhism was brought to China by Bodhidharma. In Tibet, King Trisong Detsen invited Shantarakshita and the Wisdom Vajra Master Guru Rinpoche, and the Mahayana and Vajrayana teachings flourished fully.

I hope and pray that these countries, without ignoring Bhutan, support Bhutan both spiritually and politically in maintaining its own Bhutanese tradition. Even though Bhutan is a small country, preserving the beauty of Bhutan's own qualities can benefit these large countries, just as even a few tiny flowering plants can be the ornament of a great garden. I hope that Bhutan is never misused by these large countries to cause a small sparkling fire that can burn a whole forest. Even though Bhutan looks small, it is important not to cause problems there, which could cause a catastrophe. Whatever happens in Bhutan, whether negative or positive, can easily and quickly be found on the Internet and will become an issue in other countries as well. It is not the same as in ancient times, when one may not have heard news about one's neighbors in other countries for a long time, because news can now be known instantly. Although there are many stupid people in the world, there are also many who are intelligent and can appreciate Buddhism. This appreciation can be seen these days all over the world among those who are learning about Buddhism and starting to practice, and Buddhism is receiving a lot of international attention. The most important contribution Bhutan can make to the world is to preserve the treasure of spiritual energy that comes from its Buddhist lineages.

Of course, all Bhutanese know, but I want to remind them, that if Bhutan stays as it is by continuing to be a Dharma country of Buddhists and an independent nation, it must never, never ignore Buddhist teachings and traditions, because an independent country needs a basis for that independence. Bhutan must never, never separate its politics and Buddhism, but always keep its own Buddhist culture without allowing it to fade. Bhutan's special Buddhist culture shows that it is an independent country. By showing this, no one can easily swallow it, because even though Bhutan is small, its culture is autonomous and pure. That is a provable sign of its independence, historically as well as today. It is not a problem for Bhutanese to study and apply anything necessary from modern science and technology if it is beneficial for the country and its people, but Bhutan must recognize and never, never lose its own foundation of Buddhism, as a result of the thoughtfulness of the new generation.

Whatever is practiced in Buddhism, the result must be nonsectarian to benefit other beings and to attain enlightenment. I do not want to cause paranoia, but the traditions of Buddha's speech that already exist in Bhutan, including the treasures of Guru Rinpoche and the teachings of Drukpa Kagyu, are more than enough. These traditions are vast and essential for those who can study and practice them. It is unnecessary to go outside the country to find different sects and then bring different sects back inside, using ideas about religious freedom that can cause conflict. These days, many sectarians use nonsectarian words like bait to catch fish in order to expand their own sect's authority, which has nothing to do with Dharma. Buddha Shakyamuni said that Buddhist teachings cannot be destroyed from without, but they can be ruined from within. As it is said in the sutras:

> Buddha attained the state of fearlessness,
> So no one can destroy the teachings from outside,
> But like internal bacteria that search within the lion's guts,
> They can be destroyed from inside.
> Therefore, one must remember this with mindfulness
> And abstain from whatever is negative while accepting whatever
>   is positive.

Actually, if someone wants to benefit beings, including oneself, and does not want to be sectarian, there is so much to practice in the Mahamudra and Mahasandhi teachings and *upadesha*. Going out of the country and learning the theories of different sects and bringing in many learned scholars while thinking one is progressive and exercising religious freedom can actually cause destabilization within the country. Also, wise Bhutanese Lamas and Lopöns must take the responsibility of explaining to innocent people that they should not be lured by other religions, including Christianity, and the bait they use.

I do not know about the beliefs of Bhutanese today, but I believe that previously the country of Bhutan has been in peace from the blessings of Guru Rinpoche. Bhutanese religious leaders should consider deeply the long, profound history of the teachings of the Nyingma and Kagyu that have been flowing smoothly in noncontradiction like the two Punakha rivers—Pho Chhu, the male river, and Mo Chhu, the female river—joining together and flowing together in one compatible waterway. Let them flow this way. It is not necessary to introduce many ideas about religious freedom, with proposals for the study of different religions to pretend to be nonsectarian and learned, which could cause a flood. These two rivers are more than enough. Each of Bhutan's sects of Buddhism contains all other pure Dharma, so it is not necessary to find something else to study with materialized conceptualizing.

Contradictory circumstances exist anywhere in samsara, and it is unnecessary to invent them again. For example, there are border areas everywhere in which differences in races and religions can cause destabilization. This is another reason why the people of Bhutan, especially the young people, need to be very firm in their own traditions. Without thinking that their traditions are stale or naively imitating other countries with the excuse that they should change with the times, if Bhutanese continue in the historical spiritual traditions that have existed for many generations, it will be uncomplicated and safer for Bhutan's future as a country and for the preservation of Buddhism in this world.

In Buddhism, the method of adjusting to time, place, and faculties exists in order to guide beings into the path of enlightenment according to individual capacities. Without being careful, however, just trying to adjust to new generations and new outlooks by combining Buddhism with all the Western culture and eternalist ideology of the degenerate age, and then to call this Buddhism for young people, will produce problems for perpetuating the pure traditions of Buddhism in Bhutan. I very much appreciate young Buddhists forming a group, but I am beseeching all of you with my hands clasped together not to misinterpret Buddhism by adding incompatible ideas that often originate from politics rather than spirituality, even though they seem to be very appealing. If people want to be Buddhists, they have to keep Buddhist traditions of lineage without mixing them up with nonspiritual worldly thinking. Whether a Buddhist organization is established in an elaborate or simple way, it is necessary to maintain Buddhism's purity. This is what will help the country, both religiously and politically, in the coming years.

According to a worldly level, young Buddhists are not supposed to be attracted only to the phenomena of the modern world. Of course, they can learn, accept, and develop whatever ideas can be beneficial from science and technology; but Bhutan is a Buddhist country, so even though Bhutanese can naturally learn about many worldly systems of thought and use technological advances to help their country, the main focus should be to recognize why their own culture is special, which is from the blessings of Dharma, and to carry these blessings onward. This is not only a changeable influence, like the materialization of technological development that can seem true or accurate for a while, but can be disproved later or become outdated by newer developments. Young people have to consider more profoundly the meaning of the spiritual influences in their own culture, which have been shown by previous sublime beings, including Shabtrung Rinpoche. In the past, the spiritual leaders of Bhutan have had faith in the Triple Gems, including Guru Rinpoche and his emanations as other sublime beings, and they have upheld their country very positively with their faith for many years, even though there were many problems in other parts of the world. The way that Bhutan has been upheld is only by the people of Bhutan being Buddhist and trusting in the Triple Gems and Guru Rinpoche, who is the representative and essence of the Triple Gems. It is most important to keep this ancient Bhutanese tradition without thinking that it is old and therefore should be changed to adjust to a new generation. Although technological and political changes continuously occur, since everything is naturally changing, this does not mean that a new generation is supposed to ignore old traditions of the legacy of sublime beings, expecting instant material rewards and neglecting the original source of happiness, which is spiritual qualities and spiritual teachings that open them. The young people of Bhutan have to consider spirituality and recognize that the fortunate results they now experience are from their spiritual heritage, giving careful thought to how they can be Buddhists the way previous Bhutanese have been pure Buddhists. Without examining cause and effect, but following modern theories connected only with the influence of substantialization, nothing ultimate can be gained at all. Instead, what is important, which is what is connected with Bhutan's previous Buddhist culture, can be lost or disappear, and then people will be absolutely unable to create any nonsubstantial, pure Buddhist profound spiritual qualities. So it is critical for young people in Bhutan to study Dharma, and also not only to study, but to practice at least in a simple way, to ensure that Dharma connected with one's Buddha nature can flourish continuously from generation to generation through each individual's own experience. That can be much more beneficial than anything else. Even though Bhutan is a small country, this is the way that there can be great benefit for other beings, as well as for the people of Bhutan, in the future.

If young people miscalculate what is truly meaningful and are only attracted to developing superficial phenomena, without believing in their own Buddhist traditions with faith, it is unquestionably an obstacle to practicing for enlightenment; it can even cause the disappearance of their own country's special qualities, which have come from its being Buddhist for many centuries. If this previous heritage is lost, it would be difficult to develop new spiritually positive phenomena or even analyze what is special about Bhutan, since the immaterial nature of spirituality would be beyond people's individual experience. If people become distracted by imitating superficial aspects of life in other modern countries and neglect their spiritual heritage, it is perilous. This does not mean that the technology or modernization of other countries is so meaningful that they have a great effect; it is just that people are drawn to these because they are materially obvious to them, and they can become caught up in searching for more of them. Whatever is material is compounded, and whatever is compounded will disappear, fall apart, diminish, or decay. If young Bhutanese believe in the traditions of previous sublime beings as Bhutanese have for many generations and study, pray, and practice Buddhism in a very simple way with faith, even though they do not know many extensive, complex practices, their spiritual qualities will blossom. Because these spiritual qualities are uncompounded, they will not disappear, fall apart, diminish, or decay. Uncompounded positive spiritual qualities only come from having faith in the Triple Gems, especially the sole refuge, Guru Rinpoche. Even when one is not familiar with many practices and is sometimes preoccupied with worldly life, if one still keeps faith in a very simple way without only materializing, that faith grows and blessings are received. In this way, faith and positive energy can increase in each young person's mind, so its special qualities can develop and flourish. That will create many positive results outwardly for the country so that it will not be affected or ruined by the influence of any other religion, because the capacity of other religions to influence those who are Buddhist practitioners connecting with spiritual energy will be insignificant.

Most non-Buddhist nations are developing the ideas of technology and science rather than inner qualities of mind, and the sign of this is an emphasis on instant material results, which does not cause any ultimate result of continuous happiness. From the lack of a connection to Buddhism and lack of faith, the young and old of these nations are only involved in obtaining and using material results, and they have often used material power to cause not only positive energy but many kinds of negative energy. Each nation tries to manipulate other nations, which causes war, famine, and unhappiness, as everyone knows, without opening Buddha nature through faith but only following the karma that has been previously created, and then re-creating negative karma that causes the results of war, famine, and unhappiness again. This happens through always causing contradiction and never peace. Even when there is prosperity, it is still very temporary and finishes when there is no spiritual basis of the continuity of positive energy that results from faith, belief, and creating positive spiritual appearances. If young people are intelligent and read the histories of India and China—although I do not know what is happening in these countries now that they are developing into modernized countries, and although there was war as well as peace and happiness there—they can see that in the past these countries have developed many special qualities evident in the richness of their cultures. This richness comes originally from their ancient Buddhist traditions and not from the development of materialism they are experiencing now.

If people try to make Buddhism contemporary by giving excessive attention to modern culture and its technology, politics, and values, it can gradually cause a wrong point of view and behavior because it will gradually cause a loss of the point of view and lineage of Buddhism. According to a Buddhist point of view, it is generally unnecessary to analyze what is modern and what is old, because ordinary thinking about age and even time are not ultimate. In this case, however, if the old traditions of Buddhism's spiritual lineage of ageless, timeless wisdom are sustained, it will allow Bhutan to retain the independence of its state and its religion. If historical traditions are discontinued because modern ideas are followed instead, nothing can survive in a pure way, just as a body cannot survive without a head. The necessity of this head does not mean that people must accept tyrannical dictators, but that they must rely on spiritual traditions that are based on perpetuating spiritual energy. Without relying on this essence from olden history but only depending on the wrapping of a modern cover, there cannot be a flawless, sovereign country. Expressions of modernizing Buddhism actually come from the influence of predominantly non-Buddhist culture and materialism. This is the meaning, no matter what the aspect looks like and no matter what is done or said, even if it seems to be from a religious source. Something can be called Buddhism, but if there is no essence it becomes like a Buddhist drama, which is what is happening in many Western countries.

As Buddha taught about the five defilements, the duration of life decreases; the five passions become much more gross; beings are difficult to subdue; the time is not the same as before, such as in the example of greed that results in the overuse of poisonous chemicals that change the environment; and there is perversity of view, as in a distortion of spiritual beliefs. According to the Hinayana, the cessation of the cause of suffering and its effects is attained by subduing and annihilating the enemy, passions and karma. According to the Mahayana, by realizing the selflessness of the self, and above that, the selflessness of phenomena, all phenomena are seen as magic while making magic-like merit to attain magic-like enlightenment. According to the Vajrayana, the nest of delusion is purified through the mandala of wisdom deity's practice. Instead of following these *yanas* accordingly, a perversity of view occurs when there is only a materialization of spiritual practice. Of course, scientific and technological ideas can be used in an auxiliary way for the purpose of a practitioner's progress, but the view of immaterial enlightenment must be held without grasping, no matter what yana is practiced. All yanas are for liberating beings from materialism, and are not to be relied on only for scientific research. The nature of material, no matter how powerful or wonderful, is still compounded, such as ordinary samsaric phenomena that are created by materializing, and then cause suffering from attachment, desire, and all the passions and emotions. In Tibetan Dharma terms, this is called འདུས་བྱས་ཀྱི་ཆོས་ [*duje kyi chö*];[31] in Sanskrit, it is called *samskritadharma*; and in English, it is called compounded, conditioned phenomena that have been put together, created, or produced

by a combination of causes or conditions. By only trusting these compounded phenomena, it is forever impossible to be liberated. All samsaric beings are circling between momentary happiness and momentary
suffering due to attachment to compounded phenomena. The reason
samsara is defined as circling is that it never liberates from compounded
phenomena. Of course, compounded phenomena can be used in a correct way for the accumulation of merit, but these phenomena are not
the ultimate state. Whatever is compounded, no matter how it appears
in the senses or in the mind, is material conception made by material
circumstance or dualistic mind, and causes more delusion. All of the
yanas reveal how to attain what is called, in Tibetan Dharma terms,
འདུས་མ་བྱས་པའི་ཆོས་ [du ma je pe chö];[32] in Sanskrit, asamskritadharma; and
in English, uncompounded, unconditioned, uncreated phenomena that
do not consist of parts and are not produced by a combination of causes
and conditions. But this is not like numbness or nil, as in a momentary
nihilist view, or like the nothingness of empty sky. It is great undeluded
wisdom awareness mind and its manifestation of the wisdom phenomena of body, speech, mind, and purelands. To attain that state is why
Buddha taught beings.

Wisdom's essence is emptiness, so it does not cause any dualistic
habit or obscurations, because it is the unconditioned state. At the
same time, it is unobstructed because it is wisdom, so that is why it is
manifesting as immeasurable wisdom body, speech, mind, qualities, and
activities. From that, beings are naturally benefited to be able to blossom
and expand uncompounded wisdom indivisibly and indestructibly. This
is the difference between ordinary consciousness and wisdom, and what
happens when consciousness is transformed into wisdom, which must
occur through faith by being a believer. That is the way to excel in the
qualities of sublime beings with awareness mind, accumulating merit
until attaining the uncompounded fully enlightened state, without creating compounded material theories that will delay and prevent the
opening of awareness mind by distracting beings toward the material
instead of guiding them toward the immaterial.

Of course, while still remaining in samsara, it is undeniably necessary to rely on compounded phenomena such as the five skandhas and

then to accumulate merit, but it is necessary for this to be influenced by the view of attaining immaterial flawless wisdom Buddha's body, for the benefit of the material world. In order to attain that state, it is necessary to establish a correct view with correct teachers, believing in the Triple Gems and in negative and positive karma, and trying to purify negative karma and increase positive karma through the accumulation of merit and wisdom and the recognition of the blessings of sublime Buddhas and Bodhisattvas. Then, through a human being's mind connecting to sublime wisdom in order to receive blessings the same as previous Buddhas and Bodhisattvas have done to become fully enlightened Buddhas, the perversity of view of a nonbeliever in actual enlightenment can become indivisible flawless sublime wisdom body and wisdom mind.

With freedom of religion and individual rights, anyone can find something to look for in their own way, but according to pure Buddhist theory, one cannot develop spiritually without dealing with consciousness, awareness, and wisdom, because there is no logical way to do so in order to reach the immaterial uncompounded sublime state of actual undiminishable, undisappearable wisdom. In Buddhist theory, any practices for enlightenment have to connect with beings' consciousness, awareness, and wisdom. How can beings who want to be enlightened in the immaterial state of immaterial uncompounded awareness attain that state by only relying on what they learn from science and technology instead of sublime beings' teachings on how to recognize one's own awareness mind and change material mind into immaterial wisdom? In Buddhism, whatever theory or teaching is considered is supposed to show and guide beings to the continuity of natural wisdom and enlightenment, through belief, faith, and contemplation.

Of course, the teaching of Buddha is to benefit beings both in this life and in future lives, for beings to be happy and for attaining enlightenment, but one needs to have a correct view, which is called *yangdakpe tawa* in Tibetan. From the Hinayana to the Mahayana and up to the Vajrayana, there is the path of enlightenment, as mentioned, which has the eight aspects of the path of noble beings, called འཕགས་ལམ་ཡན་ལག་བརྒྱད་ [*paklam yenlak-gye*]³³ in Tibetan, or *aryastangamarga* in Sanskrit, which are practiced and described in different ways but have one essence and are practiced for enlightenment. These eight are: right view, which is ཡང་དག་པའི་ལྟ་བ་ [*yangdakpe tawa*][34] in Tibetan, or *samyak-drishti* in Sanskrit; right intention, which is ཡང་དག་པའི་རྟོག་པ་ [*yangdakpe tokpa*][35] in Tibetan, or *samyak-samkalpa* in Sanskrit; right speech, which is ཡང་དག་པའི་ངག [*yangdakpe ngak*][36] in Tibetan, or *samyak-vak* in Sanskrit; right conduct, which is ཡང་དག་པའི་ལས་ཀྱི་མཐའ་ [*yangdakpe lekyita*][37] in Tibetan, or *samyak-karmanta* in Sanskrit; right livelihood, which is ཡང་དག་པའི་འཚོ་བ་ [*yangdakpe tsowa*][38] in Tibetan, or *samyak-ajiva* in Sanskrit; right effort, which is ཡང་དག་པའི་རྩོལ་བ་ [*yangdak petsölwa*][39] in Tibetan, or *samyak-vyayama* in Sanskrit; right mindfulness, which is ཡང་དག་པའི་དྲན་པ་ [*yangdakpe drenpa*][40] in Tibetan, or *samyak-smriti* in Sanskrit; and right concentration, which is ཡང་དག་པའི་ཏིང་ངེ་འཛིན་ [*yangdakpe ting-nge dzin*][41] in Tibetan, or *samyak-samadhi* in Sanskrit.

All of these eight aspects are coming from mind, and not from engagement between a brain and a button that is pushed. These eight aspects of the path of sublime beings are originating, developing, and functioning from the mind and to the mind until reaching the fully enlightened state. They cannot be found nor can they develop between physiological processes of the brain and material instruments that measure these processes, which can only find fragmented substance and deluded conceptions. Even though people try to investigate meditation in this way, no matter what is found, it is material, as grasping mind tries to uncover more and more subtle aspects of material conception, just as scientists have searched for the subtlest aspects of the basic constituents of matter, pointing to atoms, subatomic composite particles, and elementary particles, including quarks, leptons, and bosons. These are not final, even if they are momentarily thought to be final, since another subtler conception, such as strings or membranes, can still be found.

Just as the atoms of fuels such as uranium and plutonium can be split to produce nuclear fission for different purposes, from a negative use in nuclear weapons to a positive use in nuclear medicine, the phenomena of mind, including ego, its conceptions, and attachment to its conceptions, can be used in entirely different ways, either negatively or positively. According to Buddhism, as mentioned, all of the universe is created by mind, and sentient beings abiding in the neutrality of indifferent stupor cause ordinary phenomena. There are no phenomena that exist within ordinary appearances that are not related to other phenomena, which is relative truth's interdependence, or in Tibetan terms, རྟེན་འབྲེལ་ [tendrel],[42] which is the undeceiving interdependence of all phenomena as long as there is dualistic habit. In enlightenment, there is no interdependent relative truth or dualistic habit.

Too much sectarianism is an example of perversity of view, or ལྟ་བའི་ཕྱིན་ཅི་ལོག [tawe nyikma].[43] A pure view is supposed to be the view of stainlessness, which means I-lessness and nonattachment to phenomena, by self-sustaining selfless phenomena and sharing that phenomena with other beings through bodhichitta. If there is too much attachment to one's own ego's superiority, one makes the self stronger by concretizing it, and then its phenomena are also concretized. Even though having faith and being a believer with a correct view and accumulating merit and wisdom can make even this life comfortable and prosperous for oneself and one's country, when grasping mind becomes pressured by tremendous attachment to ego with subtle substance conceptions, it can cause an explosion of disastrous phenomena for others, and finally one's own implosion.

More than any other religion, Buddha Shakyamuni's teachings are always flawless because they are always about compassion and ultimately attaining fully enlightened Buddhahood. But degenerate beings' wrong views can seed problems among those who are inexperienced about actual Buddhism. Bhutanese must be aware of the infiltration of nonspiritual movements disguised as religion that are occurring in other countries around the world and are in the news. In Australia, Europe, and America, there have been some people disguised as Buddhists whose group has even murdered others out of their tremendous attachment to the material power of their own sect. How could an actual Buddhist kill others? I am warning that these people are beginning to plant their ideas among naively spiritual Westerners, in order to make themselves victorious over others who are turned into their victims. The only method to circumvent this is to be an authentic Buddhist, which is to be a believer in karma, to accumulate merit and wisdom, to pray to have peace for all beings, and to attain enlightenment.

In the past, the great Kadampa masters taught the four ways to aim, which are that the mind must aim toward Dharma; Dharma must be aimed toward becoming a beggar; the beggar must aim toward death; and death must be aimed toward an empty cave. In the seven holy Dharmas of the Kadampas, the body is adorned by the four wisdom deities Buddha Shakyamuni, Miyowa,[44] Avalokiteshvara, and Tara, speech is adorned by the Tripitaka, and mind is adorned by the three trainings. Also, the four special attributes for whoever is learning the stages of the path to enlightenment are that the greatness of the wisdom of the Victorious Ones is instantly realized; the greatness of the sublime speech of the Buddhas and shastras is always sacredly emerging; the greatness of all teachings is realized without contradiction; and the greatness of any bad behavior is self-ceasing. Without realizing these special attributes, they become the four attachments. Unfortunately, these teachings are not being followed by the New Kadampas, who are immersed in sectarianism and do not follow even the most basic Buddhist teachings of not harming sentient beings.

Without discriminating between old and young, or between monks or nuns and yogis or yoginis, one has to keep the Buddhist lineage, whether with vows of ordination, *upasaka* vows, or as laypeople, trusting in the Triple Gems and serving the teachings of Buddhism. Also, it is very absurd to emphasize what is modern. One is not supposed to have that kind of limited thought. Since everything is relative, any circumstances or phenomena will not continuously be the same. For example, those who are young are not always going to be young and modern; they are going to become old and change. I do not need to search for examples of aging, including myself. Among my own group, I can see how someone with a young, fresh body and innocent, pure mind has become *gomar* in Tibetan, *chaythey* in Dzongkha,[45] or *bald-headed* in English, with a haggard body and jaded mind. Whoever is born is supposed to go this way through the four great rivers equally, as Buddha said. When Buddha was Prince Gautama, he went on an excursion outside the gates of his palace, riding in his carriage with his attendant guiding his horse. From his carriage he saw the suffering of birth, aging, sickness, and death in each of the four directions, and immediately had weariness from seeing these circumstances. That is why he escaped and practiced with hardship by the river Niranjana for six years and attained enlightenment under the Bodhi Tree. So, young people are not supposed to build arrogance from the youthfulness of the body, which is compounded and does not exist continuously in a material way.

If one talks too much about new ideas without relying on logic, history, or lineage, it can cause inaccuracies such as those that have emerged in films not authentically based on the original traditions of Buddhism. By watching these, the next generation will not learn about the meaning of the actual Buddha and actual Buddhist teachings, but will receive distorted versions with obscured, impure images. For example, historically, as it is taught in the Hinayana up to the Mahayana, Mayadevi's whole body was full of bliss when Buddha was in her womb, and she had no pain when Buddha was born. This is written in many Buddhist texts and can be seen in many ancient paintings and frescoes. I have never seen anything written or painted about Mayadevi moaning in pain while Buddha was being born, or about Buddha crying at birth, as shown in one film.[46] Likewise, I also have never seen anything written about Buddha being protected by a curtain from being seen during birth, which is illogical. Buddha is stainless, so there is nothing to hide. Even among ordinary human beings, babies do not have any conception of being shy. More than that, Buddha has no conception of beings as objects. Buddha did not begin life with dualistic, grasping phenomena, checking to see if there were people nearby so that he had to be careful not to show the sign of his gender, so there is no reason for embarrassment, for hiding anything, or for Mayadevi to be depicted giving birth behind a curtain. Furthermore, Buddha was born from under Mayadevi's arm, not her secret place. This birth was not like an ordinary woman in a hospital giving birth lying down, but a sublime birth. For Buddha to be shy about birth and concealed by a curtain are ordinary ideas adjusting to and copying ordinary human attitudes and totally altering historical accounts with modern nihilist conceptions. Of course, Buddha Shakyamuni is a wisdom manifestation, but one has to base what is said about Buddha on Buddha's actual history of being born under a palasha tree, so that each new generation can understand the genuine history from the beginning. Whether or not people have the good karma to be believers with faith, it is still necessary for descriptions of Buddha to be based on Buddhist history.

Likewise, even though I am not a monk, I have read the Vinaya laws. I have never seen one sentence about monks playing guitars, as shown in another film.[47] I remember that Buddha said without question that one who has full monk vows cannot play music himself, or even go to a place where others are playing music and dancing. I also saw in Vinaya texts that there are many rules of discipline about how to step or walk. I never once saw one word written about monks kicking a football into the sky while hollering with their voices, being wild and running after it to kick it again and again until winning, but only that they should be disciplined and composed. I also saw that monks should not stare, and that their way of looking should be with serene eyes, with a limitation on how much distance ahead of themselves their gaze should extend, which is not like staring far into the distance to follow after a football's flight through the sky. This kind of performance happens from having contact with Dharma but adapting to modern thinking. I am amazed by this spectacle, like a Pygmy boy encountering an enormous Amazon in the jungle.

Perhaps intelligent young people can read the authentic histories of Buddhas and Bodhisattvas. "Authentic" does not mean something old and unpleasant, as some young people think of it, imagining they will always be young. As Kyabje Dudjom Rinpoche said:

> By relying on old history, new incisiveness can occur.

In order for one's own ageless wisdom to blossom, one has to believe in Buddha nature and go as all omniscient Buddhas have gone. Buddhas are called དེ་བཞིན་གཤེགས་པ་ [deshin shekpa],[48] or "Thus Gone," because they have gone from ordinary phenomena to enlightenment. When people do not know the actual histories of Buddhas but want to know them, it is terrible if they just watch films that show ordinary phenomena, because they can assume that what is shown in these films is the characteristic, activity, and history of Buddha. If pure Buddhist history is erased, misinterpreted, combined with interpolations of incorrect information, or changed with the thought of adapting it to a new generation, Buddhism can be transformed into non-Buddhist theater.

In the precious Buddhist country of Bhutan, the main key is for Bhutanese to recognize the great value of their history and continue to develop their own Buddhist spiritual traditions. In a brief way, Bhutan has been a very respectable country up to now, and I am happy to hear about the country's progress, but I always hope and pray that its positive phenomena will continue from reaffirming its spiritual lineage, and that Bhutanese will become more and more refined and not more and more naughty due to adjusting to new ways of thinking or commercialization for business.

Young Bhutanese have to be careful about being firm in their faith in the Triple Gems to maintain the inner strengths of their country. This is imperative. It is ridiculous to use a bias of religious dogmatism to disrupt the source of blessings of what has existed harmoniously in one's own country for many generations in the pure, awesome history of all the positive phenomena of the Drukpa Kagyu and Nyingma traditions, not muddying this with the murkiness of adjusting to shifting ordinary perspectives, but letting it continue to merge into one great pristine river in this Buddhist country from which all can drink. Dogmatism can disturb this for future generations.

Of course, I am not against democracy, but it is a laughingstock to use theories about the freedom of the individual and rule by the people in order to allow political parties to exist that represent other foreign religions, while at the same time one obstructs the religious traditions of one's own country due to divisiveness and discrimination. Without being firm in one's own traditions of the precious teachings of the Kagyu and Nyingma legacies blessed by Guru Rinpoche and Shabtrung Rinpoche, one then would have no reasoning to refute the infiltration of other foreign religions. If a distorted use of ideas about freedom of religion without limitation or discipline causes many arguments about many forms of rights, the result can be disconcerting to the country in a religious way. In implementing political freedom, young Bhutanese are not supposed to copy the examples of disbelief that exist in this world during the degenerate age, but as I hope and pray, to be happy in joy from having faith in Buddha, the sole protector. One can acquire technological knowledge and a Western education, but that does not mean that one should also ruin one's own precious culture.

The people of other countries are also sentient beings, and sentient beings need happiness, so I am not saying that Bhutanese should be Buddhist and live happily with Dharma but that it is not necessary to think of other beings and to forget about people in other countries. According to bodhichitta, whoever practices Buddhism must always dedicate its benefit for all sentient beings equally, in order for them temporarily to be happy, and ultimately to attain enlightenment. This is not like some religious traditions in which one's own group or party is supposed to be happy, but the happiness of other beings is not considered equally. If Buddhist teachings can flourish in the small country of Bhutan continuously, these positive Dharma phenomena can gradually affect other countries, which will only be beneficial for other countries and other sentient beings, harmlessly. Being Buddhist is not going to stop happiness; it is going to increase it. That is the result of what is called by the English term *merit*, or *accumulation*. The only way not to lose Bhutan's actual spiritual qualities is to keep faith and belief by being Buddhist from generation to generation, and especially to have faith unshakably in Guru Rinpoche, who is the essence of all immeasurable Buddhas and also the protector of Bhutan.

If people have faith and really believe in the Triple Gems, including Guru Rinpoche, there is no question that they can attain fully enlightened Buddhahood, which benefits all beings impartially and is the main purpose of being Buddhist. Even within this momentary life, there is nothing wrong with having faith in Buddha and Guru Rinpoche. If someone can think about Buddha and Guru Rinpoche, which are the same essence in different aspects, it only brings happiness in this life, and in a future life, according to one's practice, one can attain enlightenment. Whenever one suffers, one should remember Guru Rinpoche, because Guru Rinpoche's body, speech, and mind are wisdom, and wisdom is always and forever continuously wisdom. The meaning of that unobstructed wisdom is that it is always giving blessing, never dying, never decaying, and never falling apart, but always like stainless sky, with unchangeable positive phenomena like sunrise in the sky, bringing warmth and comfort. So, I hope and pray that young people in Bhutan will be really, really firm about being Buddhist continuously, all the time, in a simple way. Even though they are busy working to support this momentary life, they still have to remember every day in the morning, daytime, and night to continuously have faith. They have to do this under any circumstances, without searching for material results but happily with a relaxed mind, without grasping, without changing or losing faith, without ideas related to the power of materialism, and without expecting instant material rewards. This is the pivotal view. Happiness can arise according to the faith of the practitioner, as faith will definitely bring blessings and happiness. Whenever one suffers from the compounded body and the phenomena of worldly existence, if there is no faith, there is no antidote telling what to do to correct it. One can just think of that suffering again and again, and that causes more and more depression. Whenever one's life changes or difficult circumstances occur in one's family or with friends and relatives due to previous karmic debts, if one can pray and request blessings for oneself in a simple way and then be quiet with faith, one will see and know that this suffering will be cleansed. Instead of adding more suffering, suffering will be reduced and vanish. This does not cause more suffering from holding on to the residue of suffering, so suffering can gradually be totally cleansed, according to one's own practice and according to the teaching of Buddha. Then one can attain fully enlightened Buddhahood. Even if one does not have time to study or practice in an elaborate way due to worldly life, it is not a problem according to the traditions of Mahayana and Vajrayana, because one's practice can be synthesized in daily life or within one moment. That is the characteristic of the Great Vehicle, the Mahayana.

The most important point is to believe in enlightenment and Buddha, especially Guru Rinpoche, who is the essence of all inconceivable Buddhas' flawless wisdom ecstasy body, speech, and mind. The believer is one's own mind, and the object of belief is flawless wisdom body for those who have faith in all these Buddhas, including Guru Rinpoche. Nothing is ever lost by being Buddhist. I hope and pray Bhutanese parents instruct and advise their children to have faith in Buddhas and to be Buddhist, as their ancestors have done. Also, in a simple way, parents have to continuously influence their children with Dharma, even if their children go to other countries or are educated in foreign studies in order to develop their own country. It is only meaningful to be Buddhist. In this life, it brings happiness, and when one dies, it causes enlightenment. Of course, enlightenment does not have a cause or anything material, and that is why enlightenment means freedom. But while living, if one has total faith in Buddha in a simple way with one hundred percent belief, even though one is not a wise scholar or accomplished practitioner, it is extremely positive even in its effect within this life's body, speech, and mind.

When young people are drawn to the fashions of a new culture and marry people from other countries without considering whether or not they are Buddhist, they can eventually find that some religions are against Buddhism. Not analyzing this beforehand and marrying and having children with people from other religions can cause serious discord and make one's life miserable, so that one is trapped between not wanting to divorce and being unable to stay together. Even if one wishes to marry someone who is not Buddhist, if one has the capacity to help, one can decide whether or not that person can become spiritually complementary in order not to disturb this life for religious reasons, to have a comfortable life through having faith, and to finally attain enlightenment.

I do not mean to be racist, but young Bhutanese people should marry other Bhutanese, without discriminating between valleys or languages within Bhutan. Southern Bhutanese, Eastern Bhutanese, and Central Bhutanese must marry each other. Also, if it does not contribute to interference from other nations, Bhutanese can marry ethnic Nepalese from Bhutan. What is important is Dharma. So, according to a worldly level, it is necessary for Eastern Bhutanese and Western Bhutanese to intermarry, without the exclusiveness of being Ngalongpa or Sharshokpa or Bumthangpa. Ngalongpa are Bhutanese, Sharshokpa are Bhutanese, and Bumthangpa are Bhutanese, since they all belong to Bhutan even if they speak in different dialects, and whether their bodies are tall, short, light, dark, fat, slim, ugly, or beautiful. These variations do not matter; they are one country's people, so they should not divide themselves and cause conflict and unhappiness, but should think that they are of the same Bhutanese race and the same Buddhist religion and marry, having as many children as they can to increase their country's population.

Of course, everywhere in this world, ethnic groups are against each other and demanding rights. Although I have many things to say, which are not only made up or just verbalizing but come from listening to the news, what I say will be misinterpreted. I do not believe the majority of Bhutanese are narrow-minded about ethnicity. The ethnically Nepalese population living in Bhutan can have good lives and create positive circumstances, prospering and enjoying the good fortune of their karmic connection of being in Bhutan. Historically in Nepal, there have been many Buddhist lineage holders, including Newari, Tamang, and Shakya, and Bhutanese of Nepalese descent have to acknowledge Buddhism as the exalted religion of their ancestral home.

Regarding language, it is necessary for Bhutanese to study Chöke, as it is known in Bhutan, as people have done from ancient times until now, without being rigid about where this language originated. If I call it Tibetan, I do not know what old bald Bhutanese scholars are going to say, so I am saying that it is necessary to study Chöke. The reason Chöke is known by this name is that it has been the primary language for transmitting Vajrayana Dharma for many centuries, and because this language has been blessed by many sublime beings. It was established from Sanskrit for Dharma, and it is very rich. Sanskrit and Tibetan are studied in many other countries, although it is among people who are not doing this for enlightenment, because enlightenment is precious and no one understands this easily without studying and practicing. Since people still need culture, though, even many people in non-Buddhist countries who do not have faith in Buddha study Sanskrit and Tibetan in order to develop culturally, valuing these languages at an intellectual level and recognizing them as worthy subjects of study, as taught in universities around the world. So Bhutanese do not need to be ashamed of speaking or writing in Chöke. In samsara, interdependent relative truth always comes, and whatever is studied scientifically, philosophically, or spiritually is always related to everything else. If the Tibetan language is lost, Bhutanese culture cannot be as profound and deep as it presently is or survive independently, and if Bhutanese culture is affected in this way, the value of the people will be cheapened. Everything depends on the people. Their qualities of being knowledgeable, wise, expert, insightful, and very logical do not actually come from worldly culture, but from wisdom blessings and the influence of previous sublime beings. If Chöke is studied without embarrassment but with an acknowledgment of its importance for the continuation of Dharma in the world, it can be used in many positive ways even temporarily, and most importantly, it will open one's own Buddha nature for enlightenment, so it should not be ignored. Of course, young people can study Sanskrit, English, or even Chinese if it will be useful culturally, but Chöke is not only for this short life's culture. Chöke, which has so many special qualities, can temporarily be used for anything even at a worldly level, including for science or philosophy, since it is a very versatile language, but it is primarily for attaining fully enlightened Buddhahood in order not to wander in this existent world with suffering. This comes from Chöke and practice. Without studying Chöke and the scriptures of sublime beings that inspire faith, one's own wisdom, or Buddha nature according to Mahayana theory, cannot blossom. But sometimes, if someone has faith, it may not be necessary to study many languages, because opening wisdom depends on the individual's faith. Buddha is omniscient, so many different teachings are given in Buddhism according to the faculties of many different beings, including that one must study many different languages, as well as the five sciences.[49] Buddha also says, however, that it is not necessary to study many things, and that one can be enlightened from one word. Buddha adjusts in this way to beings' faculties, not with intention but because Buddha is a wisdom manifestation. The way this manifestation is perceived depends on the believer.

According to relative truth, and there are no religious theories that exist in this world that do not depend on relative truth, the doctrines that are practiced depend on beings' karma, which depends on their intention. If one reads about the history of eternalist and Buddhist cultures from China, Europe, or America, there are none that have not depended

216 GYPSY GOSSIP AND OTHER ADVICE

on interdependent relative truth. So the young people of Bhutan do not need to believe that Bhutanese culture did not come from anywhere else but was supposed to have grown from the earth like mushrooms. In this existent world, there is no culture that is not related to other cultures, so it is unnecessary for Bhutanese to consider Chöke another country's language and to think that one is not supposed to depend on it. If one does not learn anything from one's own spiritual culture, one cannot awaken one's mind and there cannot be any method to open awareness mind. If awareness mind is not opened, one cannot analyze what is wrong and what is right even for this temporary life, and then it is difficult to attain enlightenment since there is no awareness mind. The state of enlightenment only comes from awareness mind. Awareness mind must flourish from faith and devotion, accumulation, and believing in wisdom.

Of course, all Holy Dharma is precious, but if one were to try to study all the many different sects or spiritual traditions of Buddhism, it probably could not be effectively beneficial because one's attention would be dispersed by going in too many directions. Also, the result of studying depends on why one is studying and follows one's intention, whether it is actually for Dharma or for a worldly reason. Anyway, it is necessary to have the influence of Buddhism, and especially not to let the spiritual energy of Bhutanese culture diminish or decay, while also thinking carefully when one studies Dharma to do so in a spiritual way. If all of the traditions of Buddhism cannot be studied, although I do not mean that one does not need to study all of them, all Holy Dharma will be included in the study of the Drukpa Kagyu and Nyingma traditions, which are most profound and contain everything, if someone can understand them. I do not mean to be sectarian or to impose any limitation, but it is obvious and logical that they are totally complete, and as I have said again and again, it is more than enough for Bhutanese to follow their own previous sublime beings' teachings. If someone is not studying one's own precious Buddhist teachings and is attracted to other religions, cultures, or doctrines, although of course it depends on who is studying them, it often causes contradictions to form in the mind about doctrines, which can lead to negative energy in the country. Bhutan holds the essence of all Buddhist culture, so to go to another country to study something more will not result in learning anything special and could bring sectarianism back to one's own country. When one's own country contains the essence of Buddhism perfectly, it is a mistake not to acknowledge this but to try to find something else out of one's own ambitiousness for fame or power, which can cause cultural, spiritual, and even political problems in one's own country. If young people in Bhutan analyze their own spirituality and culture, they can see that there is nothing missing in its Drukpa Kagyu and Nyingma traditions. Even though Tibetan Buddhism has New School Buddhist sects, there is not one sect that exists that does not rely on the Nyingma tradition, which one can read about in Buddhist history from the time of King Trisong Detsen, Shantarakshita, and especially Guru Rinpoche, when Samye was built and Dharma was translated from Sanskrit to Tibetan. From beings' merit, at that time of the golden age of Dharma flourishing when Buddhism was brought from India to Tibet, Tibetans were not embarrassed to be learning from Indians who had different skin. Since they did not think about race, they were able to bring special holy wisdom from India to Tibet, and this holy wisdom went from Tibet to the Dragonland country of Bhutan.

When people are young and in perfect health, they are not preparing for the time when their circumstances will change. One never knows what kind of negativity can arise, but when it does, people become filled with sadness, frustration, and depression. There is no medicine that can cure this other than faith, practice, and meditation. Even though Guru Rinpoche is nonmaterial, the power of Guru Rinpoche's wisdom blessings pervades throughout the material, including for faithful beings. Spiritual energy, such as that which comes from virtue, faith, and realization, pervades everywhere and never diminishes or falls apart, because of the power of the wisdom blessings of the Triple Gems, especially Guru Rinpoche. Whenever one dies, after death there are positive phenomena that come from one's belief. While living, when circumstances change, instead of falling into depression or unhappiness, one will be comforted by thinking of stainless Buddha or Guru Rinpoche.

I very much appreciate young people being Buddhists, and I am very glad to hear about youthful Buddhists following the old Buddhist

tradition of lineage so that it can flourish for all beings, including the
people of Bhutan. It is only virtue to be serving this Buddhist country
so that Buddhist teachings can continuously flourish, without imitating
ideas of revolting against traditions that exist in other countries in the
East and the West or distorting pure Buddhist traditions with political
theories so that pure lineage and ancient teachings are lost among misinterpretations presented with pompous language and behavior. I am
not saying this because I am getting old. As everyone knows, whoever is
born has the four temporary conditions, or གནས་སྐབས་བཞི་ [nekap zhi],[50] of
compounded worldly phenomena, whether momentarily old or young.
Outer elements such as those that occur in trees, flowers, and houses,
and inner elements such as the elements of the physical body, all decay
and become old as the strength of their energy lessens. There is not one
single being for whom this does not happen. That is why Buddha taught
about and always emphasized thinking about impermanence. The
sound of this is unpleasant, but it has so much benefit, since experiencing impermanence reduces any kind of self-righteous pride and leads to
discipline, humility, faith, and compassion. These positive phenomena
will turn one's own mind to Dharma with pure strength to help one
effectively benefit other sentient beings, serve the teachings of Buddha,
and recognize one's own nature, inspiring others through one's example
and behavior. If one thinks one's youthfulness will always be youthful,
which is something that does not exist in this existent world, one can
cause pride, passions, and disrespect for what is old, chasing after what
does not exist with attachment, such as making a name for oneself. Then
the mind thinks in a way that is mistaken so that one engages in mistaken activity and behavior, forgetting that whoever is born will finally
die, whoever is gathered will finally separate, whoever is in a high position will finally fall, and whatever is compounded will finally disperse, as
Buddha taught. Having heard this thoroughly and keeping it in mind,
young Buddhists are not supposed to think they will always be young
or that anything in existence is always permanent. Youthfulness, or
གཞོན་ནུ་ [zhönnu][51] in Chöke, does not exist continuously in a material
way. Nothing compounded exists continuously.

Buddha can be anything, as tiny as the size of a sesame seed or as enormous as a mountain. That is why it is said in *The Praise to Vajra-sattva*:[52]

> The body of Vajrasattva is like sky.
> Wisdom body is unmeasurable in size and uncountable in number,
> With various powers that are indestructible.
> I bow to your vajra body.

According to tantric theory, all Buddhas, including the five Buddha families, are contained in Vajrasattva, and that is why Vajrasattva is praised. Any form of Buddha is not only little, medium, or big; it is a reflection of the faculties of beings, so there is no limitation of any particular size. Likewise, there is no limitation of age, as in being old or young. Whatever sentient beings need for happiness, Buddha reflects, so one is not supposed to materialize these reflections to be a certain way. Especially if one wants to obtain Buddha's body, it will ultimately depend on one's practice and view. Of course, if one is only thinking at a worldly level and in a nihilist way, then one may want to measure everything. All youths can look at Shabtrung Rinpoche's statues, tangkas, or frescoes to see that he has a white beard and mustache, but that does not mean they should think that he is an old, haggard Lama, and that the Nangpai Zhoennu [Young Buddhists] are always going to be young and glamorous. I hope that the youthful Bhutanese Buddhists are not going to copy limited nihilist revolutionary ideas that do not show how varied the phenomena and karma of sentient beings can be. Buddha's omniscience can reflect whatever is beneficial for beings' phenomena, so it is not necessary to limit this to being for those who are old or young. But still, if it is inspiring for other young people to see youthful Buddhists who are practicing Buddhist beliefs and holding Buddhist lineage with refined behavior and activity, even though one day they will have the signs of getting old, such as the sign of a white beard, this can be done with best intentions to help others establish their faith when they are young. These young people can also demonstrate a positive example of respecting those who are in high positions and wise, including one's own noble historical leaders in the royalty, and showing humility before respected people and one's equals, dealing with others not by competing,

which causes jealousy and negativity, but by communicating with soothing energy.

If the young people of Bhutan truly want to hold Buddhist traditions
and to let them flourish, they must learn about inner qualities, such as
having compassion toward pitiful beings and increasing faith toward
sublime beings, by studying Dharma and practicing, as shown in the
histories of previous sublime beings and Bodhisattvas. Even if they wear
the clothing of the laity's aspect, serving their country or government
with vast intention, it will be of great benefit that is beyond any age,
and gives the best example of being pure Buddhists to others in the new
generation. Whatever they do can be done with the intention of benefiting other beings, including in their own country, with respect for those
who are wise instead of what is done in the West, where families ignore
their children once they are educated and children ignore those who are
experienced and wise, including their own parents.

There is no question that the best choice for all sentient beings,
including the people of Bhutan, is for Bhutanese to sustain the ancient
traditions of the Drukpa Kagyu and Nyingma in noncontradiction in
Shabtrung Rinpoche's way, with faith in Guru Rinpoche, recognizing
that Guru Rinpoche is the degenerate time's sole protector and the manifestation of Buddha Shakyamuni. Even in this life, the least amount of
conflict within the country over religious or political issues makes the
country much safer, so it can be united and stable instead of divided with
disagreements. Just as one or two sticks can be split into pieces without
difficulty because they are fragile, but many sticks bundled together are
stronger and cannot be easily broken, if Bhutanese band together as one
in religion or politics, no one can destabilize or interfere with them.

There is a saying:

If a simple person is wise about how to abide,
Even dictators cannot manipulate him.

Internally, if the people of Bhutan unite, even people of other countries
cannot make issues out of their policies in dealing with problems inside
the country, and Bhutanese can explain that it is not necessary for other
countries to impose their ideas. Bhutan has to maintain its own culture

as an independent country. That is actually a human right. It is not only people who have come to Bhutan from other countries who have human rights; native Bhutanese also have human rights. Each nation has the right to preserve its culture and religion, so that whatever has already existed in a nation can continue, and that is a human right. For example, it is absurd for people from other nations to try to overpower Bhutan, which is a country with its own culture and laws, by imposing their ideas about their own rights. No other country would allow that to happen. It has not been permitted by any countries of the world, whether in Europe, Asia, or Africa, for insurgent groups to overtake sections of a country where they have resided, or even to secede from that country, using that country's land to form their own state. Instead of appreciating that one has been able to live and work in a pleasant country, trying to take away its land and form one's own state is considered illegal. If young Bhutanese can think in a profound way about what will not cause any problems inside Bhutan, Bhutan can maintain itself, just as when a pristine spring has not run dry but is full of underground water, it cannot be stopped by trying to cover it over with earth. It will sustain itself.

Inside Bhutan, without having a long view with foresight, but only thinking about individual power or one's position in one's own group by being nihilistic and opportunistic, conflict can ensue that will leave the country vulnerable to infiltration. Especially those religious leaders who hold power within the country have to be very, very careful not to make mistakes. I hope and pray that all young Bhutanese will further the flourishing of Dharma in whatever form they choose, whether within the monastic structure, as lay practitioners, or as laypersons in the service of the country through government office, with the essence of benefiting the country so that people inside Bhutan can have comfortable lives, and so that pure Dharma can be continuous for enlightenment. I will always pray for the long lives of His Majesty and his family, for the lives of the Bhutanese people, including its leaders, and for the prosperity of the entire country.

It is so sweet for the Young Buddhist Association of Bhutan to have distributed sweets in twenty Dzong in celebration of the birth of Lord Buddha, as I heard. Even though all of my words may not be seen as sweet like that, from the bottom of my heart, since Aum Neten Zangmo asked me to say what would be beneficial for young Buddhists, I want to tell you honestly what I think. I hope and pray that the community of Young Bhutanese Buddhists will understand this due to their insight. I am saying some unpleasant words, like a thorny cactus that could seemingly cause goose bumps, but if one reads and checks them carefully without ignoring them, one can find that a cactus sometimes has beautifully blooming sweet flowers.

Even if you think you have changed from the way Bhutanese have been in the past, I believe you still have a good lineage, better than that of any young people who are nonbelievers anywhere in the world. From my love for you, even though you may know this better than I do, I want to say simply that you can study whatever you want to study, and that there are many precious teachings you can know from the speech of Buddha and the shastras of sublime beings. But I want to emphasize how fortunate you are to have been born in a Buddhist country and to be able to learn and practice Buddhism, even though you already know this.

Thank you.

An Introduction to Dharma
Dance Offerings

Written to accompany a film of traditional dances that was directed by Kyabje Thinley Norbu Rinpoche and performed by some of Rinpoche's young dance students in the White Lotus School. The featured dances were, as translated and described by Rinpoche: (1) *The Dance of Heroes and Heroines*,[1] offering cymbals of rejoicing to wisdom Herukas, and (2) *Hung! Manifest, Padmakara, with Your Gathering of Dakinis*.[2] The latter title is the invocation beseeching the blessings of the Lord of Oddiyana, the Lotus-Born Wisdom Vajra Master Pema Kara, accompanied by gatherings of Dakas and Dakinis, offering clouds of joy to the Three Roots, who are the Triple Gems of the Vajrayana, with holy dance and cymbals.

The meaning of dance is movement. In ordinary existence, whatever is born will remain for a while and then cease. The continuous movement between being born, remaining, and ceasing is the circling dance of samsaric sentient beings, who are predominantly attached to remaining and who rely on what is not reliable, carried by the movement of karmic air.[3] Bodhisattvas are born from the movement of great compassionate intention. Seeing the suffering of sentient beings, they remain in existence to comfort beings. Their sublime dance can evoke sadness or weariness, but then it evokes inspiration, faith, and compassion, demonstrating the absurdity of samsaric activity and benefiting beings by its soothing energy, turning them toward the path of enlightenment. Whenever the performance of the illuminating activity of their hero's or heroine's dance is accomplished, they recede.

Buddhas are never born but they manifest unobstructedly, never remaining anywhere in a certain way but always abiding in the fully enlightened, unwavering state. Buddhas have no reality object to manifest since there is no reality ego, yet the quality of unobstructed phenomena effortlessly occurs and unintentionally benefits beings. Because they are free from the three states of being born, remaining, and ceasing, Buddhas' wisdom dance is forever.

In order not to circle continuously in samsara in the three states of the birth, cessation, and remaining of conceptions, we are supposed to turn the mind to Dharma through believing in Buddha's speech, to dance the Bodhisattva's dance with great compassion, in order to attain fully enlightened Buddhahood, the dance of wisdom.

The mind of sentient beings is continuous. Even if one wishes to prevent or stop it, it cannot be stopped, just as when a spring's source is deep and continuous, trying to cover it with earth and stones cannot keep it from streaming upward to emerge onto land. Since mind does not cease, conceptions do not cease, whether they occur apparently or are dormant in a state of dullness for a short time or a long time according to beings' habit. This is the circumstance that causes samsara's dance, the movement of karmic air. The manifestation of wisdom dance comes from the unobstructed movement of wisdom air.

Since mind has phenomena, the phenomena of mind cannot be denied. Each being has the choice between remaining in samsaric suffering, occupied by passions and karma without using phenomena meaningfully, or using phenomena positively for enlightenment, such as by creating virtue. This is the choice between being a nonbeliever, which means only accepting phenomena that exist in a material way and are perceived by the ordinary five senses; or being a believer, which means believing that phenomena can exist within the material or beyond the material, perceived by the ordinary five senses or beyond them and only perceived by sublime beings. Buddhas are fully enlightened with nondualistic wisdom, so there is no object to perceive or subject who is a perceiver within duality, just as stainless sky does not exist as two things. Also, this emptiness is not only like empty sky, but has inconceivable wisdom phenomena. Buddha Shakyamuni said:

The unborn is sole truth.
Infants are saying there are four truths.

If one actually enters the path of the pith of enlightenment, there is
    not even one truth,
So where are the four truths?

Nonbelievers, who do not accept what they cannot perceive due to
their lack of belief in the unobstructed quality of the nature of mind, can
become paranoid about what seems unreal to them, such as the spiritual
phenomena and history of holy dance. Although nonbelievers deny spiritual phenomena because they are not perceptible to them from reality
habit, and they thus think they are made up, they strangely still believe
in the dance of their own ordinary phenomena even when they are
imperceptible. For example, it is said in a poem:

By seeing the white light of the moon
Occurring at the peak of the eastern mountain,
From being together a long time ago,
I remember the beautiful face of my sweetheart.

As this reminiscence shows, nonbelievers can accept the ordinary
phenomena of mind even though they are not presently perceptible to
them as reality, but they deny spiritual phenomena that are not perceptible to them, due to their habit of material reality. Also, even though they
do not accept what seems unreal to them, such as thinking their dreams
are not real but only dreams, they still wish and say, "I hope my dream
comes true."

Since the phenomena of mind cannot be erased, when phenomena
occur, it is better to decide to rekindle the pure manifestation of inherent wisdom deity, which is Buddha, to attain the state of enlightenment
for the benefit of many different beings, including oneself, through
many different skillful means. This is not a nonbeliever's theory of nothingness.

The dance of ordinary worldly beings is not sublime because it is not
connected with wisdom display but with the passions of material reality.
There are countless passions, but they can be synthesized into the five
passions of hatred, jealousy, arrogance, desire, and ignorance.[4] Ignorance
is the basis of all passions, although it does not have an activity itself.

This ordinary dance exists within compounded phenomena, and whatever is compounded cannot go beyond the ordinary movement of the four finalities:

> Whoever is born finally will die.
> Whoever is gathered finally will separate.
> Whoever is in a high position finally will fall.
> Whatever is compounded finally will disperse.

All of these four finalities are dances because they are continuously moving. Sentient beings continuously move from high to low, from low to high, and from high to higher states due to changing karmic energy, which is the movement of the dance of samsaric existence. As Buddha Shakyamuni said:

> The three realms are impermanent like the clouds of autumn.
> If you look at beings' birth and death and if you look at dance, they
>   are the same, continuously moving and changing.
> Beings' life is like the sky's lightning between clouds.
> Beings' life is like a waterfall quickly descending from steep
>   mountains.

Within ordinary movement, there is movement that is uncontrollably without intention, and there is movement with intention, such as the movement of ordinary dance. This movement, which is not connected with belief in deities and offerings, does not have any positive influence of wisdom. Even though it can cause momentary happiness, excitement, or elation, it is only ordinary, temporary entertainment and distraction, so its result will be to diminish and disappear. It always occurs within compounded material conception and compounded material activity with dualistic habit, so when it finally finishes, it causes disappointment, frustration, and depression.

The other category of movement with intention, which is only positive intention, is Dharma dance, which is spiritual dance. Dharma dance is always connected with the clear view of deities, offerings, visualization, and meditation. This dance does not cause frustration or depression afterward because it is connected with wisdom manifestation, which means uncompounded phenomena, so it brings blessings and positive energy. Dharma dance has the pure object of deity phenomena and the pure subject of the one who offers, and it is practiced as a pure offering for the purification of karma and the accumulation of virtue according to the Vajrayana tradition.

The teachings of Buddha are very precious and so profound that they can be very difficult for nonbelievers to understand, yet if one understands them, they are always meaningful. Buddha Shakyamuni is omniscient, so Buddha taught sentient beings according to their faculties at many levels, manifesting according to their phenomena of time and place. All of these levels, or *yanas*, are important to categorize, but briefly, all of the immeasurable teachings of Buddha can be synthesized into the three levels of the Hinayana, Mahayana, and Vajrayana.

At the time that Buddha emanated in India, people were very respectful of royalty because they were dignified and very powerful, so as skillful means Buddha was born into the Shakya lineage of kings. Buddha had no attachment to kingdoms or race; it was only to guide beings that Buddha appeared in this aspect to teach the Hinayana, adjusting to that time. The main teaching of the Hinayana is to abandon all desirable qualities[5] that cause attachment in samsara through passions, and to discipline the five senses and body, speech, and mind in serenity to finally attain the state of Arhat. By abandoning his queens and his kingdom, Buddha taught to abstain from desirable qualities, discipline the mind, meditate, and realize I-lessness so as not to remain in samsara but to be enlightened.

Since there are many different sentient beings and those of higher faculties were not satisfied with the Hinayana, Buddha taught the Mahayana, including teachings on compassion, which is called bodhichitta in Sanskrit, and the six or ten *paramitas*,[6] for the benefit of beings who through purification and accumulation can attain the result, fully enlightened Buddhahood. According to the Mahayana tradition, one sees all phenomena as being just like magic, appearing from the interdependence of root circumstances meeting with contributing circumstances, but while they are appearing, not truly independently existing as reality or in a material way. With that point of view, one purifies obscurations and accumulates merit, without thinking that they are reality, in order to attain the state of not remaining in samsara and not remaining in enlightenment, so as to benefit other beings, not allowing them to suffer continuously and not being attached to self-peace. *Maha* means very great, and the great meaning of the Mahayana is like the sky, with no limitation, because sentient beings have no limitation, and so Buddha's methods have no limitation, encompassing all beings in the aspiration to attain enlightenment.

Many Eastern countries, such as Thailand, Cambodia, and Sri Lanka, are historically Hinayana Buddhist. Although the teachings of Mahayana are logical and proven, they are generally not accepted by these Hinayana followers, who think that Mahayana teachings are demonic ideas created by Nagarjuna and his followers and that Buddha taught only the Hinayana. People who say this still exist due to the result of the limitations of their previous intentions, prayers, and dedication. Even though Mahayana teachings were taught by Buddha with unobstructed wisdom mind, these Hinayana followers claim that Shariputra, Mongalpu, and Neten Ösung[7] were inseparable from Buddha and would have heard these teachings if Buddha had taught them. The Mahayana teaches that because Buddha is omniscient, Buddha taught according to beings' varying capacities and different phenomena in whatever way would connect with their minds, and that Buddha taught the Mahayana to those who were suitable containers in Kushinagar and many other places, including holy places in India, and that these teachings were heard by Maitreya, Manjushri, and many other Bodhisattvas. Historically, the Mahayana flourished in India and Tibet, and was brought to China by Bodhidharma as Chan.[8] In comparison to Tibetan Buddhism, which is Vajrayana, there are differences in categorizations of accepting and not accepting phenomena. Mahayana Chan Buddhism emphasizes emptiness; in Tibetan Buddhism, since emptiness and phenomena are inseparable, phenomena are used, because until one excels in the state of attaining confidence, there is mind, and mind is not only nil. Even when practitioners are abiding in the stainless state of evenness without consideration of whether there are phenomena or no phenomena, after moving from that evenness of meditation, until abiding and movement become indivisible in enlightenment, there are phenomena, so phenomena are used for purification and accumulation, without denying them.

Since there are many different sentient beings' faculties, some beings were not satisfied with Mahayana, so Buddha taught Vajrayana. For Vajrayana teachings, the omniscient Buddha openly taught Kriya and Upa tantras but did not openly teach the inner Vajrayana tantras, such as Hevajra, Kalachakra, and Chakrasambhava teachings, or Maha, Anu, and Ati, but taught them to those who were suitable containers with keen faculties when circumstances were right. For example, at the request of King Indrabodhi, who wanted to attain enlightenment without abandoning his queens, kingdom, and desirable qualities, Buddha emanated as the mandala of Guhyasamaja, and from that revelation the inner Vajrayana teachings flourished.

Dharma dance is predominantly the tradition of inner Vajrayana. The view is that the state of Dharmakaya is the forever unwavering state, but its quality of unobstructedness manifests as the state of the purelands of Sambhogakaya, always abiding in the seven branches of union.[9] From that state, for the benefit of beings, there is the manifestation of unobstructed wisdom body to guide beings, according to different beings' phenomena, in infinite indefinite aspects as Nirmanakaya's dance. According to the wishes of sentient beings, there are peaceful aspects of manifestations in the aspect of peaceful deities who manifest to beings who are attached to serenity; there are wrathful aspects of manifestations in the aspect of wrathful deities who manifest to beings who are attached to violence, which subdues wrathful beings; and there are semiwrathful aspects of manifestations in the aspect of semiwrathful deities who manifest to beings who are peaceful and also lustful and wrathful. All of these aspects of manifestation appear in Dharma dance. Peaceful dance is performed with graceful, sensual movements; wrathful dance is performed with threatening, rough movements to guide violent beings; and semiwrathful dance is performed with both peaceful and wrathful movements.

Also, all music accompanying the dance has to be performed in the same way. Each instrument and sound has meaning. For example, it is said that from the sound of the Dharma drum, wherever sublime teachers exist, they will live long lives for many eons and teach Dharma for many beings, and all precious teachings can continuously be heard by all beings so they will be released from suffering. The bell contains the body, speech, and mind of all Buddhas of the Three Kayas. The *damaru* symbolizes awakening beings from the sleep of ignorance to awareness wisdom. The sound of the wind instruments *gyaling* and *dungchen* are supposed to be the sounds of mantras. The splendorous sounds of the *dungchen* correspond to wrathful deities, and the celestial sounds of the *gyaling* correspond to Dakinis' melodies, turning beings' minds to enlightenment.

In Vajrayana, the outer tantric teachings of Kriya, Upa, and Yoga predominantly use the sounds of chanting and hand gestures with visualization and offerings. The inner tantric teachings of Mahayoga and Anuyoga, especially the teachings of Mahayoga, reveal Dharma dance, which predominantly uses the sounds of chanting and physical movements of the entire body with visualization and offerings of Buddha and Bodhisattva activities. Some of these dances are not to be revealed to others except for special reasons, but generally they can be shown publicly. They can be performed by monks and nuns, depending on the monastery or nunnery, or by laity. Sometimes they are performed inside assembly halls and sometimes outside at temples, at stupas, and in processions with invocations, consecrations, and rituals, for receiving blessings. Since they are connected with the pure spiritual phenomena of sublime beings' activities, they have to be respected as Holy Dharma.

Dharma dance clearly reveals the enlightened activities of peaceful and wrathful deities with physical movements and adornments, including the eight manifestations of Guru Rinpoche performed according to the many awesome histories of Guru Rinpoche in different times and places. One of the dances of the eight manifestations is that of Shakya Seng-ge, the manifestation of Buddha Shakyamuni, which is danced wearing robes showing that Buddha was ordained with Hinayana vows and had abandoned desirable qualities. Some narrow followers of Buddhism think that it is ridiculous for Buddha to be shown dancing because it is against the Vinaya tradition of discipline and not appropriate for the aspect of a monk. This dance is not naughty; it reminds those who see this dance of the Nirmanakaya body of Buddha Shakyamuni, in order to create faith in Buddha's teachings and activity. When the dance of Buddha Shakyamuni is performed, there are special serene movements, ways of looking with the eyes, and ways of stepping that are actually signs of discipline and detachment from samsara, and this recalls the Vinaya tradition so that one can remember Buddha's qualities.

Some followers of causal Mahayana teachings reject Vajrayana teachings from their doubt or fear by using ordinary reasoning, but Vajrayana teachings are beyond ordinary reasoning and cannot be disproved by materializing with intellectual or philosophical arguments. That is why they do not fit within ordinary people's minds. It is also why Vajrayana is secret, because Vajrayana is inconceivable sublime wisdom phenomena. The Mahayana accepts the two selflessnesses of self and phenomena, but how can the two selflessnesses be realized if Vajrayana is rejected and cannot be included within the greatness of the Mahayana view? How can immeasurable sentient beings be benefited according to their different faculties with limitless compassion and skill, as the Mahayana teaches? Logically, what is the greatness of the Mahayana if it attempts to limit the teachings of Buddha? If one believes that Buddha is omniscient, one must believe that Buddha's teachings are unlimited, because sentient beings' faculties are unlimited, so one must believe in Vajrayana. That is true greatness.

Although Hinayana denies Mahayana, and Mahayana denies Vajrayana, this denial belongs to sentient beings' dualistic conceptions and not to Buddha's teachings. If we want to attain enlightenment, we have to follow Buddha's teachings, and the teachings of Buddha are countless because they are teachings for the countless faculties of beings. Therefore, wisdom mind manifests in unending diversity.

The offering of dance is connected with the belief in manifestation. If one accepts that Buddha can manifest as anything, then one must accept Dharma dance, which is the manifestation of the skillful means of Buddhas. In the precious Vajrayana tradition in which the offering of dance is practiced, everything is turned into virtue, including all movement. Phenomena are always moving; in Dharma dance, the phenomena of the movement of forms are the wrathful and peaceful movements of unobstructed manifestation. All Buddhas abide in Dharmadhatu, and this is not dullness; infinite qualities are always manifesting as all Buddha phenomena. Dharmakaya or Dharmadhatu is the always unwavering state and the origin of the waves of manifestation, and that manifestation is the stainless movement of the dance of the manifestation of enlightenment.

In the history of religions, however, there have always been differences in interpretations of spiritual phenomena. For example, Christians say Jesus is the son of God, but Muslims say Jesus is not the son of God. Also, Christians say Jesus is the Messiah, but Jews say that Jesus is not the Messiah and the Messiah has not come yet. All of these are different systems of understanding appearances that come according to time, place, and beings' phenomena, and whatever is believed about these appearances corresponds to individual and group karmic connections. Although these beliefs are held by ordinary beings, and the perceptions and conceptions of ordinary beings cannot prove or disprove anything about the manifestations of sublime beings, these beliefs become the cause for fighting and arguing. The effort of proving, disproving, and fighting is not spiritual according to Buddhist theory because it seriously materializes and conceptualizes what followers must believe, which is the same as nihilism even though religious terms are used, and is fighting for reality. There is no actual substantial reality. Whatever is being fought for is only conception, thinking it is reality because of believing that everything exists in reality and defending that reality, and then fighting for power within materialism, with material conception. That is the essence of holding a nihilist view, although those who think this way misinterpret it as being loyal to their religious beliefs and fighting for supposedly religious purposes. Unless beings have faith in stainless sublime beings or Buddhas, they always begin with contradiction, remain within contradiction, and cause contradictory circumstances.

Manifestations of Buddha have nothing to do with reality-grasping ego because the essence of manifestation is stainless emptiness. There is no compounded substance motion because manifestation comes from the stainless state, which does not cause anything rejectable or accept-able in a reality way. That is why any manifestations are light, not heavy or dark. However the manifestations of sublime beings appear, they bestow blessings. Whether seemingly wrathful or peaceful, the essence is always flawless ecstasy.

Ordinary movement causes karma. Karma causes traps, preventing freedom. This is the characteristic of the movement of ordinary sub-stantial reality. The movement of the manifestation of Buddhas and Bodhisattvas always liberates from all kinds of obstructed phenomena, cleansing any heavy karmic energy to light energy as a result of receiv-ing the blessings of the wisdom body of Buddhas. From light energy to lighter energy to the lightest, fully enlightened wisdom performance, the state of Nirmanakaya is attained, which connects to the seven branches of union of the Sambhogakaya and becomes indivisible stainless space Dharmakaya.

Whoever carefully considers the nature of human beings, even in an ordinary way, can see that there is always movement, because the nature of mind is unobstructed. Since a self exists intangibly, dancing within tangible existence, one cannot logically deny phenomena, because phe-nomena exist since mind exists. The only problem is that all movement is materialized, which cannot cause the immaterial wisdom of liberation. Still, there is always the movement of manifestation, whether it is tem-porarily dormant or conspicuous. Since there are always phenomena, they should be used positively, such as by believing in the Triple Gems and karma, purifying negative karma, and accumulating positive karma. In the Vajrayana, one has to believe in the manifestation of the Buddha, the Guru; the manifestation of Dharma, the Deva with the blessing of ecstasy; and the manifestation of the Sangha, Dakas and Dakinis. From the Vajrayana practice of Dharma dance, heavy karmic air is cleansed and wisdom air flows.

Vajrayana practice is the realization of wisdom deity. According to the Mahayana, this is called the rekindling of Buddha nature, and accord-ing to the Vajrayana, it is called the blossoming of inherent wisdom deity to attain enlightenment. The essence of Buddha nature and inher-ent wisdom deity is actually the same; they are only different in their methods and aspect due to the unobstructed qualities of the teachings of the omniscient Buddhas. In brief, the origin of all Buddhas is Dharmakaya, which is Samantabhadra, stainless emptiness wisdom. Stainless emptiness is unobstructed, which is why all pure appearances of the Sambhogakaya five Buddha families and purelands occur with form, speech, mind, qualities, and activities, and which can only be seen by pure Bodhisattvas, not ordinary sentient beings. From Sambhogakaya occurs the manifestation of Nirmanakaya, which can appear in either impure or pure aspects according to the phenomena of sentient beings. Even though it is totally pure itself and indivisible from Dharmakaya, according to sentient beings' faculties it can be anything, so it can appear in the variety of impure aspects, pure aspects, and both impure and pure aspects simultaneously. So, with belief in the Vajrayana view of the Three Kayas, according to Vajrayana's skill, the offering of the desirable qualities of dance is made. Buddha Namparnangdze,[10] Vairochana in Sanskrit, is the aspect of appearance, which means any aspect of form of all Buddhas' manifestations, including the different aspects of the inner essence of beings and the different aspects of the outer container of the elements. These different appearances are all seen as wisdom manifestation because the origin of all immeasurable manifestation is stainless, inconceivable Dharmakaya. Even though the essence of Dharmakaya is sole immeasurable oneness, its manifestations are always appearing in different aspects, and Dharma dance is the embodiment of those aspects of manifestation.

For the dancer, it is very important not to cause any self-consciousness while dancing as in an ordinary contest for beauty or for sports, for medals or for fame, with either eager elation or cautiousness. Without expectation or worry, the dancer has to be deity, not thinking of an ordinary audience with conceptions about whether one is pleasing or not pleasing them with one's dance, such as whether one is doing well so the audience is admiring one's skill, or making mistakes so the audience is noticing one's faults. Without thinking that anyone is there, the dancer just remembers deity, dancing in the best way for offering, without thinking about the reactions of others or competing with anyone, since the intention of competition is to make oneself better and best compared to others, with passions. When the dancer does not have any self-consciousness, the dance becomes very beautiful because there is no "I" or ordinary subject, so the dancer does not pay attention to an object. It is beautiful because the dancers are centered on offerings, deities, and dancing with faith, without self-righteous ego and without losing mindfulness, because the essence of mindfulness is there in the engagement with deities. In Dharma dance, the dancer is transforming any desirable qualities into offerings with belief in deities according to Vajrayana teachings of the pure phenomena of wisdom deities, and into the generosity of giving joy to other beings according to Mahayana teachings of bodhichitta. When the dancer is offering without thinking of anything else, the dancer is released from self-consciousness and doubt and can become extremely free, so that the dance is transformed into wisdom dance and everything opens. When the dancer is free, there is no shyness, no fear, and nothing to hide, and also there is the absence of arrogance, which is the quality of not holding a self, because the dancer is thinking of deities. If there is a single dancer, the dancer can dance freely, only adjusting to the musical instruments by synchronizing each movement with each sound. When there is a group of dancers, it is very important for the dancers to be disciplined and synchronized with the body movements of the other dancers, including the mudras of expressions of turbulent wrathful deities or serene peaceful deities, as well as with the musical instruments, not trying to stand out or to be exceptional with ordinary ego, but to be like a lotus whose fresh, cool petals are all aligned with each other so that the rapturous form of the flower's beauty is clear. Then, whoever sees the dance sees it as perfect, like an undistorted blooming lotus, causing inspiration and faith to grow.

In Dharma dance, there must always be space. Movement should be continuous without ever stopping for one moment. No movements must ever get stuck anywhere, but all should freely keep going through space. Dharma dance must be like the movement of magic, not obstructed anywhere, but miraculously flowing with all kinds of round and smooth gestures that keep gracefully moving. Since Dharma dance is always connected with deities and revealing their activities, it is always special and self-secret,[11] so the dancers and the onlookers can have self-secret inconceivable phenomena. This is not because there is anything that is intentionally hidden, but because the dance itself is naturally beyond expression.

The ordinary karmic dance of sentient beings, whether done reluctantly or willingly, is done with effort, and the audience of sentient beings watches the dance with either attachment or aversion. The dance of Bodhisattvas is done with the vast, compassionate intention of fulfilling the wishes of pitiful sentient beings who are the objects of their compassion. The wisdom dance of the manifestation of Buddhas is beyond intention, purposeless, and never attached anywhere, with no differentiation between dancer and onlooker, who are indivisible.

The temporary benefit of Dharma dance is to untie knots in the karmic chakras, so the nerves and channels of the body are disentangled and the airs of vital energy are cleansed to flow smoothly, as the movement of dance grinds congested energy, including in the forms of clots or fats, increasing circulation and preventing obstruction. The body's energy becomes very light naturally by receiving blessings from enlightened wisdom body, and inherent wisdom deity can occur. The nine aspects of the wisdom bodies of peaceful deities are (1) a delicate body, which is a sign of awareness and the purification of ignorance; (2) flexibility, delicate and without hardness, which is a sign that desire has been purified; (3) suppleness, implying movement and readiness to unite, which is a sign that pride has been purified; (4) swaying, like a willow tree that moves in gentle wind without breaking, which is a sign that anger or hatred has been purified; (5) youthfulness, which is a sign that jealousy has been purified; (6) clarity, which is a sign that the defect of stains has been purified; (7) the light of radiance, which is a sign of containing all excellent qualities; (8) attractiveness, which is a sign of the perfection of the thirty-two noble marks and eighty excellent signs; and (9) splendor, which is a sign of vanquishing all. The ultimate benefit of Dharma dance is finally to attain flawless ecstasy wisdom body as the all-pervading holder of the immeasurable, inconceivable pure phenomena of the five Buddha families with consorts and their purelands.

There are many, many different traditions of Dharma dances. The dance of *Hung Zheng Shik Pema Jungne Khandrö Tsok* is the way of movement of Dakas and Dakinis, based on the history of the time when Guru Rinpoche had accomplished all of his Buddha activities in Tibet for the benefit of all beings. According to the general perception of Tibetans, as Guru Rinpoche was preparing to depart from Samye, the main place where the Sutra and Mantrayana teachings were established and flourshed, and also at Gungtang Pass, from among his many hundreds of disciples, the five disciples Namkhai Nyingpo, King Trisong Detsen, Yeshe Tsogyal, Nanam Dorje Dudjom, and the prince Lhase Mutri Tsenpo prostrated to Guru Rinpoche, circumambulated, offered mandalas, and personally requested prayers; and so Guru Rinpoche taught how to pray to himself according to each one's wishes.

As Khandro Yeshe Tsogyal requested of Guru Rinpoche:

Now, today, I, Yeshe Tsogyal, beseech you, Guru Rinpoche:
All fortunate beings including myself cannot find any other guide
    such as you, the essence of all Buddhas.
Now, today, your manifestation is departing to the country of
    rakshas[12] and to Oddiyana for the benefit of other beings,
So, for me, could you give a prayer, unelaborate and essential, with
    profound meaning and great blessings to attain enlightenment
    swiftly,
So that just by saying this prayer, blessings come like clouds
    gathering in the sky,
And whenever we Tibetans pray to you,
Your compassion manifests unobstructedly as your wisdom body
    from the power of the prayer.

When Yeshe Tsogyal requested this, Guru Rinpoche adorned himself in jewel and bone ornaments. Facing toward the southwest, raising his right hand while holding and sounding the damaru, and placing his left hand on Yeshe Tsogyal's crown chakra, he revealed the prayer of *Hung Zheng Shik Pema Jungne Khandrö Tsok*:

HUNG! Please manifest, Padmakara, with your gathering of Dakinis.
We beseech you with the Buddhas of the ten directions and three
    times to be compassionate to us.

Great Lord, Padma Tötreng Tsal,
Please come from the purelands of Vidyadharas and Dakinis
With beautiful hair upwardly spiraling and downwardly flowing
    and flowing,
Many jewel ornaments ringing and ringing,
Ornaments of the bones of human beings clanging and clanging,
Many sounds and cymbals, prolonged and profound,
Gatherings of Yidam deities resonating with the sound of HUNG,
    magnificent and magnificent,
Many of the five classes of Dakinis coming together dancing, grace-
    fully swaying and swaying,
Great Gings performing the dance of heroes, pounding and
    pounding,[13]
Many, many female Dakinis like clouds, assembling and assembling,
The eight classes of Dharma protectors acting, flashing and flashing,
Thousands in armor sounding, incessantly and incessantly,
On the right, all male deities keep coming forward and forward,
On the left, all female deities keep coming forward and forward,
In all space, holy banners and holy parasols, waving and waving,
Aromatic sweet incense, spreading and spreading,
Secret special insubstantial symbols of Dakinis, hinting and hinting,
Fierce hymns of Great Gings, whistling and whistling,
Many hymns of HUNG, splendidly roaring and roaring,
The secret special insubstantial signal PHAT, exploding and
    exploding.
Please look on me and all sentient beings of the six realms
With compassion and come here to this place.
Furthermore, coming here from your compassion,
Until we attain fully enlightened Buddhahood,
Dispel demons, obstacles, and those who lead to reversed energy.
May you bless us with supreme and common siddhis.
Please liberate us from the ocean of suffering of samsara.

This prayer was spoken by Guru Rinpoche to Yeshe Tsogyal, revealing how to invoke Guru Rinpoche from wherever Guru Rinpoche is

abiding in sacred holy places. Guru Rinpoche said to Yeshe Tsogyal, "You should pray like that. May these activities only benefit all beings. I, Padmakara, with a *samaya* connection with Tibetans, will manifest in Tibet and directly give prophecies to faithful people. When you pray, first think of the explanations of Buddha that cause faith, and when you see qualities of the Buddhas, then with clear faith, enthusiastic faith, and confident faith, you can receive blessings. When mind is free from doubt, then all wishes will be fulfilled."

Just as there are differences in any kinds of activities, there are slightly different traditions of the invocation dance of *Hung Zheng Shik Pema Jungne Khandrö Tsok* wherever it is performed. Especially in Bhutan, there are slightly different movements in the dance as it was revealed by one of the five *tertön* kings, Terchen[14] Pema Lingpa, an emanation of Victorious Longchenpa, but the origin and meaning of the dance are the same, in accordance with the prayer revealed through Yeshe Tsogyal's request. All details of the meaning and the explanation of the benefits are contained in the extensive version of the prayer of *Hung Zheng Shik Pema Jungne Khandrö Tsok*, the invocation of Guru Rinpoche with all of his retinue of Dakas, Dakinis, and Dharmapalas, with beautiful, graceful, peaceful movements, splendid wrathful movements, cymbals, drums, *gyaling*, and *dungchen*, to come to give blessings, dispel obstacles, and expand accumulation.

I often saw many different peaceful and wrathful dances in Tibet, including in Mindrolling when I stayed there for nine years. In Bhutan, my father-in-law, Lopön Sönam Sangpo, often had this dance performed for *drupchen*. There is a tradition of the performance of this dance in many different monasteries in Bhutan. Of course, I have tremendous faith in Guru Rinpoche and whatever is connected with Guru Rinpoche, so I sent a message to Kyabje Dudjom Rinpoche's student, Lama Kuenzang Wangdue, and some Bhutanese dancers who are Nyingma lineage holders, to film these Dharma dances and send them to me for my special pujas. My students easily learned to do the dances traditionally from the films.

These Dharma dances are made for invocation and offering. Whoever sees them is supposed to believe positively in the activities of wisdom deities. They are only positive and auspicious, for immeasurable accumulation. By this virtue, may all beings, including whoever is connected with these dance offerings, obtain a wholesome precious human body up to attaining the flawless ecstasy of fully enlightened wisdom body.

NOTES

Gypsy Gossip

1. The Three Kayas are the Dharmakaya, Sambhogakaya, and Nirmanakaya.
2. Skt. *upasaka* (masc.); Tib. *ge-nyen* (dge bsnyen): a male lay practitioner or lay devotee. Fem. *upasika; ge-nyenma.*
3. Tib. *getsul* (dge tshul), novice.
4. Tib. *gelong* (dge slong), fully ordained monk.
5. Mahasandhi (Skt.) is the Great Perfection of Atiyoga. The Tibetan equivalent is Dzogpa Chenpo (rdzogs pa chen po), also called Dzogchen.
6. Tib. *terma* (gter ma), a hidden treasure teaching that is revealed by a *tertön.*
7. Tib. *tertön* (gter ston), a treasure (*terma*) revealer.
8. Tib. *kyerim* (bskyed rim), the developing stage practice.
9. Tib. *dzogrim* (rdzogs rim), the completion stage practice.
10. Tib. *nyamshak* (mnyam bzhag), abiding in evenness.
11. ngo bo.
12. rang bzhin.
13. thugs rje.
14. 'byung gnas.
15. pad+ma.
16. zhes su grags.
17. The four bodies are the Four Kayas (Dharmakaya, Sambhogakaya, Nirmanakaya, and Svabhavikakaya). The five wisdoms are the wisdom of Dharmadhatu, mirrorlike wisdom, the wisdom of equanimity, the wisdom of discernment, and the wisdom of all-accomplishing activity.
18. Skt. *mudra.*
19. Skt. Vajrasattva.

Beyond East and West

1. This means qualified with the realization of wisdom.
2. "Sublime being" is Rinpoche's translation of *pakpa* ('phags pa).
3. The always noble great expanse of openness.
4. Tib. *lopön* (slob dpon), Master.
5. Shantarakshita is also called the emanation of Vajrapani, and Padmasambhava is also called the emanation of Avalokiteshvara. They are actually indivisible from each other because they are always abiding in the state of Dharmakaya.

6. I.e., materializing phenomena in the sense of misinterpreting them as only material.
7. bshad gra.
8. sgrub grva.
9. Busuku: One whose activities are eating, sleeping, and defecating. Busuku is a nickname given to Shantideva by other monks at Nalanda University because outwardly he seemed to be lazy and doing nothing other than eating, sleeping, and defecating, although inwardly he was very learned and always secretly practicing. While this name was originally an insult, it became associated with this sublime history of a hidden practitioner who quietly attained high realization.
10. Tib. *tul zhuk* (brtul zhugs). *Tul* means ceasing the previous intention and behavior of being an ordinary human being, and *shuk* means entering into a new performance of superior activity with wisdom, which is the activity of yogis.
11. *Khandrö Gegyang (mkha' 'gro'i gad rgyangs).*
12. These gods and demons are the most desirable qualities and most awful evil of grasping mind.
13. rgyud.
14. Precious teachings; pith instructions.
15. 'bri gung skyobs pa 'jig rten mgon po.
16. The Four Kayas are the Three Kayas (Dharmakaya, Sambhogakaya, and Nirmanakaya) and Svabhavikakaya, or Vajrakaya.
17. "All rudras come from beings' attachment to ego, or self, that tries to be self-victorious in the material world, which is the root of all harm and must be annihilated through realization." Thinley Norbu, *A Cascading Waterfall of Nectar* (Boston: Shambhala Publications, 2009), p. 260.
18. rang rgyal.
19. According to Kunkhyen Longchenpa's *Treasury of the Precious Doctrines* (grub mtha' rin po che'i mdzod): (1) May I be born in the realms where there is no Buddha nor even Shravakas. (2) When born, may I naturally develop the realization of the path in that same lifetime. (3) May I teach beings who are to be subdued through gestures of the body, and not through sound.
20. Unpublished manuscript.
21. "Words for the West: An Interview with Thinley Norbu Rinpoche," *Tricycle: The Buddhist Review*, Fall 1998.
22. dge slong ma.
23. thabs, skillful.
24. shes rab, wisdom; Skt. *prajna*.
25. "The Secular Buddhist Podcasts."

26. *Jampel Dzogpa Chenpo Zhi Lam Drebu Yer Mepe Don La Monpa Rigtong Dorje Rangdang ('jam dpal rdzogs pa chen po gzhi lam 'dres bu dbyer med pa'i don la smon pa rig stong rdo rje'i rang gdangs).*

27. rnam shes tshogs drug.

28. nyon yid.

29. kun gzhi rnam shes.

30. The great omniscient (Kunkhyen) Master Rongzompa Chökyi Zangpo (rong zom chos kyi bzang po); Skt. Dharmabhadra.

31. *theg chen tshul 'jug.*

32. *rdo rje bkod pa.*

33. *rten 'brel.*

34. *rgyud rgyas pa.*

35. *lang kar gshegs pa;* Skt. *Lankavatara Sutra.*

36. Skt. Angulimala.

37. An account of the 1997 murders of Geshe Lobsang Gyatso, principal of the Buddhist School of Dialectics, and two of his students in Dharamsala—reportedly with "sharp weapons"—appears at www.newsweek.com/murder =monastery=172992, accessed July 9, 2015. A number of sources accused Buddhist fanatics of the crime, but no one has ever been charged or prosecuted.

38. yar gyi zang thal.

39. Tib. *tsok kyi korlo* (tshogs kyi 'khor lo). The ganachakra puja, a ritual practice, is an extraordinary way of accumulating merit in which all the five desirable qualities and particularly all the substances of eating and drinking are blessed as flawless wisdom amrita. One offers them to the Three Roots (Lama, Yidam, and Khandro or Dakini) and also to one's own body, which in the Vajrayana tradition contains the mandala of all the peaceful and wrathful deities. This is what is called "From wisdom, having wisdom" in "The Light Rays of the Youthful Sun," in *A Cascading Waterfall of Nectar* (2009), p. 281.

40. If ganachakra puja is made in a proper way with pure phenomena, then it is the supreme accumulation.

41. tshogs.

42. *Pureland* and *Buddhafield* are synonyms.

43. rnam par snang mdzad.

44. Vairochana is the principal Buddha of the Tathagatha (or Buddha) family.

45. 'pho ba.

46. Tib. bdud rtsi; Skt. *amrita.*

47. See page 118.

48. de bzhin gshegs pa rin chen snying po.

49. *dpung pa bzang po'i rgyud.*
50. *'ja'.*
51. thod rgal.
52. *Kongshag Dorje Tollu (skong bshags rdo rje'i thol glu).*
53. rang snang ris med.
54. *skyes rabs gsol 'debs.*
55. The word *reality* is sometimes used to mean absolute truth in Buddhist books written in English, but this word actually originates from the Latin word for "thing" (*realis*), which suggests the meaning of the existent reality of relative truth that is used here.
56. The Two Kayas are the Dharmakaya and Rupakaya. The Rupakaya contains the Sambhogakaya and the Nirmanakaya.
57. Thinley Norbu, *A Cascading Waterfall of Nectar* (2009), p. 23.
58. *rin chen phreng ba.*
59. *Tonpa Dewar Shegpe Sung Yedrol Dzogchen La Ngag Pa Benduye Chun Chang (ston pa bde bar gshegs pa'i gsung ye grol rdzogs chen la bsngags pa baiDUr ya'i chun 'phyang).*

A Message for Young Bhutanese

1. Dungsey Garab Dorje Rinpoche is the son of Kyabje Thinley Norbu Rinpoche.
2. Troma Nagmo is a deity associated with *chö* (chod) practice.
3. A *damaru* is a two-headed drum held in the hand, used in Buddhist practices.
4. Tib. *chöten* (mchod rten); Skt. *stupa.*
5. dbang lung.
6. Tib. *terma* (gter ma), treasures.
7. gter gsar.
8. bka' shog.
9. tshogs drug.
10. Thinley Norbu, *A Cascading Waterfall of Nectar* (Boston: Shambhala Publications, 2009), pp. 42–43.
11. dge rtsa bcad pa.
12. bde bar gshegs pa'i snying po.
13. sangs rgyas.
14. snying po.
15. lhan gcig skyes pa'i lha.
16. chos nyid kyi lha.

17. bag chags ngan pa.
18. las ngan.
19. bag chags bzang po.
20. bde bar gshegs pa.
21. ye shes kyi lha.
22. Ngawang Namgyal (1594–1651), the first Shabtrung (zhabs drung).
23. *Dzong* refers to castles that serve as the seats of the secular government as well as the seats of the monastic spiritual authorities in Bhutan, but here the word represents the ruling occupants who are housed in them.
24. pha jo 'brug sgom zhig po (1184–1251).
25. skong bshags, a prayer of fulfillment and confession.
26. sgrub chen, "great accomplishment." The most elaborate sadhana practice in Vajrayana tradition, which usually lasts seven to ten days.
27. sgom chen. Lit. "great meditators" but used in Bhutan to mean the yogis, or *ngakpas*, who are the serious lay practitioners of Vajrayana.
28. Tib. *pakpa* ('phags pa); Skt. *arya*.
29. That is, Lumbini in Nepal, and Bodh Gaya, Kushinagar, and Varanasi in India.
30. rgyal khab 'phags pa'i yul.
31. dus byas kyi chos.
32. 'dus ma byas pa'i chos.
33. 'phags lam yan lag brgyad.
34. yang dag pa'i lta ba.
35. yang dag pa'i rtog pa.
36. yang dag pa'i ngag.
37. yang dag pa'i las kyi mtha'.
38. yang dag pa'i 'tsho ba.
39. yang dag pa'i rtsol ba.
40. yang dag pa'i dran pa.
41. yang dag pa'i ting nge 'dzin.
42. rten 'brel.
43. lta ba'i snyigs ma.
44. mi g.yo ba.
45. Dzonkha is the national language of Bhutan.
46. *Little Buddha* (1993).
47. *Travelers and Magicians* (2003), a Bhutanese film.
48. de bzhin gshegs pa; Skt. Tathagata.
49. Art, medicine, language, logic and philosophy, and inner awareness.

50. gnas skabs bzhi.
51. gzhon nu.
52. *Dorje Sempa La Töpa (rdo rje sems dpa' la bstod pa).*

An Introduction to Dharma Dance Offerings

1. *Pacham.*
2. *Hung Zheng Shik Pema Jungne Khandrö Tsok (hung bzhengs shik pad ma 'byung gnas mKha' 'gro'i tshogs).*
3. Karmic air and karmic energy are connected and cannot be divided from each other, but karmic air can be differentiated as meaning movement or change, and karmic energy as atmosphere.
4. These five are the root of the passions; emotions that result from them are branches.
5. The five desirable qualities: beautiful form, melodious sound, delicious taste, fragrant smells, and pleasing touch. They can cause attachment, as this says, in the Hinayana perspective, but they can be considered positive in Vajrayana.
6. The six *paramitas*, or six perfections, are the perfection of generosity, morality, patience, diligence, *samadhi*, and profound knowing. The ten perfections include the six perfections plus the perfections of method, aspiration, strength, and wisdom. The Sanskrit *samadhi* (meditation) is *samten* (bsam gtan) in Tibetan.
7. Neten Ösung is Kashyapa, also known as Mahakashyapa, one of the principal disciples of the Buddha.
8. *Chan* is the Chinese term; the Japanese term is *Zen.*
9. Seven branches of union: *khajor yenlak dun* (kha sbyor yan lag bdun).
10. rnam par snang mdzad.
11. I.e., inherently or naturally secret.
12. Variation of Skt. *rakshasa*; Tib. *sinpo* (srin po).
13. Gings are the retinue or messengers of deity. While performing Dharma dance (*'cham*), they are represented in the form of skeletons holding small drums and dancing with jumping movements.
14. A *terchen* (gter chen) is a great *tertön*, or treasure revealer.

BOOKS BY THINLEY NORBU